BRIAN HOEY

AT HOME WITH THE QUEEN

*The Inside Story of
the Royal Household*

HarperCollins*Publishers*

HarperCollins*Publishers*
77–85 Fulham Palace Road,
Hammersmith, London W6 8JB

www.**fire**and**water**.com

Published by HarperCollins*Publishers* 2002
1 3 5 7 9 8 6 4 2

A catalogue record for this book
is available from the British Library

ISBN 0 00 712618 2

Set in Palatino by
Rowland Phototypesetting Ltd,
Bury St Edmunds, Suffolk

Printed and bound in Great Britain by
Clays Ltd, St Ives plc

For
Charles, Lucinda,
Theodore & Rose

Contents

List of Illustrations

LIST OF ILLUSTRATIONS

The Queen opening mail. © *David Secombe/Camera Press*
The Queen poses for a portrait. © *David Secombe/Camera Press*
A picture restorer for the Royal Collection. © *David Secombe/ Camera Press*
Students from Camberwell College of Art volunteer to help with conservation at Windsor Castle. © *The Royal Collection/ HM Queen Elizabeth II*
Working on part of the Riesener Jewel cabinet. © *The Royal Collection/HM Queen Elizabeth II*
Horses in stables designed by John Nash. © *David Secombe/ Camera Press*
The Forge, Royal Mews at Buckingham Palace. © *The Royal Collection/HM Queen Elizabeth II*
The lawns at Buckingham Palace. © *David Secombe/Camera Press*
A Palace florist placing tulips in the Tulip vase. © *The Royal Collection/HM Queen Elizabeth II*
Checking fire systems at Windsor Castle. © *The Royal Collection/ HM Queen Elizabeth II*
Sister Gillian Frampton in the surgery at Windsor. © *The Royal Collection/HM Queen Elizabeth II*
Checking the Honours before an Investiture. © *David Secombe/ Camera Press*
A Guardsman cleaning a bearskin. © *The Royal Collection/ HM Queen Elizabeth II*
Footmen waiting at the entrance to the Royal Mews. *Private Collection*
William Tallon and the late Reginald Wilcock. *Private Collection*
The Van Dyck painting of Charles I, being installed in the Pennethorne Gallery, Buckingham Palace. © *The Royal Collection/HM Queen Elizabeth II*

THE QUEEN'S HOUSEHOLD

THE LORD CHAMBERLAIN

THE PRIVATE SECRETARY'S OFFICE

- Private Secretary to The Queen
- Assistant Private Secretaries
- Special Assistant
- Policy & Research Officer
- Chief Clerk
- Senior Correspondence Officer
- Secretary to the Private Secretary
- **Press Office**
- Communications Secretary
- Press Secretary to The Queen
- Assistant Press Secretaries

THE PRIVY PURSE & TREASURER'S OFFICE

- Keeper of the Privy Purse & Treasurer to The Queen
- Deputy Keeper of the Privy Purse
- Assistant Keeper of the Privy Purse
- Chief Accountant & Paymaster
- Personnel & Pensions Manager
- Management Auditor
- Information Systems Manager
- Deputy Chief Accountant
- Senior Assistant Chief Accountant
- Accountants
- Clerks

THE LORD CHAMBERLAIN'S OFFICE

- Comptroller
- Assistant Comptroller
- Secretary
- Assistant Secretary
- State Invitations Assistant
- Registrar
- Clerks
- Permanent Lords in Waiting
- Lords in Waiting
- Gentlemen Ushers
- Extra Gentlemen Ushers
- Gentleman Usher to the Sword of State

THE MASTER OF THE HOUSEHOLD'S DEPARTMENT

- Master of the Household
- Deputy Master of the Household
- Assistants to the Master of the Household
- Chief Clerk
- Deputy to Assistant
- Senior Clerk
- Clerks
- Superintendent Windsor Castle
- Assistant to Superintendent
- Palace Steward
- Chief Housekeeper

THE ROYAL MEWS DEPARTMENT

- Crown Equerry
- Administrators
- Transport Officer
- Comptroller of Stores
- Chief Clerk
- Deputy Chief Clerk
- Office Keeper

THE ROYAL COLLECTION DEPARTMENT

- Director of Royal Collection & Surveyor of The Queen's Works of Art
- Surveyor of The Queen's Pictures
- Librarian, The Royal Library, Windsor Castle
- Deputy Surveyor of The Queen's Works of Art
- Curator of the Print Room
- Registrar
- Assistant to Registrar
- Assistants to Surveyor of The Queen's Pictures
- Inventory Assistant
- Clerks

Information Officers
—
Regional Information Officer
—
Website Editor

Royal Travel Office
Director of Royal Travel
—
Assistant Director
—
Operations Manager, The Queen's Helicopter Flight
—
Defence Services Secretary

The Royal Archives
Keeper
—
Assistant Keeper
—
Registrar

Property Section
Director of Property Services
—
Director of Finance
—
Financial Controller
—
Accountant, Property Services
—
Accountant
—
Fire Protection & Health & Safety Manager
—
Maintenance Manager, Buckingham Palace & Royal Mews
—
Maintenance Manager, St James's Palace & Kensington Palace
—
Maintenance Manager, Windsor Castle and Royal Mews, Hampton Court

Royal Travel Financial Section
Director of Finance, Royal Travel

Financial Controller, Royal Travel
—
Accountant

Royal Estates & Studs
Resident Factor, Balmoral
—
Land Agent, Sandringham
—
Manager, Royal Studs
—
Deputy Ranger, Windsor Great Park
—
Farm Manager, Windsor

Gentleman Usher of the Black Rod
—
Sergeants at Arms
—
Marshal of the Diplomatic Corps
—
Vice-Marshal
—
Constable & Governor of Windsor Castle
—
Keeper of the Jewel House, Tower of London
—
Master of The Queen's Music
—
Poet Laureate
—
Bargemaster
—
Keeper of the Swans
—
Superintendent of the State Apartments, St James's Palace

ASCOT OFFICE
Her Majesty's Representative at Ascot
—
Secretary

ECCLESIASTICAL HOUSEHOLD

CHAPELS ROYAL

MEDICAL HOUSEHOLD

CENTRAL CHANCERY OF THE ORDERS OF KNIGHTHOOD

THE HONOURABLE CORPS OF GENTLEMEN AT ARMS

THE QUEEN'S BODYGUARD OF THE YEOMAN OF THE GUARD

Acknowledgements

Any author who sets out to write about the royal household and the workings of Buckingham Palace, soon discovers a major problem. It is that serving members are forbidden to speak to the media without the strict supervision of the press office and that any interviews that are granted are equally controlled. Former staff are also aware of the penalties they may incur if they break confidentiality agreements. For these reasons, many of the stories and anecdotes I have included are unattributable. The ex-footmen, chefs, housemaids and officials I spoke to, did so on the understanding that I would respect their anonymity.

When I approached Buckingham Palace with the idea of this book, I was helped initially by the Queen's press secretary, Penny Russell-Smith, who put me in touch with those members of the household who were able to discuss their departments. Ailsa Anderson, assistant press secretary, arranged briefings with the Crown Equerry, Lt Col Seymour Gilbart-Denham, and his head coachman, Colin Henderson, in the Royal Mews, and also with Edward

Griffiths, Deputy Master of the Household. David Pogson made it possible for me to attend one of Her Majesty's investitures, when the Comptroller of the Lord Chamberlain's Office, Lt Col Sir Malcolm Ross and Lt Col Robert Cartwright, of Central Chancery, explained the procedure. Oliver Everett, Royal Librarian (since retired) and Pamela Clark, Registrar, guided me through the Royal Archives at Windsor Castle and made the Royal Household Lists of 1902 available.

Jayne Fincher was kind enough to explain some of the problems encountered by photographers who are commissioned to take pictures of the royal family.

I am also grateful to James Beaton GC, Michael Kelly, Shruti Patel, Jane Sharland, David Rankin-Hunt, Michael Parker, Philip Gosling, William Evans and Peter Gwynn-Jones CVO, Garter King of Arms, all of whom pointed me in the right direction and corrected me on a number of factual details. At HarperCollins, Richard Johnson has been enthusiastic, encouraging and perceptive in his critiques, while Janice Robertson has, as ever, wielded her editor's pencil with her usual penetrating skill and unending patience. My agent, Michael Shaw, at Curtis Brown, never fails to lift me just when I need it most and my thanks go to him and everyone else who has helped in the preparation of this book.

The material quoted in Chapter Thirteen – The Good Old Days – is used with 'the permission of Her Majesty Queen Elizabeth II'.

Introduction

In many ways the Queen is a model employer. She provides uniforms where necessary, all food and drink on the premises, accommodation at the best address in the country and membership of the most exclusive organization in the world. Her staff are able to invite friends to visit them at Buckingham Palace and Windsor Castle; they get a royal Christmas card and a present from their boss – which they choose themselves in March, the value depending on their length of service – and a twenty-four hour banking service courtesy of a cash machine installed at the end of 2001. They have a subsidized bar where a gin and tonic can be bought for £1, although this, once very popular, is now fast becoming irrelevant, and increasingly underused, because the younger staff prefer the bright lights of the London club scene.

What the Queen does not offer is high wages. Well, you can't have everything.

In many ways the royal household is a throwback to another century in spite of the efforts to update certain

1

practices. They may have computers, financial experts and productivity targets in some departments, but they also employ a Yeoman of the Gilt and Silver Pantry, a Painter and Limner, a Sculptor in Ordinary and Pages of the Chambers, Presence and Backstairs: over a hundred anachronistic job titles overall. How many households today employ a Maid to the Coffee Room or a Fender Mender? Yes, there is still a craftsman with this job description as a hundred fenders remain in the Palace even though open fires are but a memory of the distant past.

In the 21st century, the servants adhere to a protocol more rigid than the royals', their status depending on that of their master or mistress. The servants' hall reflects the precedence upstairs and social etiquette remains all important. The Palace Steward looks after the domestic running of Buckingham Palace, while the valets to the male members of the royal family confine themselves to the welfare of their masters. The housekeeper is by far the most important female servant (not to be confused with those ladies who are assistant private secretaries), and the Queen's three dressers and her personal maids enjoy an intimacy with their employer shared by no one else.

The Queen is kept informed of all that goes on – the latest gossip above and below stairs – by her Page and her senior dresser, and though she wouldn't dream of discussing her own family's troubles with them, she expects, and gets, full details of every morsel of scandal, at every level. A Master of the Household once reported to the Queen that he had had to discipline a young footman who had been found in the bedroom of a housemaid, only to be told that Her Majesty had known all about it for days. Her old nursemaid 'Bobo' McDonald, who was once the

Queen's eyes and ears, may have died some years ago, but her successors have ensured that the information network she started works just as well these days. And if the Queen hears something officially which she feels should have reached her earlier via one of her 'spies' her displeasure is made quite clear. But she does this in a subtle way. She doesn't rant and rave, preferring quiet sarcasm. At a lunch party for a dozen guests she noticed one of her press secretaries resting his elbows on the table. 'Are you feeling tired?' she asked. He got the message.

It was because so many of the younger staff were 'getting together' that the old rule, which had existed for 150 years, that married couples were not permitted to remain in royal service, was rescinded ten years ago. Nowadays, several married couples, including the Queen's Chauffeur, Joe Last, and his wife, Linda, head housemaid, serve at the Palace, with Her Majesty's blessing.

Wherever the Queen goes a large part of her staff travel with her. It's part of the attraction of the job; moving around the country from one royal residence to another. But protocol is still observed, the servants all using the back doors, while the members of the household, far superior beings, enter by the front door.

There is a marked difference in the way the Queen and Prince Philip treat their 'staff' as opposed to the senior members of the household. On occasion they can be breathtakingly – if decidedly onesidedly – informal with their personal domestic servants, chatting away in a manner which could easily persuade anyone listening that they were on an equal footing. (Prince Philip talks freely with his two valets about shooting – and about their private lives, but not his own.) But rarely will they let their hair down in front of, say, the Lord Chamberlain or the Keeper of the Privy Purse. With them it is always entirely formal. And they see no contradiction in being friendly and informal one moment and stultifyingly grand the next. As a former Page to the Queen remarked, 'You never know where you are with them. It's best to keep your side of the relationship as formal as possible. Anyway the friendliness only lasts as long as you are useful. They never let you forget you are just a servant. Even the Queen can occasionally be as patronizing as the rest of her family. And where else would you have someone like Prince Edward insisting that his private secretary never enters his room with his coat unbuttoned? It's built into them all.'

The Palace is a microcosm of any town or city, with the same problems, personalities and rivalries that exist anywhere. The difference is that here over three hundred individuals live and work in close proximity and the petty jealousies and arguments can quickly grow into major rows. Where else would you see two grown men fighting because one had been given a wardrobe slightly bigger than the other? It happened here. And where else would you find a young man in tears in the bedroom corridor on the third floor, because he had just found out that his boyfriend had been betraying him – with a girl? They have also had their share of tragedies in the household. A young housemaid took an overdose when she discovered her fiancé, a footman, was in love with someone else – another footman.

Nor is the intrigue confined to the domestic staff. When the Queen appointed her first communications secretary without informing her press secretary at the time, he was furious. (He had been deliberately kept in the dark until the decision had been made.) And when he was asked to vacate his sumptuous office to make way for the new man, he simply refused, causing a minor panic in the private secretary's corridor. Eventually a compromise was reached, but it's on such inconsequential matters of 'Palace Politics' that many people who work there spend much of their time and energy.

Several rules have existed since Queen Victoria's time. Staff are not permitted to keep pets on the premises, though this is one rule that is regularly broken with kittens and even the occasional hamster finding a home in a staff bedroom. But never dogs, that would mean immediate dismissal. The difficulty arises when the Court moves and the animals have to be smuggled into the next residence. The Queen is obviously aware of the ruling, and while, as an animal lover, she might be expected to be sympathetic, she has never been inclined to extend her own corgis' privileges to the pets of any of her servants.

There is no longer a Master of the Revels to organize Palace festivities, but Buckingham Palace remains a place of great entertainment, with most of the world's top stars appearing at some time or other, either as entertainers or as guests. The royal family loves show business (Prince Philip was responsible for bringing the Variety Club to Britain in the late 'forties) and enjoys the company of many leading actors and actresses, singers, dancers and musicians. Among those who are welcome on the guest list are Luciano Pavarotti, Darcy Bussell and Billy Connolly, who played John Brown to Judi Dench's Queen Victoria in the film *Mrs Brown*. Connolly and his wife, Pamela Stephenson, have become close friends of the Duke of York and are frequent guests at Sunninghill.

5

Nor is there nowadays a Rat Catcher-in-Ordinary, or a Royal Herb Strewer, who with six maids preceded the sovereign in the procession to Westminster Abbey for the coronation, scattering sweet-smelling herbs and flowers. But there is a Poet Laureate, whose salary of £27 a year hasn't been increased since Ben Jonson was the first to occupy this exalted post in 1617, and whose predecessors include Wordsworth, Tennyson and Sir John Betjeman.

The Queen is attended by two Gold Sticks in Waiting – one of whom is her daughter, the Princess Royal, a Silver Stick in Waiting, a Field Officer Brigade in Waiting, a Mistress of the Robes – who must be a duchess – and fourteen ladies-in-waiting. She has a Standard Bearer in Scotland – and an Hereditary Carver – a Wales Herald Extraordinary and a Lord Steward, who happens to be a duke from Northern Ireland.

Inside Buckingham Palace, there are separate dining rooms for members (those right at the top of the tree), senior officials and officials (the middle-ranking administrators and clerical staff) and others for staff (domestic servants, cooks, chauffeurs and cleaners). But ladies are no longer required to wear hats to lunch in the Officials' Dining Room, as they were at the start of the Queen's reign.

Twenty-six housemaids are employed at Buckingham Palace and one of them is detailed to carry in the 'Morning Tray' to any lady staying at the Palace overnight. An inflexible rule is that no male servant may enter the bedroom of a lady while she is there, so while a footman carries the tray from the kitchens to the bedroom door, he hands it over to his female colleague. Feminism and sexual equality have little place in the routine of royal domestic matters.

The maids are given instructions in how to wield a

vacuum cleaner, which must on no account be used before 8am, so as not to disturb any royal who might still be sleeping. The carpets must be vacuumed with the cleaner walking backwards, so no footprints remain. But staff are no longer required to avert their eyes when they meet a member of the royal family, as happened at the beginning of the Queen's reign, for at that time eye contact between servant and master or mistress was strictly forbidden.

And they have grown used to the sight of the Queen running down a corridor in the middle of the morning wearing a full-length ballgown and diamond tiara. They know she is late for a portrait sitting or photographic session. When Lucien Freud unveiled his controversial painting of Her Majesty, it was revealed that he had demanded, and been granted, no fewer than seventy-six sittings, so it is not an unusual occurrence for the Queen to dress up at odd hours of the day.

The temporary Equerry in Waiting, who spends three years on attachment to the Queen from his service unit, is given a comfortable flat in St James's Palace, plenty of worldwide first-class travel and a valet to clean and press his clothes. If he is extra lucky, as Tim Laurence was during his time as Equerry, he also gets to marry the boss's daughter and move up so many rungs of the social ladder he's almost out of sight.

A great deal of modernization within the royal household has taken place in recent years, and the man responsible is Sir Michael Peat, until very recently the Keeper of the Privy Purse, but now Prince Charles's new private secretary, who is a qualified accountant with a laser-sharp financial brain. He put the finances of the royal family on a firm footing but in doing so he upset many of the longest-serving of the Queen's servants. Where once a job at Buckingham Palace was considered to be for life, Peat made it clear that this no longer applies. The 'cradle to grave' philosophy which had existed for generations of domestic servants is a thing of the past. In his view, five-year contracts are more realistic. He also encouraged applicants from industry and commerce to join the staff. This meant a slight increase in salaries at the top end of the scale but did little for those languishing at the bottom. Wages are still pitifully low for footmen and housemaids, and even senior officials with over twenty years' service rarely see their salaries jump beyond £40,000 a year, although one or two at the very top end of the scale are on £55,000 a year.

The men and women who earn the most money are those employed by Prince Charles in his office at St James's Palace and his home at Highgrove. His staff are the highest paid of all royal employees, with his previous private secretary Stephen Lamport receiving some £150,000 a year and his press secretary earning over £70,000, while her opposite number across the road at Buckingham Palace, with the infinitely more prestigious title of press secretary to the Queen, languishes far behind. All of which makes for intense jealousy between the two households. Only one senior executive in the Queen's household has a salary in excess of £200,000 a year. But this does not come out of the Queen's pocket. He is on secondment from his normal job in industry – to which he will return – and has retained his salary, much to the annoyance and thinly disguised envy of the rest of the Palace staff. He is the Queen's communications secretary – on loan from British Airways – and is said to earn some £230,000 a year, while Penny

Russell-Smith, the first woman to hold the post of press secretary to Her Majesty, is paid less than a quarter of that sum.

Most of the senior members of the royal household – and this includes those who work in the households of the family, apart from that of the Queen – actually take a drop in salary for the privilege of working at the Palace. Former service officers are expected merely to supplement their pensions, while others have private means. The prime example was the late Lord Rupert Neville who was private secretary to the Duke of Edinburgh on a salary of £15,000 a year. When he died in 1982, his will revealed that he was worth over £30 million, so his pay would have been completely irrelevant anyway.

The royal family like to say that money is a vulgar subject, and they also plead poverty from time to time. What they really mean is that for any of their staff to raise the topic is painful. The old stories about the Queen sending Prince Charles, when he was a little boy, out into the garden at night to find a lost dog lead because 'leads cost a lot of money' are true. Frugality is a common trait throughout the whole family, and one of which they are all inordinately proud but with huge contradictions in the way they like to save money and the manner in which they live.

Prince Charles enjoys the most extravagant lifestyle with no expense spared for his own or his friends' entertainment. Yet he hates waste and checks the tiniest things at home, even down to the amount of milk used in his kitchen or the number of mushrooms picked from his garden. The Queen has the best of everything in what she wears, eats and drinks, but when she heard that one of her ladies-in-waiting had spent £5,000 on a holiday in Barbados, she was horrified, asking, 'But where did you get the money?' And while she is prepared to pay many thousands of pounds for dresses she wears on official business, most of which comes from the Treasury through the Foreign Office if it's for a visit to a foreign country, she hangs on to her personal clothes for years, preferring the comfort of familiar suits and skirts to the latest fashions. When her dresses become too old for her to wear, even around the house – and that's usually after twenty years or more – she hands them to her dressers. They can keep them if they want, or give them to someone else, with one provision: all the identifying labels must be removed and those receiving them must not reveal the source. A lady in Norfolk, who was given one of the dresses because she was the same size as the Queen, wasn't all that impressed, so she passed it on to her local jumble sale – where it failed to sell.

Expense accounts at the Palace are restricted to those for whom they are considered essential and are rigidly scrutinized. Any item not thought strictly necessary for the job in hand is struck off and the person concerned made aware of the reason. Company cars are never supplied. When Sir Robert (now Lord) Fellowes was the Queen's private secretary, he could be seen most mornings cycling to his office from his home in the Old Barracks at Kensington Palace, to the great amusement of his opposite number in the Cabinet Office, who is provided with a chauffeured limousine.

But if the perks executives outside expect as a normal part of their contract of employment do not form any part of royal service, this is not to say that the conditions of employment are not congenial; in most cases they are. The members eat in an elegant dining room where they are waited on by liveried footmen; afternoon tea is served in the Equerries Withdrawing Room on the ground floor where tradition demands that nobody sits down, even though there are sufficient chairs; and if one of the Queen's more senior aides is required to work extra late, attending a function or arriving back at the Palace close to midnight, he need not worry about going home. A room is always available with another footman to lay out his pyjamas, provide him with shaving kit and, in the morning, serve him with tea and biscuits and a morning newspaper.

It's all very grand, comfortable and unhurried, with an air of dignified gentility. Yet, in spite of the country club atmosphere, the faded grandeur and slightly shabby appearance, Buckingham Palace is an efficient and smoothly operating organization which bears favourable comparison with almost any commercial company and is certainly better run than most government departments. This is due to the dedication of everyone who works for the Queen. The loyalty of the staff is unequalled, and while the royal family take for granted their effectiveness and devotion, they too realize that in the twenty-first century – when such qualities are seen by many as absurdly outdated – they are fortunate to have the services of a unique body of men and women whose only purpose is to ensure the comfort of the royals.

The main divisions of the royal household are not all that different today from those of Tudor times, except that those running the three separate sections – Below Stairs, Above Stairs and Out of Doors (which they wouldn't dream of calling them now anyway) – are nowadays full-time professional administrators. These three, the Master of the Household, Comptroller of the Lord Chamberlain's

Office and the Crown Equerry, are still nominally under the control of the Lord Steward, the Lord Chamberlain and the Master of the Horse, but, while the Lord Chamberlain remains titular head of the whole of the royal household, the others hold purely ceremonial titles. Each has a role to play, but some occupy centre stage, while others are busy in the wings. In a palace of 642 rooms, there is plenty of work for all.

CHAPTER ONE

Getting Started

Buckingham Palace is a magnet for many young men and women. They know that a couple of years' service in the royal household can guarantee much more lucrative employment elsewhere, so are prepared to put up with the poor wages and rigid discipline to obtain a reference with the Palace crest.

One former applicant, who went on to become a footman to the Queen, explained how he got in. 'I went to Thanet Technical College, which has long been a breeding ground for Palace staff. As students we were first of all made to serve the Principal in the college's restaurant, and if he then thought we were suitable material he would suggest we were used as casual footman and under-butlers when there was a State Banquet. (See Chapter Three)

'You are told to go in through the side entrance in Buckingham Palace Road and taken straight up to the Livery Room on the first floor to be fitted out. This is a bit of a pantomime as some of the livery dates back to Queen Victoria's time, so you had to find one in reasonable condition and, of course, one which fitted you. A new set today would cost well over £2,000. The surprising thing is the weight. The gilt jacket alone weighs 28 lbs [12.7 kg], so you need to be fairly fit to keep going all evening.

'We were issued with little booklets containing our instructions for the evening: where we were supposed to stand, what our duties were and how to serve drinks and food. We were given a full briefing by the Palace Steward – the boss – and he reminded us that we were going to be in the presence of the Queen and her guests so we had to be on our best behaviour. Not that there was much chance of any of us doing anything stupid; we were too nervous for that. Most of the students were restricted to serving in the State Ball Room and were confined to one area. Everything was well organized and regimented. Most of the time all we had to do was watch the traffic lights which are situated at the side of the throne. When the lights came on you walked forward, placed a plate on the table and walked back. You waited until the lights changed and then repeated the exercise, removing the plates. You didn't have to take the plates out of the room, just place them on a side table and an under-butler carried them out.'

Apart from the £24 evening's wages, there were a couple of other perks for the impoverished students who had been chosen. 'Once we had dressed in our livery and been given our orders we were allowed to go to the staff room for a meal which was free, and then to the canteen, which is run by NAAFI, and permitted to buy a subsidized drink. We could have anything we wanted, spirits or a pint of bitter, which was rather strange really considering we were about to serve royalty.'

After several months of acting in this capacity and

becoming noticed as a potential full-time footman, this young student completed his college examinations and was invited to Buckingham Palace for an interview with the Assistant Master of the Household. 'It was obvious they had checked my family background and done all their homework, and after some personal questions I was tested on my knowledge of the royal family, the order of precedence and things like that. Were there any things I was not prepared to do? Did I like travelling? Did I get sea-sick? [This was in the days when there was still a Royal Yacht.] Then they brought in an existing footman and made us stand back to back to see if we matched. This is because when we rode on the royal carriages – at Ascot for instance – it would look odd if we were at different levels. The other thing about the carriages is that Royal Mews staff ride at the front controlling the horses but a footman sits on the left rear seat handling the brake. Next to him is a royal police officer, also in livery and always on the right. We had to sit well away from him so he could easily get at his gun which was normally on his left side. He also had a small microphone and earpiece to keep him in contact with his colleagues and he had to look young. If they had used one of the older policemen it would have looked odd.'

New recruits to the household are allocated a room on the top floor of the Palace. The Footmen's Floor is not very popular as the rooms are small and the dividing walls are thin. The Pages' Floor is much more stylish with fireplaces and antique furniture. The location also reflects the relative importance of the occupants. The Pages' Floor is at the front overlooking the 'Wedding Cake' (Queen Victoria's Memorial), while the footmen are relegated to the back and side, as are the under-butlers who work in the Silver and China Pantries and also in the cellars.

The Queen employs fourteen footmen, of whom only two work directly for her; the others have duties throughout the household and with other members of the royal family. A junior footman arriving at the Palace is given a three-month trial and during that period he does not get a new set of clothes. Instead, until he has proved himself, he makes do with outfits which have been worn before. The day livery is black tail coat, red and gold waistcoat and black trousers. Once the trial period is over, the Savile Row tailors, Gieves and Hawkes, who make many of the royal family's uniforms, arrive to take measurements and supply two sets of day livery to each man. He is also provided with everything else he needs, except underwear: shoes, socks, ties, trousers and shirts. For overseas tours, white tropical outfits are provided with footmen wearing red epaulettes and pages gold to distinguish them from their junior colleagues. Since *Britannia* was decommissioned in 1997 the special uniforms supplied when domestic staff sailed in the Royal Yacht are all stored in pristine condition in the Buckingham Palace livery rooms.

The first job a junior footman is given is to man the footmen's room above the staff dining room on the northeast side of the Palace. There, under the supervision of the Deputy Sergeant Footman, he waits to be told what his duties are for the day. At first he only carries out simple tasks such as setting the table for the household members' lunch, arranging the drinks tray in the Equerries Withdrawing Room or carrying food upstairs to the Queen's footmen so that they can serve her meals. Throughout the day, the junior footmen carry government boxes which arrive at the Privy Purse Entrance and have to be taken to one of the Private Secretaries' rooms. They are also used as messengers inside the Palace, carrying letters and documents.

Once the footman has gained a little experience and confidence, he might be employed at the King's Door – the entrance used by important visitors in the inner quadrangle – to welcome the Prime Minister for his regular Tuesday evening audience of the Queen.

'In Margaret Thatcher's day I would escort her to the private secretary's office where they would have a whisky and soda and a brief chat before the equerry showed her upstairs to Her Majesty's Audience Room.' And contrary to what most people believe, this occasion was not always the most formal. 'The Queen and Mrs Thatcher [as she then was] would often have a drink themselves.'

Although the hours for the domestic staff can still be long, there is now a system whereby everyone works to a rota, and if they work long hours one day they make up for it the next. 'The Sergeant Footman and his deputy arranged the rota and it usually meant one early morning shift followed by a normal day shift. Early morning duty started at 7.15 which meant a 6 o'clock call to get bathed, shaved and have something to eat in time to carry the Queen's breakfast up to her dining room. Her personal footman would lay the table but we carried the food into Her Majesty's dining room which is next door to her sitting room. There was a round table set up for breakfast and a sideboard in front of the window where we placed the food. But the Queen always made her own toast for breakfast, we didn't do any of that. Once the food had been laid out, they liked to be left on their own. They had a television and radio in the room and Her Majesty liked to listen to Radio 4 and watch television at the same time, with the sound switched off. Sometimes, the Queen would be on her own. If Prince Philip had an early start, he would have his breakfast alone in his room in order not to disturb her. The other times we had early duty was if there was a State Visit and the royal household were having breakfast at the Palace.

'If we were not on early duty, we started at 8 o'clock and worked through until we were relieved for lunch by a footman who had been given his lunch earlier. On some days when there was a lot going on and plenty of visitors, there might be three or four staff lunches. The usual finishing time on a normal working day was 6.30pm unless there was a reception or cocktail party. If that happened, you worked until it was all over which could be very late. I have known days when I started at 6 in the morning and finished at 2 o'clock the next morning. But if that happened, the Sergeant Footman made sure you got time off to make up for it.'

At Sandringham or Balmoral, hours could be even more irregular as the royal family like to start their sporting activities early in the morning, and with 'picnic' lunches in the field and dinner parties most evenings there isn't a lot of spare time.

In the old days it was common for some domestic servants to spend their entire working lives at the Palace without ever coming face to face with a member of the royal family. Both Queen Victoria and King Edward VII were said to have recognized fewer than half a dozen of their staff and to have spoken directly to only one or two. Today the Queen and Prince Philip make a point of seeing every member of staff, even if, for the majority, it's only when they receive their Christmas presents.

When a new footman is employed, he is eased into contact with the family by serving at a small lunch. It might just be laying plates or serving vegetables but it gets the Queen used to his face – and she likes familiar faces around her. It also helps the newcomer to control his nerves and to realize that royalty are not all that different when it comes to everyday matters.

There is a strict hierarchy among the staff at the Palace and fierce competition for the best posts. The Queen's former footman explained how he climbed the ladder. 'After two years as a footman – which was quite a short period really – I was quite relaxed around the royal family and I think they grew to like me. I heard there was a vacancy coming up for a Nursery Footman. Now this had nothing to do with looking after royal babies, it's just that the Nursery Floor – and it is still called that – is where the children had their rooms, even as adults. I knew this was a promotion because this was where you got really close to them, saw them in their pyjamas and so on and became a personal servant. It also meant coming out of the footmen's room. It wasn't an easier job; in fact the hours were longer and more irregular and you still had to help out at State Banquets and receptions. But it was a step up and that's what I was looking for.'

All the staff are told how to address various members of the royal family, particularly the children and grandchildren of the Queen. 'We were instructed that when they were very young we should call them by their Christian names, and we didn't have to bow or curtsy. But once they were eighteen, they had to be addressed as Your Royal

Highness, Sir or Ma'am, and they did rate a bow or curtsy first thing in the morning and last thing at night.'

There were two footmen to look after the needs of the Prince and Princess of Wales (before they moved to Kensington Palace), Princess Anne, Prince Andrew and Prince Edward. 'Our lives were governed by meals. At first we had to push trolleys from the kitchen up to the second floor, and do it separately for each one because, in spite of them living virtually next door to each other, they wouldn't eat together. They all insisted on having their breakfast, lunch, afternoon tea and dinner on their own, so we were providing up to sixteen different meals every day, and they all wanted to eat at the same time.' Eventually, after much lobbying, a kitchen was installed on the Nursery Floor which made life a lot easier for those looking after the royal children, especially at meal times.

Their tastes might have been different but the one thing they shared was that all their meals were of simple fare. 'The Prince and Princess of Wales insisted on healthy foods, fresh fruit in the morning with cereal and toast. They all liked salads at lunch time with light fish or chicken for dinner. Princess Anne never seemed to eat enough, coffee and sandwiches most of the time, and Prince Edward was the most formal. He liked everything laid out correctly for every meal, with the best china and cutlery. He was probably the most royal of any of them and never chatted with the staff. There was one occasion though when I actually felt sorry for him. It was when he was still going through his training course in the Royal Marines. I was carrying a tray into his room to lay up for lunch and didn't know he was there. As I walked through the sitting room I noticed him fast asleep on the sofa. His feet were propped over the edge and they were red raw and covered in blisters. He was completely exhausted. This was when he was getting a bad press and later when he resigned it was even worse, but I saw the state he was in and he never once complained.

'I got on very well with his sister, who often kept other people waiting while she was having a conversation with me. You knew exactly where you were with Princess Anne, she was always the same. She could be grumpy at times, but it didn't last long, she didn't sulk. I found it easy to calm her down if something had upset her.'

As the Nursery Footman, one became used to the curious formality of life at the Palace, even between members of the royal family. 'Prince Andrew would say to me "I want to see the Queen" (never my mother). "Would you find out if she is available?" So I would telephone Her Majesty's Page to see if she could see her son and, if it was convenient, tell him the time and he would go along. There was no question of him, or any of the children, just popping their heads around her door and saying "Hello". And they had to dress properly before they saw their parents, even if it was going to be only for a few minutes. At Balmoral and Sandringham it was a bit different. Things were much less formal there and they saw a lot of their mother and father throughout the day.'

The footman also became very friendly with Prince Andrew, especially when they were alone in the Palace in the evenings. 'We would often swop videos. In those days you couldn't buy BBC classics like *Only Fools and Horses* and *Fawlty Towers*, so he would get his private secretary to ring up the BBC and they would send copies over. Once he had seen them he would swop them for my action movies. He always loved that sort of film.'

The move from Nursery Footman to becoming the Queen's Footman was via a short tour with the Duke of Edinburgh. 'I had been on two tours with His Royal Highness and also acted as his footman when he was staying alone at Graigowan House on the Balmoral Estate. So he got to know me – he called me the "blond one" because of the colour of my hair and because at first he couldn't remember my name. Then the post of Queen's Footman became vacant and the Palace Steward came to me and said, "Her Majesty would like you to fill that role temporarily." The reason was that her permanent footman had had an accident so they needed someone to stand in for a month or two. I ended up working for her for an entire year, which was the best year of my life.'

It was the closest the footman came to the Queen and Prince Philip, seeing their private apartments at close quarters for the first time. 'The Queen's page and footman would sit in a vestibule up on the first floor, opposite Her Majesty's very large sitting room. When she wanted one of us she would ring a bell. Just inside the door was a big, French screen, so you couldn't see any part of the room unless you poked your head around it. The Queen's desk was at one side of the window which overlooked the garden leading on to Constitution Hill and in front of her desk was a smaller one for her private secretary. We were warned never to move anything from her desk which was absolutely covered in photographs, knick-knacks and paperwork. The maid used to clean it very carefully. There was also an old-fashioned teletext system near the desk. The room had a large fireplace with sofas on either side and again there were masses of photographs everywhere. It was very much a working room but also extremely comfortable.'

The footman and the page were never allowed into the Queen's bedroom while she was there but they did enter on other occasions. 'As the Queen's footman, I had to go in to remove the silver items so I could clean them. I did this in my little room opposite. The funny thing is that Her Majesty's bedroom is not nearly as large as people would imagine. But it did have an adjoining dressing room and bathroom which connected with Prince Philip's rooms.'

One of the early morning chores for the footman was to exercise the corgis and help the Queen with their meals. 'Nine times out of ten, if Her Majesty was there she would feed the dogs herself. I would bring everything out; it was always fresh food, lamb, rabbit or beef plus cabbage, gravy and potatoes. They never had anything out of a tin. I would collect it all from the kitchens, bring it upstairs on an old tin tray and then Her Majesty would mix each dog's meal with dog biscuits and gravy – she always knew the exact amount and the right mixture for each one. Then – and they always waited for her to give the word – they would eat. It was either in the corridor outside her sitting room, or, if she was expecting guests, in the corgis' bedroom behind the pages' vestibule. They were fed twice a day and exercised three times. Sometimes, if the Queen was free, she would come with us and there would be just Her Majesty, me and the corgis walking around the grounds, having a chat. She obviously couldn't manage it every day, but even if it was after an interval of a couple of months, she would remember the last time we had walked together and always ask about members of my family. She has a truly wonderful memory and never forgets a face or a name.'

It has been well documented that the Queen is a firm

believer in alternative medicine and never travels without her bag of homeopathic cures. What is not quite so well known is that she uses the same creams and ointments on her dogs, as her former footman explained. 'One weekend, we were at Windsor when she called for me. She told me that Smokey (one of the dogs) was limping and asked me to find some old pillow cases. When I came back she tore them up into strips, then told me to hold Smokey on his back. So there we were, the Queen and I, both down on our hands and knees. She rubbed some of her own cream in and then bandaged up the paw as if it was a sock on the end. She did it perfectly and within two or three days the paw had healed and Smokey was as good as new. She said if it was good enough for her, it was good enough for the dogs. It was a side of the Queen that not too many people see.'

Not all the footmen have shared Her Majesty's affection for her dogs. A story is told of how one of her staff 'spiked' a corgi's drinking water with neat gin. The Queen was not amused, and the footman found himself demoted to a job well down the pecking order.

Windsor Castle is a great favourite with all the Queen's staff, partly for its location and also because the servants' accommodation is far superior to that in most of the other royal residences. 'We always looked forward to the week-end. The Queen has two footmen, so we worked every other weekend. Just after lunch on Friday, we would leave from the Garden Entrance and take some of the Queen's luggage with us in the car. We had to make sure we were there before she arrived. She travelled in one of the plain, Royal Mews cars – not a limousine – with just one police back-up car carrying the blood box. [Whenever a member of the royal family travels, a supply of their blood type accompanies them.] Our rooms at Windsor were directly above the Queen's private apartments and they were spacious, beautifully furnished and containing the most amazing antiques.'

The structure of social difference within the household was maintained at all the Queen's homes, with her personal staff accorded a status slightly higher than their grade warranted. At Sandringham, the Queen's footman was given a better bedroom than any other footman, and he ate in the Palace Steward's dining room, which was not permitted at Buckingham Palace. Members of the royal household are quick to notice the slightest nuance that distinguishes one of their colleagues from the rest. 'Everyone could see that the Queen knew who I was. She would acknowledge everyone, but she spoke to me by name and they could all see there was a closer bond. Everyone calls Her Majesty Ma'am, but with her personal staff we would refer to her as Mum between ourselves, because we were that much closer.'

But the families of staff sometimes found it much more difficult to relax in royal company, as the former footman remembers: 'When we were at Windsor, we would often have football matches between different departments, even the female grooms in the Mews had their own team. There was one afternoon when my parents came down to watch and the Queen arrived after them and parked her Land-Rover right next to their car, before she walked over to the pitch. We got back to our car, and I was talking to my mother and father through the open window, when Her Majesty came over and said, "Hello, are these your parents? How do you do?" And my father froze. He couldn't open

25

his mouth, even to answer her questions. So I had to answer for him. It was an incredible situation, with the Queen behaving just like one of our neighbours, but my father couldn't cope with it. I've seen plenty of other people react the same way. They simply don't realize that she is an ordinary human being who has found herself in an extraordinary position. The Queen likes people to relax around her. If you are nervous, it makes her uneasy too.'

Prince Philip also prefers his staff to be relaxed, but this does not mean any degree of familiarity. He demands the highest standards and, being a man who is instantly decisive himself, will not tolerate prevarication. 'When I was being trained to accompany His Royal Highness on my first overseas tour, his page warned me that if he asked a question, he expected a straight answer. No hesitation, no mumbling. For example, if he said, "Is Prince Edward in the Palace?" You had to reply either, "Yes" or "No". You couldn't say, "I'll go and find out." That wasn't what he wanted. But I soon discovered that once he accepted you, you became part of his team. He even liked to socialize with his staff occasionally. On one tour we were using the Royal Yacht as a base in the Ivory Coast, Senegal and Mauritania. One afternoon he was sunbathing on the royal deck, which was out of bounds to the rest of us, and we were doing the same thing on the upper deck. I'd fallen asleep and when I woke up I found he had moved his sunbed to our deck and was lying next to me. He obviously wanted contact with someone. He was asleep, so I didn't disturb him but when he woke up we chatted about the trip and then he said, "I'll be down to have a drink with you later."'

There were various messes on the Royal Yacht: Petty

Officers, Engineers, Seamen (who were known as Yotties) and a special Royal Mess for the household. It is a tradition in the Royal Navy that whenever a guest is invited to a Mess, even a member of the royal family, he or she should knock before entering. On this occasion, the royal staff had become used to some of the Yotties knocking on the door and walking off. The former footman takes up the story. 'A couple of us were in the Mess having a few gin and tonics, when there was a knock at the door. Thinking it was one of the Yotties, I shouted "Piss off." A voice replied, "I won't piss off, I want a drink." When I opened the door, it was, of course, His Royal Highness. He pointed at me and said, "I know it was you. I can tell your voice. You can pay for the drinks." So I bought him a bottle of Double Diamond, which is a beer he particularly likes and which is brewed specially for him to this day.'

CHAPTER TWO

❧

The Master of the Household

It has been said that Buckingham Palace is divided into a series of mini-empires, each ruled by a dictator who jealously guards his own territory.

While it is certainly true that each of the six departments which make up the royal household: the Lord Chamberlain's Office, the Private Secretary's Office, the Keeper of the Privy Purse, the Royal Collection, the Royal Mews and the Master of the Household, like to think their own section is the most important, the largest by far, in terms of number of personnel, is the last mentioned: that of the Master of the Household. In Queen Victoria's reign there were nearly six hundred domestic servants working at the Palace. Today, that number has been more than halved, but even so, the department far outnumbers any of the other offices.

And whereas most other departments, with the possible exception of the Keeper of the Privy Purse, to whom they all have to turn for money, work in comparative isolation, the Master of the Household affects every other division. When the Queen holds an Investiture in the State Ballroom it is the Master's staff who prepare the rooms, while the Lord Chamberlain's Office has overall responsibility for the ceremonial aspect of the event. If the Director of the Royal Collection decides the Picture Gallery needs a few changes, he chooses which paintings should be hung, but porters from the Master's office do the manual work. When Sir Robin Janvrin, the Queen's private secretary, wants someone to carry a document to another part of the Palace, one of the footmen is summoned, again on the strength of the Master of the Household. And there is even a connection between this office and the Royal Mews. Some of the liveried staff who ride on the back of the State coaches when the Queen attends the State Opening of Parliament are not Mews servants but footmen normally employed in a variety of duties elsewhere.

During her fifty-year reign, the Queen has been served by seven Masters of the Household, the latest being Vice-Admiral Tom Blackburn. His immediate predecessor was a Major General, and indeed, all the Masters have been former senior officers in the Army or Royal Navy. So far, nobody from the junior service, the RAF, has been appointed.

There is a very good reason why service officers become Masters of the Household. They have spent their entire careers paying as a matter of course the attention to detail that is a prerequisite for anyone aspiring to a position with the Queen. Military and naval men know that the success of operations depends almost entirely on thorough advance planning. It is also of the utmost importance when preparing a royal function, be it a full-scale State Banquet, a garden party or a more modest luncheon party.

None of the seven Masters who have served the Queen

have liked the unofficial title they are given – usually by the media – that of 'hotel manager'. They seem to think it is a derogatory term which undermines the dignity of their ancient and prestigious post. But in effect, that is exactly what the job entails, albeit at the grandest 'hotel' in the world. For the Palace has some 642 rooms, including nineteen of the most magnificent State Apartments in existence.

The Master sits at the pinnacle of a pyramid with two deputies immediately below him. One is Permanent Equerry to the Queen and looks after the private domestic arrangements of the royal family, while the other has the awesome responsibility of supervising the work of the branches 'F', 'G' and 'H', standing for Food, General and Housekeeping; and also 'C' branch which covers craftsmen and is based at Windsor. In other words the running of the Palace.

The Food branch includes the management of all kitchen and food operations. Among those working there are chefs, sous chefs, pastry and vegetable chefs and kitchen porters as well as canteen and dining-room employees, storemen and office staff. In the kitchens themselves the royal chef, Lionel Mann, reigns, and he has recently found himself with new premises. A brand new kitchen has just been completed on the site of the old one but with only half the height. The old kitchen had been there since Victorian times and the ceiling was so high that it has been possible to create above it a new part of the new Queen's Gallery, without reducing the efficiency – or floor area – of the new kitchen.

Equipped with state-of-the-art combination ovens, the use of dry and wet heat, an air cooling system, stainless

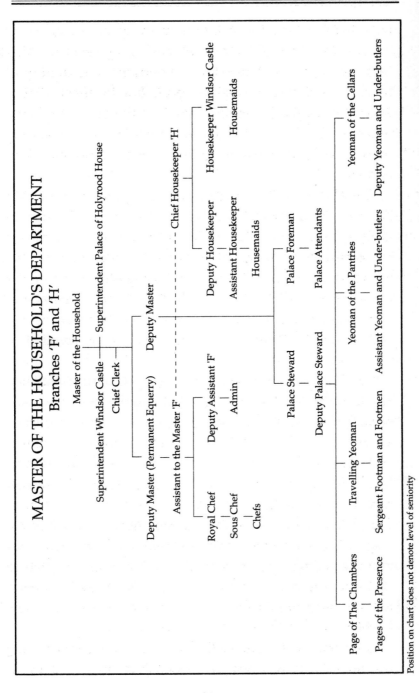

MASTER OF THE HOUSEHOLD'S DEPARTMENT
Branches 'F' and 'H'

Master of the Household

Superintendent Windsor Castle — Superintendent Palace of Holyrood House

Chief Clerk

Deputy Master

Deputy Master (Permanent Equerry)

Assistant to the Master 'F'

Royal Chef
Sous Chef
Chefs

Deputy Assistant 'F'
Admin

Chief Housekeeper 'H'

Deputy Housekeeper
Assistant Housekeeper
Housemaids

Housekeeper Windsor Castle
Housemaids

Palace Steward
Deputy Palace Steward

Palace Foreman
Palace Attendants

Page of The Chambers
Pages of the Presence

Travelling Yeoman
Sergeant Footman and Footmen

Yeoman of the Pantries
Assistant Yeoman and Under-butlers

Yeoman of the Cellars
Deputy Yeoman and Under-butlers

Position on chart does not denote level of seniority

31

steel counters for food production, it is a chef's dream. They even have dish washers, but only in the staff dining areas. All china, crystal and silver used for royal functions still has to be washed by hand. The Royal Collection advises the kitchens which valuable and fragile articles have to be specially handled as the caustic nature of certain modern detergents would be harmful.

At one time wooden sinks were used to prevent any chipping, but pantry sinks are no longer made entirely of wood. They have stainless steel surrounds and are lined with rubber, with the draining boards still made of wood. The ritual of washing the crystal glasses is rigidly adhered to and never varies. Once the glass has been thoroughly soaked and swished around in the hot water, it is rinsed in warm (never too hot) water to clean off all the suds. Finally, it is dried with a light cloth and then polished with a different glass cloth so that no finger marks or other blemishes remain. The cleaning of wine decanters is a difficult and delicate task, particularly when red wine has been decanted. Those responsible for washing up use lead pellets with an inch of water and shake the decanter for a few minutes to allow the mixture to do its work. Drying also needs careful handling as many of the decanters have narrow necks and wide bodies.

Particular attention is paid to the treatment of silver as it can easily be scratched or dented. So it is treated in a similar fashion to the crystal, washed gently in hot soapy water followed by rinsing and drying with linen cloths. Occasionally, an item might be damaged. In some cases it is taken to the royal jewellers to be repaired.

The General branch provides staff for what in a commercial hotel would be called the 'front of house': the footmen, under-butlers, pages, and Yeomen of the Glass and China, and Gilt and Silver Pantries. These two are among the most experienced servants in the royal household. Not only do they bear responsibility for the priceless collections in their charge, they are also knowledgeable experts in their fields, who can tell you the history of practically every piece of gold, silver, crystal and china the Queen owns. Guests at royal functions are often curious to know the history of the pieces used and on display, so table cards give details of the dinner services, tea plates, crystal glasses and silverware. For example, at a recent banquet the table decorations included ice pails by the early nineteenth-century silversmiths Paul Storr, Benjamin Smith and John Sharpe together with candelabra by the same craftsmen plus Philip Rundell and John Bridge. There were also two round plateaux mirrors by Philip Rundell and two square ones by Paul Storr. On the walls and sideboards were eight sconces, four with marine figures in high relief and four representing the judgement of Solomon, and four wine flagons dating to 1690 and 1828.

In the pantries below stairs at Buckingham Palace glass-doored cupboards store the priceless collection of china used for State Banquets, royal weddings and other functions. When they are brought out, the Yeoman of the China Pantry unlocks each cupboard in turn and, as he does so, marks the item removed in his record book. When the meal is over the process is repeated in reverse.

The table glass might be the set of English cut crystal in a fluted style that was made for the Queen's coronation in 1953 and is hand engraved with the cypher 'EIIR'. While the china might come from a Minton service made for Queen Victoria in 1876 with turquoise borders, panels of flowers and rich gilding around the central crown and the royal monogram 'VR'. Another service is called the 'De M. de Buffon' after the great French naturalist. Painted with birds and insects with cobalt and a gold border, it is dated 1770–89.

To many people arriving at Buckingham Palace for the first time it is the liveried staff who present the initial image of royalty. The footmen who man the Privy Purse Door (that's the one most official visitors use; it's on the right as you look at the Palace from the front) need to be smart, tactful and immaculately groomed, with a friendly, but not too familiar manner.

It is not all that difficult to get a job as a liveried member of staff at Buckingham Palace. The Master of the Household advertises in the catering industry trade papers and through the Palace website. Applications are kept on file, although there is no longer a lengthy waiting list. Nowadays the physical requirements are not as stringent as they were even ten years ago. Today they are able to accept most shapes and sizes, and the household is no longer driven 'by the size of the livery'.

Buckingham Palace is little different from any other branch of the hospitality industry in that there is an acute shortage of trained, skilled staff. But the monarchy still has a tremendous attraction for enough young people to enable the Palace to select the best applicants. They are better educated than they were, and whereas hotels and restaurants usually find their trainees from among sixteen- and seventeen-year-olds straight from school, the royal household manages to employ slightly older young men.

The most important qualification is attitude. As one of the household explained: 'Skills can be taught, but attitude is inborn. They must have a passion and great enthusiasm to serve the royal family.'

Once a man has been accepted – and passed a medical examination and vetting by security – he becomes the responsibility of the Travelling Yeoman, whose job not only involves what his title implies, looking after all the transport arrangements for the household, but also training new recruits and allocating them to their duties. The Palace has developed a programme, in conjunction with City and Guilds, leading to an NVQ (National Vocational Qualification) for Footmen, Valeting and Butlering. It is a three-year course undertaken while training 'on the job' under the care of one of the two senior footmen.

Buckingham Palace is the only official residence that maintains a full-time permanent staff. All the other homes are run on a 'property basis' rather than a full 'service basis', so only skeleton staffs are kept when the Queen is not in residence. When she moves, the Court moves with her, and the Travelling Yeoman has a special section to manage transport details for the staff.

There is a lot of travelling between residences throughout the year. Christmas and New Year at Sandringham, two months at Balmoral in the summer, odd weeks at Windsor for Easter Court, Royal Ascot and State Visits, and this is an attraction for many of the youngest members of the household. They like the idea of not remaining in one place too long.

Royal seasons are also important in the training programme. The long summer break – from August until October – is when the Queen entertains many guests in Scotland, and it is an ideal opportunity to introduce the young recruits to the ways of royal life.

A junior footman joining the Palace staff earns approximately £12,000 a year gross, or around £240 a week, after training, a substantial increase on the £7,000 he would have received ten years ago. But the number of footmen has been reduced slightly. There are now just fourteen and they are encouraged to live-in at the Palace. It is not obligatory, but it usually suits both employer and staff. The accommodation is not free. It is deemed to be a tax benefit so staff pay rent out of their salaries. Their rooms are considered to be private and respected as such. Even the Master of the Household – although he is entitled to do so – would not dream of entering without first seeking permission from the occupant.

The Palace provides plenty of opportunities for part-time casual employment. For a State Banquet, up to fifty extra footmen and under-butlers are required and the Master of the Household's department has a large pool from which to draw. Some are ex-footmen who welcome the chance to renew acquaintances, some come from the hotel industry and a few are friends of existing staff. There is never a problem in getting enough men and women. What can be a problem occasionally is the balancing of temperaments. It is a management issue that has challenged the diplomatic skills of Masters of the Household for generations. As one of them explained with commendable understatement: 'We do employ a number of "extroverts".'

Housekeeping comes under the jurisdiction of Miss Heather Colebrook, a woman of considerable experience in caring for large households, who lives 'on the job' in a beautiful apartment at the front of the Palace. She has charge of thirty-five housekeeping staff at Buckingham Palace with one deputy and one assistant housekeeper.

As with everything else in the royal household, house-keeping is conducted according to a rigid system. The maids start at 6.30 in the morning, with the major part of their work completed by mid-day. Some work straight shifts and others split shifts: several hours in the morning and others in the afternoon and evening, so that the whole day is covered. Linda Last, the wife of the Queen's chauffeur Joe, is head housemaid, in charge of a team of twenty-five maids who vacuum, dust and polish the Palace's 600-odd rooms. They are given instructions as to how each room should be cleaned, in which order and which particular items of furniture must be handled with special care. They are also given guidance on how to carry a tray when they are waiting on female members of the royal family and their guests, and their particular likes and dislikes. Several of the more experienced housemaids work exclusively in the royal apartments and, as in every other part of the household, there is an unofficial 'pecking order' among the maids which is reflected in the established career path from junior to senior level.

Few things are simple in the royal household, and this includes such mundane matters as replacing everyday items in the Palace. If the Queen's apartments need new curtains, carpets, sheets and pillow cases it's not just a case of someone going out and buying them. The process involves several different departments. Curtains and carpets come under the heading of 'G' (General) section, while the sheets and pillow cases are the responsibility of 'H' (Housekeeping). The cost of the replacements is worked out by the chief clerk to the Master of the Household, and the money comes from the office of the Keeper of the Privy Purse. Several suppliers think they can influence the Palace by offering little 'inducements' to the staff. It doesn't work, but that hasn't stopped some from pressing gifts such as miniature paintings, expensive carpets and valuable trinkets on royal servants. It is the butlers and senior footmen who are most often plied with these presents and a number of their apartments have been described as 'virtual treasure troves'. It never makes the slightest difference to the buying policy but, as one happy recipient explained: 'If it makes them feel better, what's the harm?'

In fact the housekeeping budget is strictly controlled and divided into two sections: operational and capital. If a major article of furniture, including curtains or carpets, needs to be replaced, it comes under capital expenditure and both the Master of the Household and the Keeper of the Privy Purse are consulted, with the Queen being kept informed. These are not part of the Housekeeper's responsibility. But if everyday items such as towels, blankets and linen have to be bought then the housekeeper is able to do so out of her own budget.

One unusual side of the housekeeper's responsibilities is the buying of Christmas presents on behalf of the Queen. The process starts in March when Mrs Colebrook circulates a form to every member of staff asking them what they would like Her Majesty to give them that year. There is a limit: gifts to the value of £28 for the newcomers, which is then increased according to length of service. Once the list has been completed, Mrs Colebrook does the buying and in December they all gather in the Bow Room at the Palace where the presentation takes place. Members come first, followed by senior officials and officials, with staff bringing up the rear. The entire business takes a whole morning and the organization is yet another tribute to the skills of the

Master of the Household's department. So far, no one has received the wrong present. But it is something of a pantomime, with the Queen and her staff all playing their parts. When they receive their gifts each expresses delight – and surprise – even though everyone knows the gift was chosen by the recipient nine months earlier. One or two of the longer-serving servants and officials use their Christmas allowance to build up collections of china and crystal. The record is held by an official with thirty-two years' service, who is able to have a single cup and saucer or dinner plate every year, and is still hoping to complete his collection before he retires.

Everyone who works at Buckingham Palace recognizes that this is the pinnacle. You cannot get any higher, even if the money is not necessarily as good as elsewhere. To work for the Queen is the ultimate ambition for many people, and some of those older retainers who have spent a lifetime in royal service are perfectly happy with their lot. It's what they hoped for when they started, in some cases, thirty or forty years ago, and they have realized their ambition, and have a sense of achievement.

The Palace Steward, who supervises all the liveried staff, has reached a level comparable with the House Manager of any five-star hotel. If he wished, he could easily leave and join a catering establishment at home or abroad, and double his salary overnight. But his loyalty, and that of his colleagues, has never been called into question. No Palace Steward has ever left the Palace to take up better paid employment, even though there have been plenty of opportunities. They have all remained faithful to Her Majesty until they retired. And she, in turn, appreciates this loyalty and realizes how fortunate the royal family is to have the services of so many experienced and devoted servants.

When preparations are being made for a State Banquet, the Queen will arrange to view the room as it is decorated and the table laid. If a lampshade is crooked or a lightbulb missing, she will notice straight away and draw attention to the fault. In this way, she lets her staff know she is not taking them or their efforts for granted. There is only one standard – perfection – and she has a reputation for not missing a thing.

CHAPTER THREE

❦

Invitation to the Palace

The preparations for a State Banquet at Buckingham Palace are programmed down to the tiniest detail, and everyone involved, including footmen and cloakroom attendants, is given a full briefing and written instructions by the Master of the Household's department.

Preparations begin early on the morning of the banquet when the gold cutlery (it really is solid gold) and silver gilt plates are brought out of storage and thoroughly polished, as is the table, which runs to 160 feet (48 metres) when measured around its horseshoe shape and takes six men from 'G' department three hours to assemble its seven leaves. It is so wide that footmen with large dusters on their stockinged feet shuffle over it to maintain its sheen. Everyone knows the stories about the Palace Steward checking the distance between place settings with a ruler – and it's true, because if he didn't, they might get to the end of the table and find themselves a place short. Altogether they use 1,350 knives, forks and spoons and 850 crystal glasses (five for each place setting). The tables and corners of the room are decorated with seasonal flowers. In summer they might be lilies, pinks, alstromeria, gerberas, freesias, roses and sweet peas.

Banquets always begin at 8.30pm with the first of the 170 guests arriving an hour earlier. Five footmen are on duty at the Grand Entrance to welcome guests, with three more to open car doors and an extra footman if a guest is using a wheelchair and needs assistance. Another footman takes up a position on the first floor at the door leading from the Picture Gallery into the Music Room and remains there until required later in the Ball Room. Yet another has to stand behind the Lord Steward in the Music Room at 8 o'clock to take Presentation Cards from those guests who have been selected for presentation to the Queen or Prince Philip and are now directed towards the White Drawing Room. Meanwhile two of the footman's colleagues assume positions in the Blue Drawing Room (said to be the most beautiful of the Palace's State Rooms) to direct guests to the Ball Room. Another is stationed at the entrance to the Silk Tapestry Room, and the briefing note adds that all these footmen should make sure they know the location of every cloakroom and toilet, while specially selected house-maids – usually the more mature ladies – are on duty near the ladies' cloakrooms with safety pins and spare pairs of tights.

Royal guests always use the Garden Entrance on the north-west Constitution Hill side of the Palace, and two senior footmen are ordered to be on duty there at 7.45pm, while the Duke of Edinburgh's Page waits at the top of the Queen's private lift to conduct them to the Royal Closet where they have their own pre-dinner drinks.

Although the guests are not expected before 7.30 a

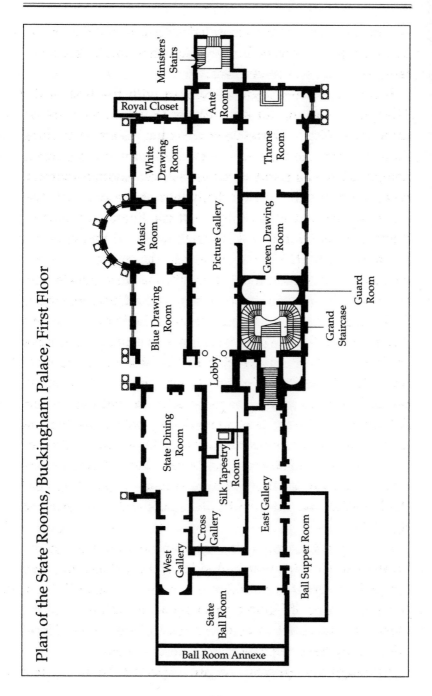

Plan of the State Rooms, Buckingham Palace, First Floor

number of footmen and under-butlers are on duty in the Throne Room at 7 o'clock to prepare drinks with three men delegated to dispensing them when the first guests arrive. Nine footmen report to the Throne Room at 7.30 to hand pre-banquet drinks into the Picture Gallery. Two hand around cigarettes. At 7.45 the Officer of the Guard arrives in the Grand Hall and is escorted upstairs to the Blue Drawing Room via the Silk Tapestry Room. The footmen are resplendent in scarlet livery decorated with gold braid, scarlet plush knee breeches, pink stockings and black buckle shoes; while senior staff wear black livery with gold braid, fine white wool cloth breeches and black pumps.

For the meal itself, those serving are split up into nineteen groups, number one being the royal service. There are four men to each service: one page, one footman, one under-butler and one page on wine. Services ten and eleven are considered important for the staff as these are directly opposite the royal service and in the Queen's eyeline. Pages waiting the banquet report to the Palace Steward in the Ballroom at 7.45, those on wine service to the Yeoman of the Cellars at 7.15. Footmen waiting the banquet have to be on duty in the Ball Supper Room at 7.45 and under-butlers in the Ball Room Annexe at the same time. The pages who pour the wine also ladle the soup while the under-butlers hand out croutons. Pages on food duty are responsible for taking petit fours around after handing the sweet dish.

Pages, assisted by footmen, serve each course; wine butlers serve gravy, under-butlers serve potatoes and bring in all food from the Annexe. Under-butlers remove food dishes and cutlery to the Cross Gallery. Footmen enter with clean gilt plates and leave all dirty plates (including china) at the East Gallery Door of the Ball Supper Room. Wine butlers bring in wine from the Ball Supper Room. Pantry assistants take away dirty dishes and cutlery through the East Gallery, Silk Tapestry Room and Service Lift. The Plate Pantry Yeoman instructs an under-butler to warn the Palace Steward that the food is up. The Palace Steward instructs the Yeoman for plates to enter by the green light signal in the Ball Supper Room. The Palace Steward instructs the Yeoman for food to enter by the green light signal in the Ball Room Annexe. All this is controlled by a system of 'traffic lights' in the State Ball Room that is operated not, as supposed, by the Queen, but by the Palace Steward. As the written service arrangement states: 'On the Amber light signal in the Ball Room plates are brought forward and on the Green light plates are placed in front of guests.'

The procedure is repeated for the food, with a Green light only for soup. Those taking part in serving the banquet are instructed to 'BE SURE TO WATCH THESE LIGHTS'. Six more instructions follow, including the fact that port must be handed clockwise and that wine pages are to report to the Yeoman of the Royal Cellars in the State Dining Room after the port has been handed. Menu booklets and gilt cruets are to be left on the table. These booklets are invariably taken away by the guests as souvenirs and even one or two cruets have been found missing. When dessert has been handed, the Palace Steward makes sure all pages and footmen leave the Banqueting Room and go to the State Dining Room or Ball Supper Room. Strict silence must be kept in the entire area outside the Ball Room whilst Her Majesty and the visiting Head of State are speaking.

A State Banquet is something like the well-known adage of a duck on water – all is calm above while underneath

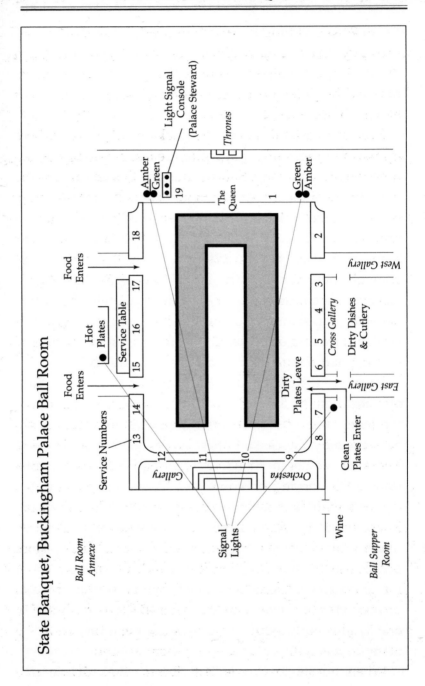

State Banquet, Buckingham Palace Ball Room

the duck is paddling like mad. In the Ball Room, the footmen are the very embodiment of serenity while beyond the serving doors all is a frantic rush that seems the epitome of panic, but it isn't because everyone knows exactly what he has to do.

Even in an establishment like Buckingham Palace, where events are programmed down to the last detail, things can occasionally go wrong. Shortly after the Queen came to the throne, one of the guests at a State Banquet was the actress Beatrice Lillie (who in real life was Lady Peel), and an unfortunate footman accidentally spilled soup over her brand new Paris fashion evening gown. Before he could apologize, she came up with what has gone down in Palace legend as the best one-liner ever heard: 'I will thank you never to darken my Dior again.' He managed to keep a straight face and she carried on throughout the meal as if nothing had happened.

Pages are instructed when they are to return to the Banqueting room to draw chairs back, but footmen remain in the State Dining Room or Ball Supper Room. Coffee will be served by pages and footmen in the White Drawing Room, Music Room, Blue Drawing Room and State Dining Room. The serving of coffee and liqueurs is equally disciplined with four teams to serve in the White Drawing Room and Music Room from the Throne Room, while three under-butlers act as back-ups with coffee cups. More people use the Blue Drawing Room and State Dining Room for coffee so six teams are on duty with a further three to provide the cups. Five men look after the liqueurs, but only one is allowed to pour; the others carry the trays into the State Rooms with three handing them around.

When guests leave the Ball Room, they divide into

groups, some going into the State Dining Room and the Blue Drawing Room and others to the White Drawing Room and Music Room. Five more footmen hand around cigars and cigarettes. Twenty-three of those who have waited at table during the banquet are delegated to 'Replenish Glasses'.

During the banquet, the orchestra of one of the Guards Regiments has been playing in the gallery, and after the main part of the evening the Director of Music is provided with refreshments in the Household Breakfast Room at 10pm, attended by a single footman. The Officer of the Yeomen of the Guard, who have also been on duty, is given his dinner at the same time. The Yeomen have theirs later. Meanwhile seven footmen in State Livery report to the Grand Entrance to 'See Out' the guests while two seniors wait at the Garden Entrance to assist the royal guests into their cars.

The visiting Head of State always stays in the Belgian Suite on the ground floor of the Palace. He is accompanied to his rooms by the Duke of Edinburgh, and two footmen sit up all night outside his rooms in case they are needed. A further two are on the same duty in the Principal Corridor, where any guests accompanying the State Visitor have suites.

Back in the reign of Queen Victoria it was the custom – it still occasionally is – for certain Heads of State to bring their own personal servants to attend to all intimate requirements, particularly regarding meals. When the Shah of Persia was staying in the Belgian Suite in 1873, one of his servants used to lie across the doorway to his bedroom every night to make sure no one entered. He wasn't supposed to sleep but one night the Shah woke in the early hours to find the man snoring. In his anger, he ordered another of his guards to beat the recalcitrant servant. Apparently the guard was a little too enthusiastic and the poor man was killed. Then, to avoid a scandal, his body is supposed to have been buried secretly in a far corner of the Buckingham Palace gardens near Hyde Park Corner. True or false? It makes a good story and is told and retold – and perhaps embellished – with each generation. It was this same Shah who was highly amused at the sight of his first indoor lavatory. What was then regarded as modern plumbing had apparently not reached his realm and it was his practice to relieve himself on the floor of whatever room in which he happened to find himself, expecting one of his retinue to clear up after him. He saw no reason to stop this practice at Buckingham Palace and it is a tribute to the imperturbability of the royal household of the day that they didn't turn a hair at this unconventional behaviour.

As the nation's hostess the Queen is the recipient of a multitude of 'thank-you' letters. After a diplomatic reception, a private audience or a State Banquet, she might receive several hundred. Her guests often telephone the private secretary's office to ask if it is in order to write and, if so, how should the letters be addressed. They are all told the same thing. She prefers the letters to be addressed to her personally, and not to her private secretary, and she reads every one. If she is a guest at someone's house, she will always write personally to thank them and she appreciates the same gesture.

When Tony Blair writes to her, whether it is officially as Prime Minister or in a personal capacity after a private dinner party, the letters always begin and end (as should those from anyone else) in the same way: 'Madam, with my humble duty' then the text followed by 'I am, Madam, Your Majesty's most humble and obedient servant.' Letters from members of the Government are hand delivered and those intended for the Queen personally have the writer's initials on the lower right-hand corner of the envelope.

The ladies who handle the Queen's mail have a private 'Rogues Gallery' of amusing letters that have followed a State Banquet. Plenty ask for a particular recipe, which they receive by return, while some ask to borrow the Queen's military orchestra. This is an easy one as the army encourages its musicians to take on work outside and there is a standard rate for private parties. They will provide anything from a trio to a full-size 'Big Band' with all the trimmings at a cost of some £3,000 for an evening just as the Royal Marines did when there was a Royal Yacht, and that too was with the knowledge and consent of the service authorities. Perhaps the oddest request the Palace has received though was from a gentleman who claimed his dinner jacket had been ruined by a fellow guest's cigarette. He wanted to know if Her Majesty was going to pay for a new outfit. He received a polite brush-off in reply.

CHAPTER FOUR

∽

Behind the Green Baize Door

The late Diana, Princess of Wales was the most popular of royal employers and occasionally also the most disliked and feared. She could be generous to a fault, friendly to the point of familiarity, then suddenly change into the most imperious and demanding prima donna. Her staff rarely knew where they were with her from one day to the next. She inspired devotion perhaps only matched in the royal household by the redoubtable 'Bobo' McDonald, the Queen's nursemaid for over sixty years, who worshipped Her Majesty and could never see a fault in her. Similarly, Diana had a couple of servants, her butler, Paul Burrell, being the one most widely recognized, who simply adored her and who put up with her tantrums because they felt her other qualities outweighed the occasional nastiness.

The relationship between the royal family and their servants is not easy to define. You do not get the easy familiarity that exists in many aristocratic families between employer and old retainer, for the royals appear to be reluctant to ever allow anyone too close. It is a fear allied to suspicion. 'Bobo' was the exception, but the Queen's dressers, who are the personal servants closest to her, who see her in the most intimate circumstances, are not held in anything like the same regard. Nor is either of her two pages or her housemaid who brings the morning tray and runs her bath. The Queen knows that if any of them were to leave, a replacement would be found within the hour, so a closeness is never allowed to develop.

Nowadays servants no longer remain in their posts for life. Some leave for better jobs elsewhere or, because they cannot get on with their present member of the royal family, ask to be transferred. Or perhaps a particular royal has demanded that they should be removed. The most famous occasion when a royal retainer was taken on by another member of the family was at the time of the Abdication. Crisp, King Edward VIII's valet and most valued personal servant, refused pointblank to accompany his master into exile and he was quickly offered a job, which he accepted, by the new sovereign, King George VI.

Usually, the only time there is a major, wholesale change is when a member of the royal family dies. When Prince Henry, Duke of Gloucester, died in 1974, his entire staff were dispersed to work in other departments of the household, and the death of Diana, Princess of Wales, in 1997, caused a major upheaval among her staff. Diana's apartment in Kensington Palace has been emptied of all her possessions and everything associated with her. Some of those who looked after her moved to other households within the royal family, others to jobs outside.

Anne Beckwith-Smith, Diana's closest companion and personal secretary for fifteen years, is now working for the Arts Council based at the Tate Gallery. Mervyn Wycherley, who was the Waleses' head chef until a year before she died, has found a new and successful career, running a profitable business catering for many of the most exclusive corporate functions in the capital, including several for the royal family. Princess Margaret's son, Viscount Linley, is among those who use his services for a special dinner party. His successor at Kensington Palace, Darren McGrady, who was famous for his bread-and-butter pudding, has also landed on his feet. He now cooks for a Texas oil millionaire in Dallas where he earns over $75,000 a year. Diana's private secretary, Michael Gibbins, returned to the world of high finance as a director of Singer & Friedlander, and is also earning far more than he was paid in royal service.

Several of the Princess's office staff joined the Memorial Fund – her former personal secretary, Jacqueline Allen, in public relations and another colleague, Jane Harris, in administration. Jo Greenstead, who handled much of Diana's correspondence, was recruited to provide support for future grant applications.

The highest profile member of Diana's staff was her butler, Paul Burrell, whom she described as 'my rock'. In the days following Diana's death, Paul took control of her private affairs, sorting out her wardrobe, safeguarding her jewellery and later travelling to the USA to appear at society functions connected with her charities. Paul then became Head of Fundraising for the Diana, Princess of Wales Memorial Fund, though he did not get the job he wanted, chief executive of the entire operation, a post that carried an annual salary of £75,000. After a disagreement with the people who run the Fund he left and published a coffee-table book on etiquette which was an immediate best-seller in Britain and the United States. He also found an agent to manage his affairs which includes bookings on the lucrative US lecture circuit. But he had to give up his elegant 'Grace and Favour' apartment in Kensington Palace, so his wife – who was employed as a maid in the household – and family now live in Cheshire, where he has recently opened his own flower shop. In January 2002 Burrell and another royal servant, Harold Brown then working for Princess Margaret, were charged with stealing several hundred items belonging to Diana and at the time of writing were awaiting trial later that year.

Paul's assistant at Kensington Palace, under-butler, Craig Weller, returned to work for the Prince of Wales at St James's Palace while Diana's dresser, Angela Benjamin, joined the late Queen Mother's staff at Clarence House.

One of the longest serving of Diana's domestic staff was Lili Piccio, the housekeeper. When she found herself out of a job she was snapped up by Diana's neighbours at Kensington Palace, the Duke and Duchess of Kent. As a parting gift, she asked Paul Burrell if she could have a signed picture of the Princess. When she was told they had all gone, she asked Paul to sign one with his own name instead. Two other domestics, Filomena Ferreira and Maria Silva, were found positions in the royal household, where there are often vacancies for housemaids. Diana's former staff still keep in touch with one another and meet once a year to remember their late boss.

The pecking order within the royal household at Buckingham Palace, is carried over into the relationship between the households of the other members of the family. When Prince Charles and Princess Diana first lived at Kensington Palace, their staff enjoyed friendly relations with most of their neighbours, as long as the others realized that those who worked for the Waleses were superior to anyone else in the royal compound. The exception were those servants who were employed by Prince and Princess Michael of Kent. As Charles and Diana never socialized with Prince Michael and his wife, they let it be known that they would prefer their staff to keep a distance too. They did not want any loose gossip being bandied around. There was a lot of social intercourse with the staff of Princess Margaret, who got on extremely well with both Charles and Diana in those early days. But when Charles moved out of Kensington Palace and his wife lived there alone, she was cut off from all contact with Princess Margaret and there was a certain amount of frost in the relations between their respective servants. However Princess Margaret remained on the best of terms with her nephew Charles (on her death, he spoke movingly about his beloved 'Darling Aunt'), and they never ever disagreed, so their servants remained friendly also. A mark of the late Princess Margaret's loyalty to her staff was displayed when, on the death of Princess Diana, she immediately offered butler Harold Brown a job in her household, and she kept him on even after he was charged with the theft of some of Diana's belongings.

Princess Anne's staff tend to stay at her country home, Gatcombe Park, in Gloucestershire, so they do not have many opportunities to meet their colleagues, apart from those who travel down to Highgrove with the Prince of Wales, while those who work for the Gloucesters and the senior branch of the Kent family at Kensington Palace rarely meet any of their neighbours. They are not forbidden to do so, but they recognize that if their principals don't mix, it would not be suitable for them to establish close friendships. The servants who feel most left out are those working for Prince Edward, Earl of Wessex, at his home, Bagshot Park. He is easily the most status-conscious royal employer and there is rarely any relaxing informality. Unlike his brother, Prince Charles, Prince Edward would not dream of taking all his staff out for a meal, and his servants do not expect such generous and spontaneous gestures.

Apart from working directly for the Queen, which is the ultimate in royal terms, the most popular employer is far and away the Prince of Wales. All the domestic staff – and many of the officials – prefer to work for him. One of the reasons is that he pays better, the other is that his household is run with more style than those of his siblings or cousins. True, he has more money than all the others put together, so he can well afford the extra wages, but the working conditions are a vast improvement over those at other royal residences.

A former chef explained what happened before he moved from the Queen's household to that of the Prince of Wales. 'As a single man, at first I was given a room on one of the servants' floors at Buckingham Palace. There are different floors for different grades: pages' floor, footmen's floor. But as a chef I was regarded as a professional, a cut above the footmen, so I was allocated a room on the pages' floor. It was a very comfortable bedsitting-room equipped with large Victorian furniture of which there is a huge store in the Palace. There was also quite a lot of petty jealousy among the staff, so if one of us had a better room than the others thought we should have there would be a huge row. Everyone knew where they stood in the pecking order and woe betide anyone who moved too quickly out of his place. We also had a network which told us who was going to move or retire, so when we knew that a better room was becoming vacant we would all try to be first in the queue to get it.' None of the staff bedrooms at Buckingham Palace has its own bathroom; they all have to be shared. Two footmen apparently took this quite literally when they were found sharing a bath in 1995. They claimed they were doing it to save money – as directed by the Keeper of the Privy Purse who had ordered stringent household economies. They were allowed to keep their jobs.

Much of the social life for those who work for the Master of the Household takes place on the footmen's floor. They hold what they call 'Corridor Parties' when someone will find out who's staying in that night and tell them to bring a bottle or two. Music is provided by the one who has the best collection of records and no one objects if the festivities go on until the early hours. Sometimes, when he was younger and lived in the Palace, Prince Andrew would come up from his rooms on the second floor and join in. He wasn't expected to bring a bottle, but he did sometimes provide a little music.

It isn't only in the allocation of rooms that the rigid order is maintained. 'We chefs were thought of as being higher up the ladder than the ordinary liveried servants so we were allowed to eat in the stewards' room, which was one up from the servants' hall, but one below the officials' dining room.' There was one occasion when the situation became ludicrous. 'The officials' dining room was being decorated and the senior officials, who had their own room, wouldn't hear of their slightly more junior colleagues eating with them. So they had to suffer the indignity of moving down a peg to eat with us in the stewards' room. But they refused to join us at the same time; separate lunch and dinner times had to be scheduled. One day, even this could not be arranged and we had to all eat together. The officials demanded – and obtained – permission to erect a screen down the middle of the room so they wouldn't have to see us.'

Another peculiarity of the pecking order was the way in which senior servants would not mix socially with the lower orders when they were off duty. At one point in the 1980s the Queen's butler warned his assistant that he had been seen having a drink with a junior footman. 'Remember your position,' he was told, 'and do not lower the dignity of your privileged post within the royal household.' The assistant never again made the same mistake.

Rivalries between members of the royal family are reflected by their respective staffs. The Prince of Wales is known not to care too much for Princess Michael of Kent, and as we have seen when he lived at Kensington Palace he discouraged his servants from having anything to do with the Michaels' staff. The Gloucesters, who are above the Kents in the order of precedence, also do not socialize with Prince and Princess Michael, nor do their staff, but they do mix with the senior branch of the Kent family, the Duke and Duchess. The footmen, chauffeurs and cooks all take their cues from their royal bosses. If the principals aren't friends neither are their staff.

And the chauffeurs make sure the order of precedence is maintained when the royals are leaving for the same function, such as the annual visit to the Chelsea Flower Show. It is always the Prince of Wales first, followed by the Duke and Duchess of Gloucester, the Duke and Duchess of Kent, with Prince and Princess Michael bringing up the rear. Prince Michael doesn't appear to worry too much about his lowly position in the royal rankings, but Princess Michael has been known to chafe at the apparent discrimination.

Many of the domestic staff at Buckingham Palace are not assertively heterosexual. Indeed in the early days of the twentieth century there was a policy of recruiting only homosexual footmen. The reasons were twofold: they were unlikely to marry and leave, and also there was little risk of their getting any of the housemaids 'into trouble'. The policy has changed but the royal family still has a relaxed attitude towards homosexual men, although not towards women of a similar persuasion. The Queen now allows her servants to bring partners of the same sex to the annual Christmas staff dance, but she does not care to see them dancing together. Married couples are now permitted to remain in royal service, but until very recently, if a domestic servant married another, one would have to leave. This applied to even the most long-serving and valued members of staff. A former Palace Steward, Cyril Dickman, married a housemaid. She was forced to leave.

Even today some new recruits turn up for work expecting to meet the Queen on their first day and to be working for her directly. It doesn't happen that way. As the former chef told me, 'When I was interviewed for the job, it was by an official from "F" branch. I didn't even see the Head Chef; as far as the rest of us were concerned he lived on another planet. And when I started, he didn't even know I was part of his team. I was quickly told that as there were over three hundred people working at the Palace, there was no chance I would be cooking for the Queen or any other royal for at least three years. The majority of staff at the Palace are employed looking after other staff. In fact, it wasn't until I had been working at the Palace for five years that I even saw a member of the royal family, apart from when we went upstairs to receive our Christmas presents.'

He went on to explain how cosseted life is, even for those who work below stairs. 'We were thoroughly spoilt. Our rooms were cleaned every day by a maid, she made the bed and changed the linen and provided fresh towels. The laundry was collected once a week, free of charge, and we could buy a large gin and tonic for about £1. We were allowed to invite friends into the Palace as long as we signed them in and out, and they couldn't stay after midnight. But a certain amount of surreptitious smuggling went on, especially at weekends.'

New boys experience a certain amount of 'dormitory ragging'. One young footman, who went on to become a valued member of the household, arrived at the Palace and on his first night his colleagues made him an 'apple-pie' bed, folding the sheets up to half their regular size. Next morning they found him sleeping with his knees tucked under his chin, the bedclothes still as they had left them the night before. When they asked him why he hadn't remade the bed, he replied, 'I thought that was the way they were supposed to be and the household was trying to save money on the sheets, so I thought I'd better leave things as they were.'

Another footman found himself regularly recruited by the Queen to perform an unusual task at Balmoral. 'In the late afternoon, it was quite common to see Her Majesty call for a butterfly net so she could catch the bats which infest the upper reaches of the castle. She would catch them in the net, hand them to me and tell me to let them go outside. She was very strict about them not being harmed.

Of course, the next day, they would all come back again and we would go through the same routine. I think she enjoyed it.'

It was also at Balmoral that a junior footman found to his cost that one should never expect the royals to do anything for themselves. The family planned a barbecue one afternoon and the footman laid out all the necessary equipment and food and then, as required, retired from the scene so that Prince Philip could take over and pretend that he had made all the preparations. It was one of those occasions when royalty likes to believe it is roughing it. Unfortunately, one vital ingredient was missing. The poor footman had forgotten to bring a box of matches. No one else in the royal party had any means of lighting the barbecue fire, so the footman was despatched with all haste, and a flea in his ear, back to the castle – a journey of some miles. On his return, Prince Philip didn't spare his wrath. A few choice naval expressions flew around.

As today, when the Court moved from London to Windsor or Sandringham or Balmoral, the staff went with it. 'The moves became part of everyday life,' the former chef explained. 'We were always told well in advance where we were going. At weekends the Queen leaves on the dot of three on Friday afternoon for Windsor, so as soon as lunch is over we would pile into a coach and be driven off down the M4. You would leave your suitcase outside your door at Buckingham Palace and by the time you arrived in Windsor, it was waiting, again outside your door. The baggage had been loaded onto an Army truck and in my time they never lost a single item.'

Windsor is regarded as the favourite royal residence, not only by the Queen but also by her staff, 'because it's right in the middle of town, so as soon as we had finished work, we could step straight outside for a night out.'

But it is in London that the staff are able to make a little extra money. This is where the 'moonlighting' teams come into their own. If you want your dinner party catered by staff of the royal household, nothing could be simpler. Footmen are often prepared to serve meals at private dinner parties with numbers from eight to forty. A 'fixer' in every department at the Palace will quote a price: currently it is £60 a man for footmen and £100 for a chef. They will even arrange music, with a trio from the band of the Household Brigade costing around £150 a night or a 10-piece orchestra £1,000. And it's all in cash. The one thing the footmen won't do is use their royal uniforms. They all have smart outfits of their own which they keep for private functions. The Master of the Household is fully aware of these extra-curricular activities and turns a blind eye, feeling it not only helps the lower paid staff to supplement their wages but also gives the younger, newer men an opportunity to gain useful experience. In fact, various members of the household utilize their colleagues' services for their own parties, but they get a discount, paying on average around £16 a night for a footman and £30 for a chef. Until fairly recently there was also a thriving 'black market' in food and wine with the 'moonlighters' prepared to find the ingredients for a dinner party from the royal kitchens. But this has stopped with the introduction of new security measures and computerized controls. Footmen are, however, still willing to attend houses in the neighbourhood of Buckingham Palace once a week to clean the master's shoes and perhaps press his clothes. The going rate for this service is £20 a time. The 'private' car-cleaning service operated at weekends in the Mews costs around £10 a car, but for that you get your vehicles hand-washed and polished and any minor mechanical faults are corrected.

New staff often found it strange, unless they had come from one of the few great houses still occupied in Britain, to find that royal residences had so many rooms with different uses. Breakfast, lunch, afternoon tea and dinner were all taken in different rooms, and there were special rooms reserved for cleaning silver, brushing clothes, hanging game, making pastry, ironing, keeping guns and washing dishes. There were rooms for dressing and undressing and rooms for writing letters. The Queen's father, the late King George VI, liked to relax at Sandringham by reading the Game Book in his favourite conservatory. When this was happening, everybody kept clear as he hated to be disturbed. The outside staff learnt that when they were approached by a member of the royal family, they were to touch their hats, if they were wearing one, but if a conversation took place, they were to remove the hat altogether.

Working in the royal kitchens gives one a unique look at the way royalty lives, even today. Pheasant, partridge, quail, plover, woodcock and snipe, all shot on one of the royal estates, are served to the Queen and her guests. But the meals do not compare with those of earlier reigns, particularly those of Edward VII and, to a lesser extent, George V, when twenty-four extra French chefs might be brought over to help prepare a State Banquet. Or two hundred pheasants cooked for a single meal and fifty shoulders of lamb brought specially from Wales. But they still enjoy the hot-house grapes grown at Windsor to garnish the fish dishes. Some of the recipes in use today are eighty or ninety years old, but they draw the line at using twenty-four bottles of brandy when they make their mincemeat at Christmas, as happened in what the cooks still call 'the good old days'. One impressive dish remains a favourite. It's a raised pie which contains a boned turkey stuffed with a chicken, which is stuffed with a pheasant and finally stuffed with a woodcock. The meat is then encased in pastry and eventually served cold. Prince Charles is said to enjoy this particular creation.

Nowadays a posting to the Prince of Wales's household is seen as a good career move. Not only is the money better, but the working conditions are also an improvement, and the Wales establishment is seen as the most exciting. A one-time member of his staff, who also worked for the Princess of Wales for a time, explained the attractions. 'They were much younger, more vibrant and, at first, enjoyed entertaining on a grand scale. There were celebrities from all walks of life, particularly show business. We saw all the biggest names in music, films and theatre. Prince Charles loved to entertain the leading actors and musicians while Diana used her unique position to invite her favourite pop stars, like Michael Jackson, and rock groups to Kensington Palace. Of course, they all had to "sing for their supper" – there really is no such thing as a free meal with royalty.'

Apparently Diana loved to hear all the latest gossip, including the juiciest details of the various love affairs that go on inside the Palace walls. As one of her staff explained, 'She had to hear the lot, four-letter words and all. It was as if she wanted to be shocked. The only trouble was you never knew where you were with her. One day she would walk into the kitchen, kick off her shoes and sit on the table saying, "Right, let's have the latest gossip." The next she would ball you out for some imagined minor fault and be very grand. It would have been better if she had stayed on her side of the green baize door. Then we would all have known where we stood.'

Nowadays Charles has a large staff of eighty, but this includes a substantial number of office workers as well as the domestics at his 75-room residence in York House, St James's Palace and at Highgrove. The Queen Mother had a total of eighty-three staff, with the bulk, around sixty-five, manning her five homes. At Clarence House alone there were a housekeeper, six housemaids, two pages, four footmen, three chauffeurs, two gardeners plus another fifteen to help clean and maintain the property. Three lady clerks handled her correspondence, with a press officer and an assistant to deal with the media. There was a Lord Chamberlain, a Comptroller, a Clerk Comptroller to the Household, an Apothecary to the Household, a Treasurer, a Page of Honour, nine equerries and a factor (or farm manager) at the castle of Mey.

Every member of the Master of the Household's staff who aims for promotion and a career in royal service starts as a footman before working his way up. And as a footman he sees the royals in a variety of circumstances, not all in their most favourable light. A former footman to both the old Duke of Gloucester and later the Queen, who has now left to earn more money elsewhere, told a revealing anecdote. 'On one occasion, when Prince Henry (the Duke of Gloucester) was living in York House at St James's Palace (where Prince Charles now lives) we still had coal fires. One day His Royal Highness was sitting, dozing in his chair by the fire, when a live coal fell out of the fire onto the carpet. It started to burn a hole in the rug, being completely ignored by the Duke. A couple of minutes later I walked into the room, saw what was happening and rushed over, seized a pair of tongs and put the coal back on the fire. The Duke said, "Where the Hell have you been? I've been waiting for someone to do that for five minutes." It simply would not have occurred to him to pick it up himself.'

A former butler to the old Duke of Gloucester revealed that he insisted that one of his favourite brand of cigarettes should be placed beside each ash tray in every room in the house so that he would not have to look for one himself. He further demanded that a match box should be left with one match peeping out so that he did not have to open the box and search for one. His staff found nothing unusual in these orders: they were used to the detailed instructions the royals took for granted.

Another occasion involved the Queen herself. Her footman had set out the meat and vegetables for the daily ritual of feeding the corgis. Her Majesty mixed the food herself, as she always does, and her servant remarked that it was a 'nice piece of fillet steak, I wouldn't mind it myself.' As soon as he spoke he realized he had overstepped the mark. Her Majesty didn't say another word, but turned and walked back into her sitting room.

Two of the most desirable domestic posts within the royal household are those of the Page of the Backstairs. These are senior footmen who have served in the Master of the Household's department for many years and who wait personally on the Queen. They work on alternate days, attending Her Majesty in her private apartments on the first floor facing Constitution Hill. The Pages act as a conduit between the Queen and the rest of the Palace. If anyone wants to see her, they will first telephone her Page to see if it's convenient for them to call on her. The Pages are also skilled at gauging Her Majesty's moods, so old hands in the Palace use them to find out if this would be the right moment. Pages are also the channel between various members of the royal family. All messages are passed through them. Through them the Queen's family can find out where she is at any time to avoid infringing on her privacy. For instance, if Prince Charles is staying at Sandringham at the same time as his mother and he wants to walk in the garden, his Page will first of all ring his opposite number in the Queen's household to find out if she is in the garden. If she is, Charles will remain out of sight. They all know the Queen likes to be alone when she is walking in the grounds. Similarly, at Buckingham Palace, no one goes in the garden when the Queen is there with her corgis.

All the men who have become Palace Steward, the senior domestic servant, responsible for all the liveried staff, have been Page of the Backstairs before promotion to the top job. There are three sets of Pages: Page of the Chambers, Page of the Presence and Page of the Backstairs. The Page of the Chambers is also the Deputy Palace Steward, number two in the domestic hierarchy. His responsibilities include allocating the right number of footmen, cloakroom attendants and nurses for duty when an Investiture is being held. As each of the recipients are allowed to invite three guests to witness their honours being presented, a large number of staff is required to cope. Through long experience, the Page of the Chambers has perfected the art of shepherding over five hundred people through the Grand Entrance and into the State Ball Room with the minimum of fuss. Alongside the Ball Room is a fully-equipped first-aid station with qualified medical staff on duty as fainting incidents are common. An ambulance is standing by near the side entrance to the Palace in case anything more serious occurs.

The Queen receives foreign emissaries at Buckingham Palace, even though they are accredited to the Court of St James's, and when an ambassador or high commissioner is due to present his credentials on his appointment, the Page of the Chambers liaises with the Royal Mews in making the arrangements. The diplomat is collected from his residence in a carriage drawn by a pair of horses and attended by two liveried footmen.

The third set of Pages are the Pages of the Presence, who, despite their title, do not work as personal servants to the sovereign. They provide services to the senior members of the household, such as making sure a fresh supply of stationery is placed on the desks of the private secretaries every morning. They also supervise the footmen who look after the Grand Entrance – when it is in use – and the Privy Purse Door. This is the entrance used by the members of the household and also by all official visitors below diplomatic rank. An important part of a Page of the Presence's role is to smooth the path of any visiting household when a foreign Head of State arrives at Buckingham Palace or Windsor Castle. He ensures that his opposite number is made comfortable and knows his way around. He also spends part of his off-duty hours showing the guest's servants the sights and telling them where the best shopping bargains are.

The footmen work under the Pages but are allocated to different duties most days by their foreman, the Sergeant Footman. He was the first to interview them on their original application, and he makes out each day's rota, giving the men numbers, one to six. Footman number one works under the Pages of the Backstairs, doing all the jobs, the footmen claim, that their seniors don't like. As most of the Palace staff loathe the Queen's corgis, the Pages usually pass on to the junior footman the task of exercising the dogs – and cleaning up after them. Footman number one also carries the food from the kitchens to the first floor for the Queen and Prince Philip, where he hands it over to the page. A housemaid delivers the morning tray to the Queen, but the footman carries the Duke of Edinburgh's coffee and biscuits, just after 7.30 in the morning. The lift they use to bring up the food, not only for breakfast, but lunch and dinner also, connects the basement with the third floor. First thing in the morning the staff may use it to get from their rooms to the servants' hall. But they are forbidden to use the lift when it is needed for the royal food: between one and two o'clock and again between 7.30 and 8.30 in the evening.

The number one footman spends the rest of his shift doing whatever the Page of the Backstairs tells him to do. It might be running errands, carrying messages to various parts of the Palace or just standing by in the little pantry opposite the Queen's bedroom in case he is needed. It can be very boring on occasions; at other times, particularly when a State Visit is in progress, rather hectic. But working as number one does give the footman the opportunity of observing the Queen at fairly close quarters and learning how to gauge her moods for future reference. So the job is seen as a definite leg-up.

Footmen numbers two and four – no one seems to know why they sandwich number three – look after the needs of the senior members of the household. And because of this they are also the source of many of the stories that emerge about the royal family. Most of the leading tabloid newspapers have contacts among the footmen and pay handsomely for any tips that lead to a good story. So if footmen two and four keep their ears open when they are attending the members in their dining room or carrying messages between offices, they can often pick up titbits which provide them with that extra income. One famous columnist was once asked by a press secretary who his 'mole' was. He replied, 'I have eleven in the Palace.' That's what happens when wages are so low.

Members of the household generally converse in English, but if the Queen and Prince Philip want to discuss something, or someone, when one of the servants is present, they will invariably turn to French which they both speak fluently. And when Prince Philip talked on the telephone with his last surviving sister, Princess George of Hanover, known in the family as 'Tiny', who died in December 2001 at the age of eighty-seven, they always spoke in German. German is also used by Prince and Princess Michael of Kent in their homes at Kensington Palace and Gloucestershire whenever they want secrecy. Prince Michael is easily the best linguist in the royal family, being fluent in French, German and Russian. Prince Charles once tried the same linguistic tactic, using French to talk privately to Princess Diana, but it was a complete failure as she couldn't understand a word.

Footman number three has the easiest job of all. He is positioned just inside the King's Door on the west side of the inner quadrangle. It is still known as the King's Door on the orders of the Queen, out of respect for her father, King George VI. This is the door used by members of the royal family – but not the Queen, who uses the Garden Entrance – and also by the Prime Minister when he arrives for his 6.30 appointment every Tuesday evening. The footman has a timetable telling him who is expected and when, and in between guarding the door he also carries any documents and letters from Sir Robin Janvrin, the Queen's private secretary, upstairs to her sitting room when required.

As he is not overworked, the Sergeant Footman may also make number three replenish the drinks tray in the Equerries Withdrawing Room or find out for the kitchens how many of the household will be in for lunch. Everything stops for tea in the Palace and footman number three brings the sandwiches, cakes and tea into the Equerries Room every afternoon. This is where most of the gossip is exchanged as the members meet to chat over the day's events and to sound out their colleagues when something is being planned.

Footman number five is the Palace dogsbody. He is right at the bottom of the ladder and consequently given the most menial tasks. One of his duties is to act as valet to the Equerry-in-waiting during his three-year stint on secondment to the Palace. The equerry is given the use of a pleasant but small ground-floor apartment at Friary Court in St James's Palace, where his front door is exactly opposite that of Princess Alexandra. The apartment is furnished from the royal storerooms in the grounds of Windsor Castle and is directly underneath the Brick Balcony from which is read the acclamation of a new sovereign. The footman makes sure the equerry's shoes are brightly shone and, as they are all service officers, the standard is extremely high. He also inspects uniforms and suits to check that no buttons are missing and whether they need cleaning or pressing.

But he does not have to carry a morning tray and newspaper as he did when the equerry lived in at Buckingham Palace. And these days he is allowed to speak first. Not all that long ago, he was not permitted to open his mouth unless he had been spoken to.

The footmen can tell tales about the various equerries they have waited upon. Some have been pleasant and easygoing, others have been affected by the belief that they are somehow more important than anyone else because of the position they hold. And all the footmen hate it when the equerry who has been to a late party throws his clothes in a heap, expecting them to be picked up and in pristine condition first thing the following morning. One footman told me of one such occasion. 'His clothes were strewn all over the floor, so I left them there. He summoned me and said, "What the Hell do you think I left them there for? Get them sorted out or I'll sack you." I told the Sergeant Footman what had happened and he said to leave it to him. The next thing that happened was that the equerry apologized and promised it wouldn't happen again. The Sergeant Footman had given it to him straight and threatened to report his behaviour to the Queen. He wouldn't have, of course, but it did the trick and I never had trouble with him again.'

When Tim Laurence was equerry, his room was on the same floor as the Princess Royal's suite – this was when she had rooms in Buckingham Palace – and the women in her office would often see him passing the door on his way to his position downstairs. He occasionally passed the time of day and even dropped in to ask a favour, such as having shirt button sewn on. They were happy to oblige, but it quickly became apparent that he knew his position and the relationship soon became more distant. He wasn't un-friendly; he just kept things at arm's length. This was, of course, long before anyone knew of his romance with their boss.

Footman number six is not always employed, but when he is it is because an important guest is expected and the Grand Entrance is in use. Number six has the privilege of opening the car door for the visitor. There have been occasions when this duty has been highly rewarding. One Middle Eastern ruler handed over a small bag containing rubies and diamonds as a tip, while an American statesman slipped a fifty-dollar bill into the unsuspecting, but ever-ready, hand. Guests of the Queen are not always the most generous tippers, but most are expected to leave a twenty-pound note behind when they leave the Palace or Windsor Castle after a night's stay. It's strictly against the rules. Indeed, the Master of the Household leaves a note asking guests not to leave any gratuities, saying, 'The staff neither expect, nor are allowed to accept money from Her Majesty's guests.' A few respect this request, but the majority know the servants expect a little something extra, and are happy to oblige.

These then are the so-called lower level of servant at Buckingham Palace. But just because they are involved in the domestic chores of the royal household, it does not follow that they are servile in any way. In fact, there is a certain amount of arrogance attached to the more senior servants, who have the ability to deflate pomposity in self-important visitors without any apparent effort, and without causing offence. It is a skill that has been acquired over many years of dealing with a variety of people, some of whom believe that simply because the man who opens the door wearing a tail-coat is obviously a servant, he is not worthy of respect. These are, of course, the exception. But they still turn up occasionally, and when they do the footmen and pages are ready for them, masters of the royal put-down. One visitor who arrived at the Privy Purse Door demanded to use the lavatory immediately, without a please or thank-you. There is a well-equipped cloakroom just to the left of the entrance hall that most visitors are directed to. On this occasion, the duty footmen guided the ill-mannered visitor through a labyrinth of corridors and down into the bowels of the Palace where he was shown one of the staff lavatories. The man didn't even realize he was being given the run-around.

CHAPTER FIVE

ﻖﺨ

Nannies, Nursemaids and Dressers

Three categories of royal servant consider themselves different from all the others and infinitely superior. The nannies, nursemaids and dressers who look after the royal family from birth occupy privileged positions in the household. And the family come to regard them as indispensable supports without whom everyday life would be unthinkable. They are privy to royal secrets and witness both male and female members of the family in moments of extreme intimacy. The Queen's three dressers, headed by her chief dresser, Angela Kelly, a former soldier in the Women's Royal Army Corps, see her first thing in the morning and last thing at night when she prepares for bed. They help her to dress and undress and when she is being measured for a new outfit, it is they who pass the tape measure around the royal bosom. Neither Sir Norman Hartnell nor Sir Hardy Amies, now in his nineties and who has designed clothes for Her Majesty for fifty years, ever once saw their most famous client in her petticoat. They entrusted the measuring and early fittings to one of their female assistants and the Queen's dressers. The only couturier allowed to see Her Majesty undressed is Maureen Rose, who holds a Royal Warrant for her services to the Queen.

But although the dressers are among the most loyal and devoted of all royal servants, there have been occasions when one has slipped up. A young temporary dresser – not one of the Queen's – had been invited out by her boyfriend to a special celebratory dinner. She didn't feel any of her own dresses were suitable for the evening so she 'borrowed' one from her mistress. Normally, dressers know exactly where their boss is going to be every day and every evening, so they can lay out the appropriate clothes. This time it went wrong and both turned up at the same restaurant. The princess whose dress it was made no comment at the time, but the following morning the 'temp' was told her services were no longer required. However the dress has been worn by its royal owner on numerous occasions since. Clearly she did not feel the need to throw it away simply because it had been worn by a commoner.

The reliance that the royal family place on their servants is quite extraordinary. On one occasion, the Queen was staying with the late Earl and Countess of Carnarvon at their home in Wiltshire. One morning Her Majesty's dresser was taken ill and was unable to attend the Queen, who was so unused to fending for herself that one of the other Palace dressers had to be driven to Highclere at high speed as a replacement.

Royal nannies are a law unto themselves. They do not regard themselves – nor are they regarded by others – as being on the same level as any of the domestic servants. They are not required to eat in the servants' hall; they do not make their own beds, clean their own shoes or carry their own meals. Frequently they become the most important fixture in the lives of those they look after, and the relationship can, in some cases, last for long after the nanny has outlived her working usefulness. Prince Charles had two nannies, Helen Lightbody and Mabel Anderson, both of whom became so close to him that the relationships bordered on obsession. And he, in turn, came to depend on them to such an extent that when he had to go away to school, it was not his parents he cried for but his nanny.

The most famous nanny, who started work as a nursery maid and went on to become the Queen's dresser and closest confidante, and who reigned supreme over Her Majesty's personal staff for sixty years, was the late Margaret 'Bobo' McDonald. She was a fierce guardian of the Queen's image and no one in the household, no matter how senior in rank or grand in title, dared cross her. She refused to socialize with any other members of the Queen's household, apart from her own sister, Ruby, who was as devoted to Princess Margaret as Bobo was to the Queen. A young footman joining the Palace staff was instructed 'not to speak to Miss McDonald if you meet in one of the corridors unless she addresses you first'. Apparently it was her custom to ignore everyone other than royalty. This included all the household, even those employed in the Queen's private office. It was Bobo who told the Queen what to wear and when and accompanied her whenever she made a private visit to stay with friends. And the friends, among them Countess Mountbatten, made sure Bobo was happy with her accommodation and had everything she needed during the stay. They knew that if Bobo was unhappy then the Queen would quickly become aware and the visit could be ruined and was unlikely to be repeated.

But Bobo was unique. No other servant in history, with the possible exception of John Brown, Queen Victoria's ghillie, and the scourge of her household because of his arrogance and appalling manners, has carried so much weight. Bobo ruled over a personal fiefdom with a rod of iron. She had her own servants to attend to her every need, and the finest network of informers among the staff to tell her everything that went on in the Palace and at all the other royal residences. They were her eyes and ears, and she relayed all the Palace gossip to the Queen.

Even when bedridden during the last years of her life and confined to her quarters immediately above the Queen's apartments in Buckingham Palace, Bobo knew everything that was going on, and if by some chance she was not the first to hear an item of gossip or scandal, her fury was felt throughout the Palace. Working on the basis that information is power, she intimidated many of the household, even those occupying positions far above her own. Successive Lord Chamberlains shied away from confronting Bobo, knowing that she had the ear of the Queen, and Her Majesty, in turn, would never hear a word against her old retainer; so they trod very carefully when dealing with this little old woman who treated her so-called superiors with barely concealed scorn.

In more recent times, Tiggy Legge-Bourke became almost as close to Prince William and Prince Harry as first their nanny and, later, as companion. Her proprietorial attitude attracted controversy, and it was said that she was thought of in many ways as an 'elder sister' rather than a paid employee. She also made an implacable enemy of the late Diana, Princess of Wales, who alleged that Tiggy had tried to usurp her place in the boys' affections.

But long before Tiggy came on the royal scene, Barbara Barnes attracted a huge amount of attention as the first nanny to Prince William. Pictures of her carrying the infant prince down the steps of the aircraft at the start of a visit to Australia made her a familiar face on television and in newspapers throughout the world.

Before being appointed to care for William, Barbara Barnes had been working for the Glenconner family, and Princess Margaret, a close friend, suggested to Lady Glenconner that Barbara should apply for the position of nanny to the baby that the Princess of Wales was expecting. Barbara was summoned to Buckingham Palace – being driven there by Lady Glenconner herself – and allowed to enter via the Privy Purse Door, unusual in that employees are normally expected to use the side entrance in Buckingham Palace Road. She was taken up to the first floor and asked to wait. 'The Princess was late back from an engagement and when she came in she was friendly and quite informal. We said goodbye and two weeks later I received a letter offering me the post.'

Barbara took up the job when William was just four weeks old and stayed with him for over four years. At that time the Wales's office was at Buckingham Palace and there was only a small staff at Kensington Palace: one chef, one valet, a dresser for the Princess, a butler and a Gurkha orderly on attachment. They didn't even have their own chauffeur. If one was needed, they would get one from the Palace Mews.

Right from the start, the regimented routine that characterizes all royal households was implemented, with the entire family and staff moving from palace to country house to Scottish castle on the appointed day. Bags had to be packed and ready to go at exactly 2.20 every Friday afternoon, so they could be collected and taken to the waiting cars. They had to leave at precisely half past two for the journey to Highgrove. On Monday they would be driven back to London, leaving at the same time and arriving on the dot. If they were going to Balmoral, they would have to make sure everything was organized so that the aircraft could leave when it was scheduled to take off. Just because they belonged to the Queen's Flight, there was no chance of making them hang around for half an hour. Everything worked to a rigid timetable and the Prince of Wales insisted on punctuality.

Looking after the child who is destined one day to become King was not just a full-time job, it was all consuming. Seven days a week, twenty-four hours a day. As William became older, his nanny or nursemaid began taking him around London, to all the usual places that children like. They would stop in local parks so he could play on the swings and roundabouts and he was never recognized. The chauffeur didn't wear a uniform on these occasions so they could blend in, and no one thought anything of it when the policeman lifted the pram or buggy out of the boot of the car just like any father. The only rules were that they should not take the same route or visit the same place two days running. The security office had to know where they were going – they were in constant touch with the car anyway – and there was always a backup vehicle close behind. The Queen took a great interest in her grandson; as a future heir to the throne, she would naturally be concerned about his progress, apart from the fact that she was a loving grandmother. William was often taken to see her and he also went to Buckingham Palace most days so he could swim. He learnt at a very early age, as all the royal children do.

The Queen and Prince Philip were not unlike most grandparents of their generation and class in that they were pleased to see their grandchildren, but nothing was allowed to interfere with their normal routine. Whatever was planned for that day, they would carry on with it, even when the children arrived, scrubbed and polished.

There was a strict pecking order, even for the royal children. At tea-time they all trooped down to the drawing room where the adults waited for the children to join them for tea. A footman opened the door and a sea of famous faces was revealed as the entire royal family sat at small tables having their tea. As well as the Wales children, there were the two youngsters of the Princess Royal, and the children belonging to the Gloucesters, the Kents and Prince and Princess Michael. All had to line up with the Wales children at the front, followed by those of the Princess Royal, then the Gloucesters, the Duke and Duchess of Kent and finally the children of Prince and Princess Michael of Kent who brought up the rear, all arranged according to the order of precedence. The strange thing was even the youngest knew their place, without quite knowing why they had to stand in a certain order. After bowing or curtsying to the Queen the youngsters joined their parents while the nannies hovered in the background, ready to resume charge of the children when required. It was a surreal scene. Royal children are taught manners by their nannies from an early age. Both William and Harry were made to bow to the Queen, the Queen Mother and Princess

Margaret almost as soon as they could walk, but they were not required to bow to their father, as he was to his own parents.

The children's relations with other members of the royal family depended on how the adults got on. Sometimes, as with Prince Charles and Princess Anne, there was a lot of coming and going. With others, such as Prince and Princess Michael of Kent, it was not so frequent. There was a lot of contact with Peter and Zara Phillips. They would travel to Highgrove every week when they were small, where they would have lunch or tea in the nursery and play with their cousins for a couple of hours. Quite often Prince Charles would be working in the garden and the Princess might be lying on a sunbed or doing her tapestry. They would chat for a few minutes, then carry on with whatever they were doing. A return visit to Gatcombe Park was then arranged. There the nursery is on the top floor. It is a large, pleasant room but the outlook is spoiled by the fact that the stone balustrades obscure the view from the windows. If Princess Anne was around on these occasions, there wasn't a great deal of smalltalk. She tended to keep to her own part of the house.

Although Prince and Princess Michael of Kent also lived in Gloucestershire and their home at Nether Lypiatt Manor formed the 'royal triangle' along with Highgrove and Gatcombe Park, their house was rarely included in the children's visits. A record was kept and organized so that each household only issued the same number of invitations as it received.

When William was still in his pram, his nanny or nursemaid would take him for walks in Kensington Palace Gardens and they would sometimes meet the late Princess

Margaret who, before her illness, was a firm believer in long, vigorous walks. When they met she would always stop and look at the child, but even though she was an interested great-aunt, 'She did not care too much for personal physical contact with small children.'

If one of the nannies of the royal children was staying at one of the Queen's residences she would be treated more like a guest than a servant, being waited on by footmen and maids. The maid would bring morning tea in bed, while the footman would carry in the breakfast and place it on a hotplate and, in Scotland, where it was always cold even in high summer, a fire was lighted in the nanny's room and a teapot placed in the hearth to keep warm. In Scotland the staff are given lessons in Highland dancing so that they do not put a foot wrong at the annual Ghillies Ball.

It was at the Queen's Highland home that some of the staff had a rare opportunity to see Her Majesty in her night clothes. It happened at Balmoral where, one evening, some of the staff were holding a party which went on rather late. In the early hours of the morning – around two or three o'clock – a footman who was slightly the worse for wear, accidentally leaned on the emergency bell-push and the fire alarms went off. All over the castle everyone knew the drill, and at that time of morning it couldn't be a practice. The Queen joined her staff in her dressing gown and nightie and they all stood around until they were given the all-clear.

A similar incident occurred at Sandringham when a member of staff also sounded the fire alarm. Again Her Majesty trooped downstairs in her night clothes to discover another false alarm. She was not amused.

When the royal family are in Scotland they like to have

picnics in the grounds. But they are not like any picnics ordinary people enjoy. Footmen lay the tables and arrange the food, cutlery and china and then move to a discreet distance where they can keep an eye on things and be within calling range if needed. The Queen pours the tea, but that is the extent of her culinary efforts. Everyday domestic chores are not part of the daily routine of any member of the royal family, young or old. As one former nursemaid says, 'I don't think any of them has ever run his or her own bath or hand washed any of their clothes. And they don't pack suitcases; they wouldn't know how.'

Another aspect of royal life that servants see but which is denied outsiders is how regimented their daily routine is. 'One could never imagine the Queen or any of the others asking for a cup of tea or coffee if it wasn't the right time of day when they usually have one. The idea of eating and drinking between meals just wouldn't occur to them.'

The Queen, Prince Philip and the Prince of Wales all have reputations for impatience. They demand impeccable service and when things go wrong they are not the most understanding of employers. Princess Anne's short temper has been well documented, and both the Duke of York and the Earl of Wessex have inherited their parents' occasional tartness with servants. At the same time, all the royal family are appreciative of hard work, and when they return from a particularly arduous overseas tour during which they know their staff have had to put in extra effort, will always send a hand-written thank-you note. Another perk for some royal servants is that many firms send gifts to their principals. For instance, the late Princess of Wales was often given presents of expensive perfume and make-up, in the hope that she would like them so much she would informally promote these wares. She invariably distributed these gifts among her female staff and, in the days when Princess Margaret was the most glamorous lady in the family, she did the same.

The fact that nannies held and, in some cases, still hold a special place in the hierarchy of the royal household has given a few a severe case of 'Red Carpet Fever' – the belief that they are as important as the royals they serve. Helen Lightbody, Prince Charles's first nanny, was said to be as imperious as old Queen Mary, insisting that footmen who carried the child's food to the nursery referred to him as 'His Royal Highness' even at the age of eighteen months, and rarely speaking directly to any of the domestic staff. Occasionally nannies and other carers become so besotted with the children they look after that they cannot cope when they are no longer needed. Prince Charles's first governess, Miss Peebles, known to him as 'Mispy', was devastated when he left the Palace schoolroom to attend Cheam, his first preparatory school. She had looked after him for five years, and had almost become obsessed. Although Miss Peebles remained in charge of Princess Anne, she was aloof and seemed totally disinterested, and two years later she was found dead, alone in her room at Buckingham Palace. Charles was deeply distressed when she was discovered. Princess Anne said later that her only reaction was guilt because she didn't feel anything. The verdict was natural causes, but Mispy had been known to have developed a fondness for the bottle after Charles had left, and people in the household who knew her at the time said she had simply willed herself to die.

There have also been cases of former nannies and governesses falling from grace, the most notable being Miss

Marion Crawford – 'Crawfie' as she was called by the Queen and Princess Margaret to whom she was governess. Crawfie had devoted her life to the children, but when, on her retirement, she wrote a book, *The Little Princesses*, about her royal experiences, she paid the penalty. The book, which was a saccharine account of life with the family, contained no salacious revelations, indeed it was simply a fond tribute. But the royals virtually airbrushed Crawfie from the scene. She was ignored for the rest of her life – taken off the Christmas card list (so important to former servants) and even when she died there was no forgiveness. The family felt she had betrayed their trust and as far as they were concerned, she had never existed.

There is a long tradition of nannies, nurses and governesses coming from Scottish stock, and at one time there was also a great deal of traffic between the various branches of the family, with nannies being passed from one to another when children got beyond the age of needing nursery staff. These days, though, the initial introduction to a royal household is more usually through the same channels by which anyone else recruits staff. Prince Charles's favourite nanny, Mabel Anderson, who started out as Helen Lightbody's assistant, actually advertised her services in a nursing magazine and the then Princess Elizabeth replied and eventually offered her a job. Other members of the family advertise themselves, usually hiding their identity under a box number.

They say no man is a hero to his valet and the same might equally be asserted of nannies, who see royalty in more intimate circumstances than anyone else. As one famous nanny commented, 'You have to understand they are famous but otherwise ordinary, normal people in an unreal situation. That's the only difference really. It would be strange if they did behave like everyone else, when you consider the way they have all been raised, to expect everybody to treat them with deference practically from birth. So, it's no wonder they behave in an imperious manner, that is what they have all been brought up believing is their natural right.'

CHAPTER SIX

❦

The Royal Valets

'The aim of a valet is to know the personal requirements of the gentleman whom he is valeting and to work unobtrusively to provide the services necessary to meet these requirements.' These are the words of a Deputy Master of the Household introducing valeting duties to footmen who are training to become valets.

When unpacking a visitor's case the trainee is told to 'remember to place the suitcase on a trestle table', because suitcases have been put down on dirty station platforms and on pavements and roads, and it is a crime to put them on clean, even valuable, bed covers.

When clothes are put away in the wardrobe and drawers, collars, ties and handkerchiefs should be placed in the top drawer of the dressing table. Socks should also be in an easily accessible place.

Valets are instructed how to hang suits correctly by making sure the sleeves are hanging straight – most particularly the sleeve nearest the back of the wardrobe.

Before being allocated to work for one of the royals, a

new valet is assigned to look after members of the household and then visiting guests of the Queen. It is a tough school as senior members of the household can be harder to please than any member of the royal family. When working for guests the valet is told to find out the likes and dislikes of the visitor by asking him, for example, when he likes to have his bath. He should also make sure the visitor knows the location of the bathroom as few bedrooms in royal residences have en suite facilities.

Then the valet should find out when the guest would like to be called and should this be with early morning tea or fruit juice, biscuits, etc? The valet should explain how he can be contacted at any time and a typed card bearing his name will have been left on the dressing table.

The laying out of evening clothes is a special skill and the valet quickly learns the system employed at Buckingham Palace, Windsor Castle and Balmoral. He is advised to imagine he will be dressing himself in them. That way nothing is likely to be forgotten. First there must be careful final brushing of the dinner jacket, for black shows every speck. He should then undo the shirt buttons and, if the shirt is wrapped in laundry paper and cardboard, remove this and any pins and throw them away. If collar studs are required, he should put them in position.

One of the most important duties of the valet is to run a bath for his gentleman, which he should do about an hour before the time of dinner. The bath should be filled to two-thirds with hand-warm water and never with water that is too hot. This can always be added later if required. And it is vital to run a little hot water into the bath first. The reason is to warm the bath, 'otherwise it will be cold to sit in'.

The routine to be followed when calling a gentleman in the morning is also quite precise. 'Open the door as quietly as possible. If a light is needed, try to switch on one which does not shine into the gentleman's eyes.' Any tray should be placed on a chair or table near the bed where it can be reached easily. Then, after drawing back the curtains and shutting any open window, he should gather up the evening clothes, taking first the jacket, then the trousers – in their creases – shirt and underclothes. Socks and bow tie are tucked into one of the shoes. (In this way they are not so likely to be lost on the way to the pressing room.)

'Up to now you have not spoken. This is as it should be!' But if the valet does not know which clothes to put out he may ask, then lay them on a chair – jacket over the back; trousers across the seat; vest, pants and shirt (in that order, so that they are presented in the order required). Before leaving the room the valet should tell the gentleman the time, what the weather is like and, of course, take away the evening clothes.

Rules are laid down for the removal of clothes for valeting. The first one is: empty all pockets before removing clothes. Then, if possible, leave braces on trousers, unless the gentleman only has one pair, then they should be left in his room. Cuff-links should always be left on the dressing table, and when carrying a suit or dinner jacket and a pair of shoes, care should be taken that shoes must never touch other garments. This is because 'the soles of shoes pick up traces of dirt, engine oil or messes one has walked over and the uppers will have polish on them.' A good valet will arm himself with bags to put shoes in for removal. Valets are also warned that guests at Sandringham or Balmoral will probably have a 'hairy tweed jacket' which will not need pressing or brushing, so it can be left in the gentleman's cupboard.

Brushing and pressing are carried out according to a set of rules laid down by the Deputy Master of the Household who advises that: '. . . no Savile Row tailor sends out suits with creases in the sleeves.'

When pressing coats valets should use sleeve bolsters and always press the lapels from the back, to create a 'roll' effect. Particular attention should be paid to the lower back where creases from sitting can occur. Trousers should not be over pressed, but often enough for a sharp crease to be maintained, and brushing is best done firmly using long strokes and a good quality brush which should be regularly washed.

Surprisingly it is felt in royal circles that shirts, socks and underwear can sometimes be worn again. The guide notes indicate that evening wear does not necessarily need washing after being worn only once, and part-worn underwear should be kept in a spare drawer and never mixed with clean clothes.

Shoes which may have become wet through tramping through the fields or gorse should be stuffed with newspapers to absorb the moisture and never dried in excessive heat.

When a guest is leaving, his valet packs his bag in the following order: trousers and waistcoats first, followed by shirts, underwear on top. Plenty of tissue paper should be used to minimize creases in suits, the aim being to pack so that clothes come out of the case in a fit state to wear immediately. Hair oil bottles should be wrapped in a plastic bag inside a waterproof sponge bag. Boots and shoes should go into shoe bags and be placed so that, when the case is picked up, they will be at the bottom. Lastly the valet should label the case with the name of the person and his destination.

When a valet is attached to a senior member of the household who is also a service officer, he is instructed in the various uniforms the man has to wear, on what occasions, and how to lay them all out.

For example, the 'U.1' ceremonial uniform, which is worn when new ambassadors and high commissioners arrive at Buckingham Palace to present their credentials, consists of: a blue tunic, overalls and braces (with the overall – or trouser – straps fastened tightly under the instep), boots and spurs, aiguillettes on the right shoulder, a gold sash, gold sword slings, a sword with gold knot, large medals, gold-edged shoulder straps, a white collarless shirt and a cap and white gloves if it is an outside engagement.

The method of laying out is important because if it is done out of sequence, the whole rigmarole has to be started again. First the aiguillettes are attached to the tunic, then the shoulder straps and the medals. Valets are then instructed to hang the tunic on a chest of drawers, 'box' the overalls and place them in front of a chair. These skin-tight breeches worn by cavalry officers are so close fitting that they have to be turned inside out and laid on the floor so that the wearer can step into them. It is the only way he can get them on. The valet should then insert the cufflinks and place the folded shirt on the chair. The sword, sword belt and sash go on the bed with the cap and gloves if these are to be worn. The medals, spurs and cap badge must be polished each time the uniform is used, and the welts of the boots must also be polished even if the boots themselves are patent.

At investitures the uniform is comparatively simple, just a blue frock coat, overall trousers, boots and spurs, aiguillettes, a crimson sash, white sword slings and a collarless shirt – or even a tee shirt.

Service dress is worn by the military for outside engagements when civilian members of the household are in lounge suits. It consists of a khaki jacket, trousers and braces, khaki shirt, tie and socks, brown shoes and a Sam Browne belt, which must be 'spit and polished', gold aiguillettes and a blue cap if it is a royal engagement or a khaki cap if not.

When the Crown Equerry attends the Trooping the Colour Parade or the State Opening of Parliament, he wears a scarlet tunic with the other accoutrements of U.1 uniform, plus a bearskin cap and white kid gloves. The valet is warned that medals, spurs and tunic buttons must be polished, and that the white piping on the tunic has to be whitened with chalk – but this may only be carried out under the supervision of the Sergeant Footman or his deputy.

The two valets (pronounced to rhyme with mallet, not ballet) each man in the royal family employs, take it in turn to attend their master, and as his closest personal servant, they enjoy much prestige. Prince Philip's valets live in comfortable apartments immediately above his rooms at Buckingham Palace overlooking Constitution Hill, where they have bedroom, sitting room, bathroom and a shared brushing room to deal with HRH's clothes. They have no other responsibilities apart from looking after the prince and they are regarded as privileged beings by the other domestic staff.

Valets have usually come up through the ranks of footmen, and they are always selected by the royal concerned.

It rarely happens that a valet has not been known for years to the man he is going to serve. They work in such close proximity and in a degree of intimacy not experienced by any of the other staff that it is imperative that master and servant get on well together. The late Earl Mountbatten took his old naval Chief Petty Officer Steward with him when he retired from active service and William Evans carried on in civilian life performing the same role for many years. No one knew Mountbatten better than his valet. He dressed him, knew where every decoration should be worn and in what order, and kept his collection of eighty uniforms in pristine condition. Lord Mountbatten later said that his shoes had never been shined as well as when 'Evans looked after me.'

As Colonel of the Life Guards, Mountbatten was also Gold Stick in Waiting to the Queen, and in this capacity he rode immediately behind her at the Trooping the Colour parade. William Evans describes the way he prepared his master for the ordeal. 'First of all I would run his bath to relax him and make his body supple. After drying him I would dust him liberally with talcum powder so that I could pour him into his buckskin breeches which were so tight I had to make him lie flat on the bed so I could pull them on over his cotton underpants. Then a soft vest was put on and ultra-thin cotton socks. I stood him up so I could pull a shirt over his head. The shirt was specially made and there was no collar because the neck of his tunic needed to be buttoned up tightly around his throat. But the arms had to be extra long so that the cuffs, with Life Guards cuff-links, could protrude beneath the sleeves of his tunic. Next came the neck decorations. They were put on before the tunic and every one had to be in the correct order. They were on adjustable ribbons with the ribbon hidden inside the tunic, which came next, before the heavy steel cuirass – or breast plate – on which I had had tiny clips welded so that the back of the medals and decorations could be attached in order that they wouldn't swing about. Getting the thigh boots and spurs on was a problem because Lord Mountbatten could not bend, so I knelt on the floor and forced the boots on with two hand-held clamps. As he was going to be mounted during the parade, I had to make sure the rear buttons of his tunic were undone. If it had been an unmounted attendance, they would have remained fastened. The final touch was to add the Garter sash, his ceremonial sword belt and make sure his staff of office, the Gold Stick, was in perfect polished condition. I also had to powder his hands to enable him to wear the tight gauntlets and place his steel helmet, complete with white plumes, known as the onion, on his head.

'Buckingham Palace sent a limousine to fetch him and to get him into the car he had to lie back in a practically horizontal position as he couldn't bend at all with all this paraphernalia on. For the journey to the Palace he lay back stretched out across the two seats in the rear, and in the quadrangle, when we arrived, he again had to be manoeuvred out very carefully.

'By the time the parade was over several hours had passed, and when I met him at Buckingham Palace on his return he was soaked through and through with sweat. Every item of clothing had to be stripped from him and taken away to be laundered. I had already brought a fresh suit, shirt and underwear and, after getting his bath ready, dressed him for the rest of the afternoon.

'To make sure he was fully prepared for the parade, he

had private rehearsals in the grounds at Broadlands, his family home in Hampshire, where he would dress in full uniform and ride through the grounds several times to get used to being on his horse in full dress uniform. One misty morning, the local milkman came in and told me he thought he had seen a ghost, a figure in armour riding a white horse through the trees. I didn't have the heart to tell him it wasn't a ghost, but the master of the house having a practice.'

The Mountbattens, Lord and Lady Louis, seemed to attract problems wherever they went, but they never allowed any to interfere with their plans, particularly if they involved the Queen. There was one occasion when they were travelling to London from their home in Hampshire, to prepare to accompany Her Majesty to the State Opening of Parliament. Lord Louis was in full naval uniform, before changing into his parliamentary robes at the Palace. Their car broke down on the A30 near Staines. Immediately, they jumped out, flagged down a passing Green Line bus and asked the driver to drop them off at Buckingham Palace. He willingly obliged, apparently not in the least put out at seeing two strangers in what must have seemed like fancy dress, and he even altered his route to accommodate them. Another transport hiccup occurred during a visit to the naval base at Rosyth in Scotland. Mountbatten, as Admiral of the Fleet, was due to inspect the base and a full guard of honour was standing on parade waiting to salute him. Again, his car broke down *en route*. Just then an electric milk float passed by, so Admiral of the Fleet, Earl Mountbatten of Burma, commandeered it and ordered the milkman to drive to the base. When they arrived he then insisted that they carry on to the saluting dais. He then performed his inspection of the parade as if it was the most natural thing in the world to turn up in such an unconventional manner. Many of the officers present dined out on the story for years afterwards – and most were never believed.

All the men in the royal family like to shoot; it's a pre-requisite for inclusion in weekend country house parties, and they like their valets to accompany them. So an extra duty which, in theory, is purely voluntary, is to know how to load the guns. What happens is that the valet is asked if he would like to go shooting with his boss. If he agrees – and so far none has declined – he is then sent on a short course to Purdey's or Holland & Holland where he is taught the rudiments of loading the shot-guns. He is also measured for a suit of clothes to be worn in the field.

The valet learns all the little tricks necessary to keep the royals happy. Prince Philip and Prince Charles like to use a favourite fountain pen wherever they are, so when they are travelling by air their valets remove the pens from their suit pockets and keep them in a special case lined with blotting paper; fountain pens have a habit of leaking at high altitude.

They also carry spare pairs of reading glasses and fully charged cordless electric shavers which can be used if required on board the aircraft. Prince Philip is fair and doesn't need to shave twice a day, but Prince Charles has a heavy growth and after a long flight he will always shave just before landing. The valets carry a comb but these are rarely used as all the royal men, Philip, Charles, Andrew and Edward, use silver-backed hairbrushes. King Edward VII once ordered a guest at Sandringham to leave immediately when a comb fell out of his pocket. In those days, no gentleman would even own such a thing. To comb one's hair was the mark of a 'cad'.

One valet had the unusual task of packing tiny sardine sandwiches in a special pouch that could be hidden under State robes, so that when his master was waiting for the Queen to emerge for the procession to the House of Lords during the State Opening of Parliament, he could stave off the pangs of hunger. This habit continues among courtiers today who, both male and female, hide food in their clothing to avoid fainting during long functions. Her Majesty is said to be fully aware of this little idiosyncrasy and is highly amused.

When travelling abroad every royal valet packs a suit of morning clothes, so that, should a death occur in the royal family, his master will return to Britain suitably clad. Another useful item of equipment is a tin of whitening powder. On trips to hot countries where tropical uniforms are worn, it is easy to mark the white uniforms when getting into or out of aircraft or ships. The powder comes in handy for cleaning off black stains.

One thing the valet has to learn very quickly is the significance and order in which decorations are worn. Once again they are given a short course of instruction at Spink, the royal medal suppliers, who show them how both large and miniature decorations should be worn.

Prince Philip and Prince Charles both have dozens of uniforms belonging to many different service units, so their valets have to know the correct way to attach the appropriate decorations, and also how to lay their hands on them quickly. Each has his own system of keeping the medals and ribbons catalogued and is particularly careful when dealing with foreign orders. Political instability in many parts of the world, and rapid changes of government, even in the Commonwealth, make it imperative for no senior member of the royal family to be seen wearing a decoration awarded by a previous regime which is no longer recognized.

Valets become used to the idiosyncrasies of royalty, both British and foreign. When Prince Philip's aunt, Queen Louise of Sweden, Earl Mountbatten's sister, came to stay at Buckingham Palace she would always carry a card in her handbag on which were printed the words 'I am the Queen of Sweden.' When she was asked why she did this she replied: 'I often wander around London on my own. If I was knocked down by a bus, nobody would know who I was. So when they looked in my handbag they would find out.' She must have been the only monarch in the world to feel she needed to carry such identification.

When a male member of the royal family is single, he relies more on his valet than when he has a wife. The late Stephen Barry, who was valet to Prince Charles for twelve years, became indispensable – until his boss married. Then his position changed. No longer was he regarded as a close confidant, and when Diana's influence on her husband's wardrobe began to clash with Barry's (and Prince Charles's, though he would never admit it) ideas of style, the end was in sight.

In the period when Charles travelled the world as the most eligible bachelor on earth, it was to his valet he turned for honest advice – about girlfriends (though Barry was homosexual) and how he should dress for particular occasions. It is a common misconception that because the royal men always look immaculate and perfectly dressed, they choose their own suits, shirts and ties. The truth is that not one of them has the slightest idea of how to dress themselves and, just like their womenfolk, would be helpless if they were suddenly left without professional assistance. In exactly the same way that the Queen and Princess Anne depend on their dressers to select their outfits for the day, Prince Philip and his sons are equally dependent on the servants who look after their clothes.

The Prince of Wales, who is regarded as one of the most self-reliant of the royals, cannot manage without the assistance of his two valets. Stephen Barry told of the morning when he laid out three ties and asked the Prince which one he would like to wear. Charles told him, 'You choose, that's what I pay you for.' It was also Prince Charles who wrote a note to Barry complaining that his toothpaste had not been squeezed on his toothbrush the correct way, '... and the handle of the toothbrush is facing in the wrong direction. You know I'm right-handed.'

Prince Philip disagrees with his two valets about the way he chooses to wear a handkerchief in the top pocket of his suit. They would prefer him to have it loosely tucked in, as most gentlemen do, and to vary the colours. He insists on a white handkerchief at all times, and worn absolutely square, with half an inch showing, which they claim is the mark of someone not out of the 'top drawer'. But Prince Philip is unlikely to change even if, privately, he agrees with them. He has been wearing his handkerchief in his own way for years and that's the way he intends to remain.

Valets see their masters in the most intimate circumstances. When Prince Charles is being dressed in his uniform for the Sovereign's Birthday Parade – Trooping the Colour – his valet hands him his underwear to put on himself. But thereafter he is dressed in every single item.

Without the help of his valet, the Prince – or any of the others for that matter – simply could not cope. This is an extreme example of the value of having a valet, but in everyday life also, because of the complicated and strenuous programmes the royals undertake, they still need someone they can rely on totally, to make sure they are appropriately dressed on all occasions.

Prince Charles is associated with over three hundred organizations, military and civilian, and almost every one has its own tie. In any one day he might have three or four engagements, and it is important – and good manners – for him to wear the appropriate tie. So if the first engagement of the day is, say, at the Royal Automobile Club, he will pay them the compliment of turning up wearing their tie. If the next one happens to be at the Welsh Guards Depot, and he is not expected to be in uniform, the correct tie will be placed in his car so that he can change en route. When he is outside London and not able to return to St James's Palace, all the appropriate ties are placed in his car by his valet and his personal police officer hands them over at the right moment. The record for Prince Charles is believed to be eight different ties in a single day.

A good valet knows all the tricks of the trade and also which accessories should be worn with every military and naval uniform. There was one occasion when Prince Philip's regular valet was ill and his opposite number on leave, so a new man had been brought in to help out temporarily. His Royal Highness was being dressed in his uniform as an Admiral of the Fleet when he noticed that the servant had put out black, toe-cap shoes. Philip knows as well as, if not better than, his staff the correct dress and he pointed out that black patent boots should be worn. The following day his usual valet returned to work and discovered the error. He was horrified as, if the Prince hadn't noticed the slip in time, despite his absence he would have felt responsible.

As valets move up the career ladder in the royal household, their status is recognized in subtle, and sometimes not so subtle ways. A former royal valet recalled how when he was working for one of the minor royals, he was allowed to eat in the stewards' hall at Windsor Castle – a great step up from the servants' hall – but even here there was a strict order of precedence. 'On the first day I found the Palace Steward sitting at the head of the table, with the Queen's second dresser on his right. The first dresser refused to eat with the rest of the staff and had her meals served in her private apartments. I was invited to sit on the Palace Steward's left. The next day I found I had been moved two places farther down the table because the Queen Mother's pages had arrived at the Castle. The following day I was even lower because Princess Margaret had turned up and her servants took precedence over me.'

A skill every valet learns is packing. One of them always accompanies his principal on overseas visits and every eventuality is catered for. An extended world tour, such as those undertaken by Prince Philip in his early days in the royal family, could mean as many as forty-three countries in six weeks. This could involve his valet packing winter uniforms, summer whites and jungle greens for three different services, plus outfits for various levels of formality. Mess kits for service dinners, dinner jackets for civilian affairs and full evening dress, white tie and tails, for those formal occasions which warranted the style. Then there were all the decorations which had to be numbered in their own cases so the valet could lay his hands on them at a moment's notice. There was one occasion when His Royal Highness arrived by air in South East Asia, expecting to be greeted by a high-level government official, so he dressed in his tropical uniform with medals. As his aircraft taxied to a halt, he noticed that his host waiting on the tarmac was a member of the royal family wearing full regalia. Philip's valet quickly found the appropriate sash and decoration of the country they were visiting, and by the time the doors were opened Prince Philip was ready to be welcomed and a possible insult was avoided. His valet had saved the day.

Once Lord Mountbatten's valet passed on an invaluable tip to his opposite number in Prince Philip's household. They were on a trip to the Caribbean and the Prince wanted to go snorkelling. Mountbatten's man remembered that the sun in that part of the world can be particularly fierce even under a few feet of water, so he suggested that Prince Philip's valet should persuade his boss to wear a pair of old pyjamas. It took some doing but when Philip heard that his Uncle Dickie always took this precaution, he agreed. At the end of the afternoon, he was the only member of his party not to have a bad case of sunburn.

There is a special bond between the royal men and their valets. If Prince Charles is travelling in his car with one of his two valets, they know he likes to listen to classical music and they place the right tapes and CDs in the vehicle. But sometimes he will ask them if they mind the music being played and if they would prefer to hear something else. None of them has yet told him they can't stand his kind of music – with royalty democracy goes only so far.

CHAPTER SEVEN

Likes and Dislikes

Newcomers to the royal household are quickly appraised of the likes and dislikes of the royal family. The Queen dislikes facial hair, so beards are out and moustaches are frowned upon. Apart from her liveried servants, she does not care to see men in three-piece suits, so waistcoats are discarded very rapidly. Similarly, she prefers traditional black lace-up shoes to brown shoes or slip-ons. And she can spot a made-up bow tie at a dozen paces. She once mentioned to her then Lord Chamberlain (Lord Maclean) that he should advise a particular official to learn to tie his own bow tie for Palace functions.

The royals all enjoy ice in their drinks but they do not like the sound of ice-cubes grating against each other. So a special machine has been installed to make ice-balls, which apparently produce a softer, more pleasant sound. Footmen soon learn also that Her Majesty will not drink sparkling water; she prefers the still variety, preferably Malvern, bottles of which accompany her everywhere at home and abroad.

The Queen bathes morning and evening but the temperature of the water changes. In the morning it is lower because she does not wish to soak; her ablutions take a minimum amount of time as she wants to get on with the day's work. In the evening, however, she likes to relax in a hot bath so the water temperature is increased slightly. And the towels are always white with a slightly rough texture.

The only napkin rings at Buckingham Palace are those used by the household. The Queen and Prince Philip do not need them because there is always a fresh napkin for every meal. The Queen's grandfather, King George V, was once amused to find a napkin ring beside his place-setting when he dined with friends at a private house. 'What's this?' he exclaimed. 'It's far too big for my finger.'

The royals call their policemen, pages, chauffeurs and older servants by their surnames. Junior footmen and personal valets are addressed by their Christian names. The exception was Princess Diana, who called everyone by their Christian name, or nickname if she knew it.

Her Majesty does not like strangers trying to pet her corgis – as many do to ingratiate themselves, and new staff are warned about this possessive attitude. She dislikes anyone trying to get too close to her pets, and they are more than likely to snap at any hand that attempts to pat them. There is no dogs' cemetery at any of the royal residences; instead the corgis are all buried at various spots on the Sandringham estate, usually near a favourite tree, with a small stone marking the grave.

Whenever the Queen needs attention, someone always comes to her, not the other way around. Doctors are summoned, hairdressers are on hand, pedicurists cut her toenails in the privacy of her own room. The only time she goes out to see a professional consultant is when she visits the dentist – and that's because all the necessary equipment is available in Harley Street where her dentist – who is a part-time member of the royal household, with the title of Surgeon-Dentist – has his rooms. Prince Philip has a fully-equipped barbershop attached to his suite where his hairdresser comes to cut his hair once a week.

The Queen's correspondence file is massive. She receives thousands of letters every week, but one thing she is loath to do is dictate the answers. Instead, if she cannot write back personally, she will order one of her private secretaries to reply in her name or, if it is to a child or elderly person, the duty lady-in-waiting will write the reply. Together with every other member of the royal family, the Queen cannot bear to listen to long, rambling speeches, so when she is expected at an official engagement, those in charge are told in advance that they should make sure all speeches are kept to a minimum. Twelve minutes is regarded as the optimum time.

Tennis is not one of the Queen's favourite sports. The last time she went to Wimbledon was in 1977 – the year of her Silver Jubilee – when she presented the women's championship prize to Virginia Wade. And many years later the sportswoman related that, behind her dark glasses, the distinguished spectator was glancing at a copy of *Sporting Life*. Racing is her favourite sport and she names all her own horses herself.

Unlike Prince Philip and Princess Anne, the Queen has never been a fan of sailing. Her husband and daughter are skilled in the sport, but Her Majesty prefers dry land even though she is an excellent swimmer. Another sport which has never held any attraction for the Queen is skiing, although when she was younger, the late Princess Margaret was an enthusiastic and excellent water-skier.

Chefs who join Prince Charles's household are told he prefers fish to meat, and he especially likes cold dishes such as salmon and prawns. Potatoes must be kept to a minimum, and he never eats chocolate puddings or anything with nuts in it. By contrast the Duke of Gloucester is a chocaholic. He loves chocolate in every form, as a dessert, in drinks and in bars. He will eat any kind but prefers dark to milk chocolate.

No one may touch Prince Charles's shoes except his orderly from the Welsh Guards, who comes in every morning to polish them. And when the Prince visits the United States, which he loves, his aides are instructed to tell his hosts not to address him as 'Hi Prince'. He hates it and would prefer a plain Charles if they cannot manage his full title.

In the early days of the Queen's reign, it was not considered polite ever to turn your back on her, so everyone who was granted an audience would walk across the room to meet her and then, when the audience was over, retreat backwards, sometimes to the amusement of Her Majesty. She realized how ridiculous this was, and how uncomfortable it could be for some of the more elderly men and women, so she abandoned the practice early on. Today the only people who still walk backwards are the Lord Chamberlain and the Lord Steward, at State Banquets, when they follow the pattern of the carpets to keep in a straight line, and the Lord Great Chamberlain, who follows the same tradition at the State Opening of Parliament.

Footmen and police officers are warned that when they

ride in one of the royal limousines or on one of the carriages, they must not on any account look around. Eyes front is the order of the day and several men have found it difficult on the journey to Windsor or Sandringham to avoid looking out at something that has attracted their attention.

Before men and women are introduced into the royal presence, either in the Queen's sitting room if it is a private audience, or perhaps at a garden party when certain guests are chosen from the crowds to be presented, they are told by one of the equerries the normal routine. Some ladies still believe it is essential to wear gloves when shaking the sovereign's hand but this is no longer a requirement; nor do they need to curtsy if they do not feel inclined. Gentlemen should give a short neck bow, but again this is left up to them.

When the Queen is expected to pay a visit on an official engagement, her hosts often telephone the Palace to ask if there are any special items she likes or things that should be made ready. The most frequently asked question is, 'What happens if she wants to go to the lavatory?' The answer is that her lady-in-waiting should be made aware of the exact location of the 'retiring room', and it should be reserved for Her Majesty's exclusive use if required. Some hosts go to extraordinary lengths when a royal guest is expected, installing brand new, expensive toilet suites, which are generally never used. They also occasionally ask ridiculous questions like, 'Will she pull the flush herself?' but the Queen likes as little fuss as possible and is quite capable of completing her own ablutions. She uses an old-fashioned bristle toothbrush, not an electric model, and she does not care for the longer-lasting nylon variety.

The Queen likes to drive herself around the estates at

Sandringham and Balmoral, but she refuses to wear a safety belt. Similarly, when she rides, which she does almost every morning at Sandringham, she will not wear a hard hat, preferring a silk head-scarf.

Before the Queen goes to the theatre, she likes a light supper of smoked salmon and scrambled eggs. She says it's too late to eat afterwards.

She never uses a thesaurus when doing a crossword – she thinks it's cheating – and one way to tell if she disagrees with some remark is when she replies 'How fascinating', a phrase she says in a variety of tones. Her favourite news-paper is the *Racing Post* which is delivered to her every morning wherever she may be.

The Queen has often turned a blind eye when one of her favourite servants has appeared to be slightly the worse for wear. She's sympathetic to their having a little too much to drink, but only the men, not the female staff. She herself does not drink champagne. If a toast is proposed at a royal banquet, she merely pretends to take a sip.

The Queen, other royal ladies and their ladies-in-waiting, do not normally wear black unless they are in mourning. The length of the mourning depends on which of the four types it is: General, restricted to the death of a sovereign; Court, observed only by the royal family and their households; Ser-vice, when the armed forces wear black arm bands; and Family, observed only by the royal family. Nowadays, the length is decided by the Queen and is generally expected to last no longer than one month. For the death of her sister Margaret the Queen wore black only until the funeral six days later, and when the Queen Mother died on 30 March 2002 family mourning lasted until 19 April.

Her Majesty does not like a duvet on her bed. She prefers

linen sheets and woollen blankets. Her sheets are six inches longer than Prince Philip's, because she likes a deeper 'turn-back'. She has never rung a door-bell in her life. Whenever she is expected as a guest, someone telephones her exact time of arrival so her hosts are always waiting at the door.

The Queen does not like the appearance of Buckingham Palace to be spoiled by odd windows being opened – so they are never opened at the front of the building, even in high summer. An exception to this rule was made on the Nursery Floor when the Queen's children were small. If it was very hot the windows were opened a little to let in some fresh air, but never fully. Similarly, none of the net curtains at the front are ever drawn back so as not to damage the 'chocolate box' effect.

Her favourite Prime Ministers were Harold Wilson and James Callaghan, while Margaret Thatcher and Tony Blair are said to be among the least popular. But a former footman to the Queen denies that she and Margaret Thatcher did not get on, saying: 'They always gave me the impression that they liked each other. I certainly never felt that Her Majesty disliked Mrs (as she then was) Thatcher.'

One custom that was begun by Queen Victoria and of which the Queen thoroughly approves is the practice of holding all Privy Council meetings standing. It results, she says, in shorter gatherings.

Her Majesty will not allow thirteen people to sit down to lunch or dinner. She says it is not because she is superstitious, but some of her guests may be. However she does throw spilt salt over her shoulder – just in case. And at 'First Footing' on New Year's Eve at Sandringham, one of the footmen is delegated to hand around a bag containing forecasts for the coming year. Each member of the royal family takes a 'Lucky Dip' and if their particular forecast is not very favourable the poor footman gets the blame.

Unlike most people, the Queen's Christmas decorations are not taken down on twelfth night. She likes them to remain throughout her stay in Sandringham, which is usually until just after the anniversary of her father's death on 6 February.

The royal family is the same as any other group in having its preferences and its aversions. The difference is that where their servants are concerned, there is no redress. Although the domestic staff belong to a trade union there has never been industrial action at Buckingham Palace, and in practice staff have no right to complain about bad behaviour, ill temper or even sexual harassment should that occur. (No case has ever come to the knowledge of anyone outside.)

If the Queen or Prince Philip, or any of the other royals, wants a footman or maid moved, the Master of the Household is informed, and the offending servant is discreetly told they are being allocated to other duties. They are not told the reason and neither is there any appeal. Sacking is rare in the royal household. Serious theft or, even worse, talking to the press, are the usual reasons why staff suddenly are 'let go'. One of the most important things a royal servant has to accept is being able to swallow the fact that they are little more than any other possession. In some cases, not even as useful and certainly not as valuable. Priceless articles of furniture cannot be replaced; servants all know that should they disappear, within an hour someone else will arrive to take their place.

The Queen uses a system when appointing her servants – and this applies all the way to the top, not just at the lower level – which gives her a tactful 'get-out' clause. Whenever a new aide is being given a job, she invariably says, 'Let's try it for a couple of months to see how we get on. Then if either of us can't stand the other, we can call it a day.' It's a clever ploy, which her servants realize is really a one-way street. No one who has been appointed to work personally for Her Majesty has ever told her at the end of the trial period that they don't like her and want to leave, and, in fairness, there have been few occasions when she has had reason to end the relationship. But it does give her the option should she wish to exercise it, and on those rare occasions when it hasn't worked out the new man or woman is able to leave without feeling humiliated.

The Queen's personal staff tend to stay with her for many years, mainly because they have worked their way up from the lower ranks, so they 'know the form' and what is expected of them. Dressers, valets, pages and footmen are all chosen personally, and they enjoy an intimacy no one else in the household shares. The Queen knows the Christian names of all her immediate staff and always uses them. So her three dressers – Angela Kelly, Carol Grave and Julie Thackray – are all used to being called Angela, Carol and Julie. Similarly, Pat Pentney, the flower arranger, who sees the Queen nearly every day, is addressed as Pat, even though she is Mrs Pentney. Her Majesty wouldn't dream of calling Paul Whybrew, her page, anything other than Paul and he would think he had done something very wrong if she did.

Prince Philip's two valets work only for His Royal Highness, and the Palace Steward and Sergeant Footman, who in theory are higher grades, wouldn't dream of trying to tell them what to do or allocate them to other duties. If they did, the valets would simply refuse and, if it came to a showdown, they know that Prince Philip would back them. He is the most considerate of bosses, in spite of his reputation for impatience, and his staff are, without doubt, the most loyal in the Palace. He demands complete obedience and utter professionalism; in turn he gives them his protection in all things. Even the Queen's private secretary, supposed to be the most important person in the royal household, has found himself having to stand and take a verbal roasting from Prince Philip, when he has had the temerity to challenge something one of the Prince's staff has done.

This doesn't mean that all is sweetness and light in Philip's household. If he thinks something is wrong, which he often does, he will blow his top and blame the nearest person regardless of whether they are to blame or not. But he doesn't bear grudges. Once his tantrum is over, it's forgotten. And he will not stand for anyone talking back; neither will any of the royal family. Right or wrong, they are always right. But Philip's attitude to his staff differs slightly from that of the Queen's in that when one of his carriages turned over during a competition, his first concern was for the coachman sitting with him. The Queen's initial worry would have been for the horses.

Animals figure largely in the royal family's life and none more so than Her Majesty's corgis. On one occasion a footman had been carrying a tray laden with tea things into her sitting room when he became entangled with two of her corgis. They nipped at his ankles and finally caused him to fall, dropping the tray as he did. He is a big man and fell heavily, twisting his leg under him. Her Majesty immediately ran over but, ignoring him, fussed over the dogs. He was in some pain but the yapping of the dogs was of more concern to the Queen and he was left to limp out of the room by himself. When he told his colleagues the story they laughed and asked him, 'What did you expect? We're just part of the furniture around here.' Prince Philip takes a paternalistic attitude to his staff; they are on his team, he's the captain, but as long as they give him one hundred per cent, he returns their loyalty in full measure.

Although the Queen loves to hear gossip from her staff, she still keeps them at arm's length. No one, since Bobo McDonald, has been allowed to get close and it's a relationship both sides prefer. At least with her they know where they stand and there is never the slightest chance of any familiarity. There may be friendliness – of a sort – but no one is ever left in any doubt that the boss also happens to be the sovereign.

Prince Charles has a large staff: over eighty at Highgrove and St James's Palace, and they soon learn that he has a habit of checking food stocks to see that there is no waste. When he stays at Craigowan, the house he often uses on the Balmoral estate, he will walk into the kitchen and see how much milk is in the 'fridge, and then work out how many people it is for. He once did the same with the number of chickens in the freezer, only to be told, when he questioned why there were so many, it was because 'You do like your vol-au-vents'.

Every year His Royal Highness takes his staff out to Christmas lunch at the Ritz Hotel (to whom he awarded a Royal Warrant at the end of 2001). Nothing is denied them, they can eat and drink whatever they want and expense

One of the daily duties of the Queen's footmen – and one they don't all care for – is taking Her Majesty's corgis for a walk in the grounds of Buckingham Palace, morning and evening, rain or shine.

At 9 o'clock every morning the Queen's Piper parades in Highland dress and marches on the terrace beneath her window playing some of her favourite Scottish tunes. The ceremony lasts for fifteen minutes and Her Majesty enjoys every second.

The cleaners start work at 6 am and everything is usually finished by noon. The housekeeping staff all work under the supervision of the chief housekeeper at the Palace, who believes there is nothing to beat good old-fashioned 'elbow grease'.

As with everything else in the Royal Household, there is a strict routine for vacuuming the carpets. The cleaners must not be switched on before 8 am in case any of the royal family are still asleep and the vacuum cleaner must be used while walking backwards to avoid leaving footprints.

The Queen's Royal Body Guard of the Yeoman of the Guard is the oldest active military corps in the world, having been created by Henry VII in 1485. They are not to be confused with the 'Beefeaters', who are the Yeomen Warders at the Tower of London.

There is only one way to polish a table that is over one hundred feet long and ten feet wide and that is for a footman to wear dusters on his feet and walk about. It is also the most convenient method of placing the heavy candelabra.

Yes, it is true that at a State Banquet each place setting is measured with a ruler. And for a very good reason. With one hundred and twenty guests, if they didn't measure every setting they might get to the end of the table and find there wasn't room for them all.

It can take up to seven hours to assemble and set the table for a full State Banquet with particular attention paid to the glasses, gold cutlery and spectacular floral displays.

Once the table has been laid, the Palace Steward will inspect it. If he is satisfied, the Master of the Household checks it and finally the Queen herself comes in to see that everything is in order.

The decanting of wine is a special skill learned over the years by the Yeoman of the Wine Cellars. Note the candle being held to warm the bottle to the correct temperature as it is being poured.

The vegetable chefs are highly skilled at making sure that each carrot, sprout, potato and garden pea is exactly the same size as its neighbour.

Behind the scenes the senior footmen in their ceremonial uniforms wait for the festivities to begin while the kitchen hands – in less formal attire – bring the food up to the ante-room adjoining the State Ballroom before it is carried into the banquet.

Nobody but the chefs are allowed to touch any food that is going to be eaten at the royal table. One of the dessert chefs arranges fruit prior to a formal dinner at Windsor Castle.

is no object. The Prince is equally generous when it comes to entertaining at home; his guests enjoy the delights of one of the finest tables and cellars in the country. But his own tastes are simple, bordering on the frugal. He is not a big eater and his drinking is restricted to a couple of glasses of white wine. He is often offered a glass of vintage champagne when he visits friends' homes or at public functions, but he actually doesn't like champagne and only takes the occasional sip to be sociable.

Prince Philip is another who does not care for champagne. He likes sweet German wine or a bottle of beer. The brewery firm of Ind Coop and Allsop used to market a beer called Double Diamond. It was enormously successful thirty years ago following an advertising campaign that claimed 'A Double Diamond works wonders.' Prince Philip obviously thinks it still does and the company now bottle it just for him even though they have discontinued brewing the beer commercially. Footmen at Buckingham Palace are taught how to pour the beer from the bottle to a glass so that a perfect head is obtained, and more than one has felt the rough edge of Philip's tongue when he hasn't achieved quite the right touch.

The Princess Royal is generally regarded as the most 'no-nonsense' member of the family and outsiders would be surprised at how regal she can be with employees. There is no familiarity at all, or even much friendliness. Strangely, she always seems to be more relaxed with the young footmen who bring her morning coffee, occasionally chatting informally with them in her sitting room.

Her own personal team – including the female petty officer from the Royal Navy she gets for nothing on attachment – can recognize the signs of her moods and react accordingly. When she enters a room they always stand. She will usually tell them to sit down, but if they did not stand in the first place they would be made aware of her displeasure. She doesn't mince words. If she has something to say she will say it, but again, like her father, she does not bear grudges and she doesn't sulk. Once it is over, it's over as far as she is concerned. Her policemen are the ones who spend more time with her than anyone else, but none gets very close. There was a rumour over twenty years ago that one of her bodyguards became emotionally involved with her. There was never any direct evidence to prove the allegation but he left the Royalty Protection Department soon after. When she is driving to and from an engagement in her private Bentley, the policeman sits alongside her but he is never allowed to take the wheel; she hates being driven. One of his duties before they set off is to make sure CDs of her favourite music are in place. She doesn't care for small talk, preferring to listen to popular records. She is not a lover of classical music.

Her chef knows her tastes to perfection. They rarely change and anyway she eats like a sparrow. Her figure – a slim size 10 – is the same as when she was first married in 1973, and her staff say if she could take a tablet instead of food, she would gladly do so. She regards daytime meals as taking up valuable time which could be used in other ways, but she does enjoy small dinner parties, both as hostess, at which she is brilliant, and as a guest at the homes of her circle of close friends such as Andrew Parker Bowles or Sir Jackie Stewart, who first met her when they were voted sports personalities of 1971. They never have the problem of deciding which wine to offer her; she doesn't drink alcohol, sticking to mineral water.

For a while after her marriage to Tim Laurence in 1992 they rented a small apartment in Dolphin Square in London's Pimlico. The idea was to make him feel independent of royal ties. But security was difficult and Anne in fact spent only one night there. They gave up the lease in 1995. Nowadays the Princess has two homes: Gatcombe Park, in Gloucestershire, which the Queen bought for her and Mark Phillips in 1976, and which she retained after their divorce, and an apartment in St James's Palace, where her nearest neighbour is her brother, the Prince of Wales. She has servants at both places and an office staff at Buckingham Palace, to whom her behaviour is usually correct – unless she thinks something has gone wrong – but rarely cordial. The one thing her staff all agree on is that they know where they stand with her. Or, as one of them put it: 'If we expect the worse, we're never disappointed.'

CHAPTER EIGHT

All the Queen's Horses

When Queen Victoria was on the throne, the horse was the main form of transport and she kept two hundred in the Royal Mews at Buckingham Palace and the other royal residences in London. A further hundred were stabled at Windsor Castle, and all her residences had scores of their own horses, which remained at that particular spot throughout their lives. The only horses that moved residence with the Queen were those she rode herself. Her favourite was a pony on which she walked through the grounds at Osborne House, her home on the Isle of Wight, invariably led by her ghillie, the fearsome John Brown.

By the time her great-grandson, Bertie, was crowned as King George VI in 1937, cars had replaced horses as the day-to-day mode of transport, and fewer than one hundred horses remained in the entire royal household, including those in Scotland. At Buckingham Palace, only seventy-five were stabled permanently and their main tasks were for ceremonial duties and delivering mail and packages between the royal family's homes in central London.

Today the number has been reduced even more, with some twenty Cleveland Bays and ten Windsor Greys – so called because their home was once in the Mews at Windsor Castle. The thirty horses live in immaculate conditions in the Mews located in the south-west corner of the Palace grounds, and when they are required at other places, such as Windsor for the ceremonial procession at Royal Ascot, they are transported by horsebox.

The royal children have all been taught to ride in the Mews riding school, which is seventy-five yards long and laid with a firm surface over a six-foot-deep foundation of faggots and peat. There, in order to get the horses used to the conditions they are likely to encounter in processions through the busy streets of London, recordings of loud military music and crowds cheering are played, and flags and bunting are strung across the school, vigorously waved in case it is windy when the horses are on ceremonial duty.

The Crown Equerry, who commands the Royal Mews, takes no chances and when Prince Charles was being invested as Prince of Wales at Caernarvon Castle in North Wales in 1969, the horses were rehearsed in a variety of conditions. They even had soldiers throwing buckets of water under their hooves as they pulled the State Carriages up the steep incline of the approach to the Castle in case it rained on the day. It didn't, but the men in charge of the Queen's horses were not about to be caught out. The stable lads are also encouraged to shout and bang dustbin lids as loudly as they can, to simulate the noise made by the crowds who line the routes they take. And, in these days of possible terrorist attacks, the horses are made familiar with the sound of guns being fired.

When the Queen used to ride her horse Burmese in the

Sovereign's Birthday Parade, her skill as a horsewoman, and Burmese's capability under fire, were put to the test when a man fired blank cartridges at Her Majesty as she turned from The Mall into Horseguards. Neither horse nor rider flinched.

These days, no member of the family rides for pleasure in London. Rotten Row in Hyde Park, which was at one time a very popular venue, is now left mainly to local riders and members of the Household Cavalry exercising their mounts from their stables in Knightsbridge Barracks.

When the Queen rides at Windsor, as she still does most weekends, her own horses are available as they are kept there along with others which Her Majesty sometimes offers to guests if they want to ride. When President Ronald Reagan stayed at the Castle, he enthusiastically joined the Queen on a number of occasions riding in the grounds and said that, although he was more used to riding 'Western' style, as he did when he was a film star, he found the Queen's choice of mounts to be perfect in every way.

Buckingham Palace has been described many times as a village, and the Royal Mews is a tiny self-contained hamlet within that village. It is a very tight-knit community whose inhabitants keep to themselves. Those who live and work within its walls are the grooms, stable-lads, coachmen, chauffeurs and upholsterers, all under the supervision of the Crown Equerry, who is responsible for all travel by road that the Queen and her family undertake. When Her Majesty leaves Buckingham Palace on Friday afternoon for her weekend at Windsor Castle, she is not driven in one of the State Rolls Royce limousines, preferring to travel in her own personal car, a dark green Jaguar. It is more anonymous and does not attract anywhere near the same

THE ROYAL MEWS DEPARTMENT

Crown Equerry

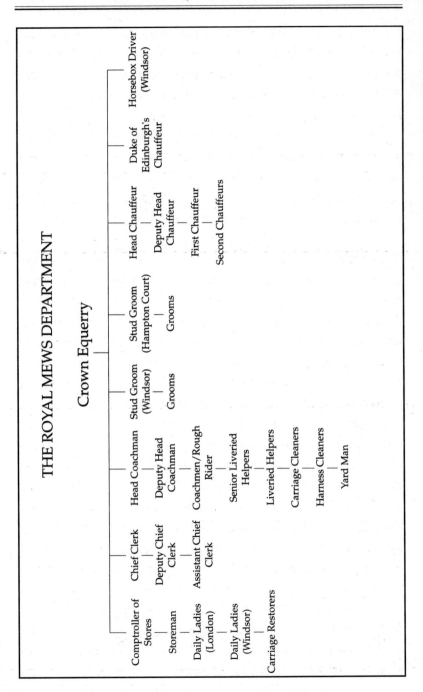

Comptroller of Stores	Chief Clerk	Head Coachman	Stud Groom (Windsor)	Stud Groom (Hampton Court)	Head Chauffeur	Duke of Edinburgh's Chauffeur	Horsebox Driver (Windsor)
Storeman	Deputy Chief Clerk	Deputy Head Coachman	Grooms	Grooms	Deputy Head Chauffeur		
Daily Ladies (London)	Assistant Chief Clerk	Coachmen/Rough Rider			First Chauffeur		
Daily Ladies (Windsor)		Senior Liveried Helpers			Second Chauffeurs		
Carriage Restorers		Liveried Helpers					
		Carriage Cleaners					
		Harness Cleaners					
		Yard Man					

attention – and that is how the Queen likes it to be. The Crown Equerry, Lt Col Seymour Gilbart-Denham CVO (the post is invariably held by a former senior army officer), is a full-time member of the household. He lives in a splendid residence which is tied to his job, so he will have to vacate it when he retires; and he pays a significant proportion of his salary in rent. It is just inside the gates of the royal mews, where, in theory, he is able to keep an eye on anyone coming or going.

The three-storey house is far too large for the average family these days, dating as it does to the time when Queen Victoria owned all those horses and employed hundreds of men to look after them. The rooms are enormous and need massive furniture to fill them. But the most intriguing part is the basement, where the old kitchens were located. Cast iron coal-burning ranges weighing several tons – so heavy they cannot be removed safely – are a reminder of the days when Queen Victoria expected her Crown Equerry to live in some style and allowed him ten servants, all paid by herself.

The Royal Mews is built around a quadrangle and dates from 1825. King George IV commissioned John Nash to design it and its layout is mainly the same today as it was nearly two hundred years ago. The entrance is in Buckingham Palace Road with the Crown Equerry's house on the immediate left and his office directly opposite. The horses are stabled on the north and west sides, with the east side reserved for the state coaches and carriages. The south side has been converted to accommodate the royal limousines and the private vehicles of the Queen and the Duke of Edinburgh. Apart from Her Majesty's Jaguar, she also has a Vauxhall estate car. Prince Philip has a Discovery and a

London taxi. He used to travel around the capital in an electric-powered vehicle, but there were too many difficulties with charging the batteries and also, because the car was practically silent when it was running, the drivers of other vehicles could not hear it and there were a number of slight accidents, so it had to go. Prince Philip retains his passionate commitment to the environment by insisting that his vehicles are equipped to run on LPG (Liquid Petroleum Gas) in order to restrict pollution.

All the private vehicles are in 'Edinburgh Green'. This is the family colour of the Queen and Prince Philip and was adopted in 1948, a year after the couple were married. It was in 1953, Coronation Year, that His Royal Highness confirmed to the College of Arms that this shade of green was to be his official livery colour.

A story circulates in the garages that originated in the early days of the Queen's reign. Apparently she and the Duke of Edinburgh were being driven back to Sandringham from a private dinner party late one evening. This was in the days when the royal limousine travelled unaccompanied by a police back-up vehicle. As they drove through a remote village, at what the local policeman thought was excessive speed, he stepped out into the road and demanded that they stop. When they obeyed, he saw that the car had no number plate or road tax disc – an offence for any other vehicle – and asked the chauffeur for his driving licence. Whereupon the senior police bodyguard sitting beside the driver said: 'Do you realize we've got the Queen and Prince Philip in the back?' The local man replied: 'Yes, and I'm Roy Rogers [this was in the 'fifties when Rogers was a famous cowboy film star], and this [referring to his bicycle] is my horse Trigger.' Then the

Queen popped her head out of the rear window and said 'Well, you and Trigger had better let us get on our way.' Some days later the police officer received a commendation for his actions. The Queen and Prince Philip had seen the funny side.

There are a number of houses and apartments in the Mews where married couples are allocated pleasant quarters which, if they were rented commercially, would fetch astronomical sums. On the first-floor gallery which runs around the Mews, one can usually see children's toys lying around. The Queen has no objection to small children living on her premises, and while they obviously have to be kept out of harm's way at all times, their presence gives the place a homely atmosphere not apparent in other parts of Buckingham Palace. Her Majesty always makes an appearance at the Mews' annual children's Christmas party, when a horse-drawn sleigh enters the yard and Father Christmas hands out presents.

The Royal Mews is open to the public throughout the year and frequently visitors ask where the 'real' Mews is, believing this one is kept purely as an attraction. But this is very much a working stables and garage with a routine that rarely varies and a regime that is controlled with military efficiency by the man in charge. The Colonel is supported by an assistant and a senior administrator with responsibility for all the stores, the fabric of the buildings, all repairs and the accounts. The place is now big business with over 100,000 visitors passing through its doors every year. The garages, which are separate from the stables, are looked after by a transport officer. Apart from making sure the cars of the Queen and Prince Philip are always kept in immaculate condition, he arranges the transport for any incoming State Visit, including those at Windsor. He has only one brief: to get the right people to the right place at the right time. And even though he has performed the task many times, his file for a State Visit is still several inches thick.

The administrator is in effect the Royal Mews' senior clerical officer, who works from an office immediately above that of the Crown Equerry. They are in constant communication, and even though the administrator is not a member of the household but an official, the relationship is marked by an easy informality occasionally but not often found in other parts of the Palace.

Many of those who work in the Mews were formerly employed in other stables; The King's Troop Royal Horse Artillery and the Household Cavalry are fertile recruiting grounds, but equestrian agencies are also becoming more and more involved, making the establishment roughly 50/50 military and civilian. On the Queen's express orders, there are no female 'lads' in the Mews at Buckingham Palace. But the Master Saddler is a woman, so too is the horsebox driver and there are female grooms in the stables at Windsor. Days start early when the single young men who are stable lads and grooms are woken at 5.30 in their dormitory. They have to report for duty at 6am prompt for morning stables, and their first duty is mucking out and checking that the two horses each looks after, have eaten their overnight feed. If they haven't, the foreman, Colin Henderson, who is also the Head Coachman, is informed so that a report can be made to the veterinary surgeon.

Grooming is the next order of the day, and this takes around an hour. At 7 o'clock there is an hour's exercise – usually in the riding school. If the horses have passed inspection by the Head Coachman, the lads are allowed to eat their own breakfast, which is served at 8am, and it is always something substantial. A 'Full English' of eggs, bacon, beans and fried bread is the usual fare, washed down with mugs of hot, sweet tea.

After breakfast, which lasts for half an hour, the men change out of their mucking out overalls into their smart working riding gear: black coats, dark breeches, highly polished boots and riding helmets, a necessary precaution against injury. The horses are saddled and taken in a string across to Hyde Park for their morning exercise in Rotten Row. Although everyone connected with riding knows it is a hazardous sport, for the Royal Mews horses, the most dangerous part of their day is crossing the roads. They turn immediately left on leaving the Mews and move into Buckingham Palace Road, around the Queen Victoria Memorial in front of the Palace and ride up Constitution Hill. They are no longer accompanied by a police escort to see them safely across Hyde Park Corner, one of the busiest intersections in London. And as the exercise takes place at nine o'clock, right at the height of the peak period for traffic, it can be very difficult to negotiate a safe route. Irate drivers rarely give way to horses these days so, as Colin Henderson says, 'We take our lives into our hands every morning.'

Back in the Mews after their period of morning exercise, the animals are inspected to see if they have suffered any injury. If all is clear they are rubbed down and given their morning feed. By this time it is normally around eleven o'clock and the staff take their mid-morning break. Half the team then start to prepare the Mews for its daily opening to the public. It is one of the most popular attractions in

London and remains open throughout the year, unlike the State Apartments at Buckingham Palace, which are open only for eight weeks while the Queen is in Scotland.

Although the horses in the Royal Mews are kept mainly for ceremonial duties, certain tasks have to be fulfilled on a daily basis. People who live and work in the vicinity of the Palace are used to the sight of the claret-coloured Messenger Brougham being driven every morning, carrying the mail between Buckingham Palace, Clarence House, St James's Palace and Kensington Palace. Until recently, the brougham also called at Coutts, the royal banker's in the Strand. But negotiating Trafalgar Square with its nightmare flow of fast moving cars, buses, vans and motor cycles proved too difficult. As the Crown Equerry explained: 'Some drivers didn't seem to realize that a nineteenth-century brougham is not equipped with disc brakes.' The situation became so fraught that Col Gilbart-Denham advised the Queen that Coutts should be removed from the route and she, reluctantly, agreed.

The name Brougham came into being when Lord Brougham had a light carriage built to be hauled by a single horse and capable of carrying two passengers. They have had one in constant use at the Royal Mews since 1843 and the coachman and his assistant both wear plain livery of black top hat, black coat and black breeches in the summer. In winter they are equipped with a heavy fawn 'drab' coat which is guaranteed to keep out anything: hail, rain, wind or snow. The Messenger Brougham has become something of a tourist attraction in its own right, and the coachmen, although they dare not show it, are quite delighted to be photographed as they sit proudly on the box during their rounds.

There are over one hundred and fifty diplomatic embass-
ies and High Commissions in London (manned by nearly
4,000 staff), and each one has to be accredited to the Court
of St James's – still the official seat of monarchy; Buckingham Palace is only the official London residence of the
sovereign. So whenever an incoming diplomat has to present his credentials to the Queen, the Crown Equerry
arranges the transport, normally three carriages. The first
is for the ambassador and his wife (who travel in the State
Landau) or high commissioner (Semi-State Landau), and
who are always escorted by the Marshal of the Diplomatic
Corps, the member of the royal household responsible for
maintaining links between the Queen and diplomatic missions. The other two carriages are used for relatives and
members of the diplomat's staff who are invited to accompany him to the Palace and who are presented to Her
Majesty at the short ceremony. The Foreign Office employs
a lady in the protocol department, one of whose duties is
to instruct the wives and daughters of new diplomats in
the correct way to curtsy when being presented to Her
Majesty.

Because there are now so many foreign missions in
London – in Queen Victoria's reign only six foreign ambassadors were based in the capital – and there is a frequent
turnover of personnel, presentations take place up to three
times a week. The duty of carrying the diplomats is very
popular with Mews staff as it starts around ten in the morning and finishes by lunchtime. An extra perk is that there
is usually a celebration in the residence of the diplomat
once the formal part of the morning is complete, and the
coachmen and carriage attendants are often invited in for
a quick drink. But the days when lavish hospitality was

expected and accepted are long gone. The Queen used to see the carriages arriving back at the Palace and noticed how long they had been away. She wasn't too concerned about the coachmen and attendants having a drink, but she did not like the horses being kept standing still for too long.

Because there are now so many foreign delegations in London, and everyone has to be accorded the same courtesies, it has been necessary to impose a three-mile limit – or half an hour's driving time – from Buckingham Palace, on the 'ambassador' pick-up. Traffic conditions simply will not permit them to travel any farther. Even so, London is unique in its practice; the Royal Household of The Netherlands in The Hague has a similar system, but they will only collect ambassadors from a central point, not from each residence.

Most afternoons are free in the Mews except when there is a need for training or for working on the horses. At 4pm they start preparing the stables for the night. Two grooms are on duty throughout the night, checking the horses, picking up droppings and seeing there is plenty of fresh water.

The Mews no longer has an in-house farrier. It's more economical to hire a contract man who comes in whenever he is required. But even so some sixty-three staff are employed, including twenty-five in the stables, two carriage restorers, a saddle and harness maker and a storeman who maintains the livery and the washing machines, while a daily lady comes in to handle the laundering of breeches, shirts and socks. An enormous amount of cleaning is carried out, particularly when the Mews is open, when the carriages have to be cleaned every day, instead of just once after a state occasion and then returned to their carriage houses until the next time they are required. Included in the exhibition at the Mews are the Irish State Coach and Australian State Coach, either of which can be used when Her Majesty attends the State Opening of Parliament, and the Ivory Mounted Phaeton which is used by the Queen when she is being driven to Horseguards for The Sovereign's Birthday Parade.

The stores in the Mews contain all the uniforms the liveried staff wear on ceremonial occasions. They do not all have their own set, so the storeman numbers each one and keeps a record of the measurements of every member of the staff so that when they need to be fitted out he can select the right size. Some of the postillion jackets from Queen Victoria's time cannot be worn for the simple reason that they are too small. In those days, the majority of liveried staff were ex-jockeys – all of diminutive stature. By today's standards, they would just about fit the very smallest jockey types. This shortage of uniforms is a limiting factor when the Head Coachman, Colin Henderson, is deciding who does what job on a State Visit, 'We are, however, each year having larger uniforms made, but this is a slow process in view of costs,' he says. A State Visit means all stops are pulled out. Everyone is on duty and all thirty horses are involved. The Cleveland Bays are home-bred at Hampton Court Royal Paddocks, the oldest stud in Britain, but the Windsor Greys are bought in.

Both the Queen and the Duke of Edinburgh have a keen eye for detail, with His Royal Highness making his views known in his own forthright manner. As a man used to competition driving when speed is of the essence, he is occasionally impatient at the more sedate pace necessary when being driven back from a ceremonial duty such as the State Opening of Parliament. The Head Coachman has on more than one occasion been urged by Prince Philip to 'get a move on'. It's usually said in a semi-joking tone and the Head Coachman doesn't mind. As he says, 'It keeps us on our toes.'

An important part of the Royal Mews is the garage which houses the State limousines. Five Rolls Royces, recently joined by another (a Bentley) as a gift for Her Majesty in Golden Jubilee Year, are used by the royal family for official duties. And at every State occasion where there is a carriage procession, the Crown Equerry follows at the end of the line in a car, just in case there is a mishap with one of the horse-drawn carriages and alternative transport is required. He is in constant radio contact with the Queen's personal police officer up ahead. Colonel Gilbart-Denham tells the story of one German State Visit when the car he was being driven in was very nearly wrecked. 'A horse of the Household Cavalry suddenly kicked up and backed into two of the Queen's horses which were pulling the 1902 State Coach. I was bringing up the rear in one of the Rolls Royces when the horse then reared up and both horse and rider came over backwards, missing the car I was in by inches. It was the closest shave in fifteen years as Crown Equerry.'

The State limousines are all painted in what is described as 'Royal Maroon Livery', and while the Daimler limousines used by other members of the royal family on official occasions carry registration plates like every other car in Britain, the Rolls Royces do not. Until 2002 the youngest model was a Rolls Royce Phantom VI, presented to Her Majesty in 1978 by the Society of Motor Manufacturers and Traders to mark her Silver Jubilee the previous year. The oldest car is another Rolls Royce, this time a Phantom IV built in 1948, when the Queen was still Princess Elizabeth. There are two identical limousines built in 1960 and 1961, and they, together with the Phantom VI, have removable roof coverings so that the Queen can be seen through the transparent perspex lining underneath. The interiors are also illuminated by fluorescent light which is switched on when the Queen is being driven to an engagement at night.

While the royal family's private cars are garaged in the Mews, they are not maintained there. When one of them needs a service, Jaguar, Rover or Rolls Royce are telephoned and they come to collect the vehicle and then return it afterwards. The coaches and lorries which transport staff members and their luggage between different royal residences are not housed in the Royal Mews. These belong to the Army and are kept at nearby barracks. But two luggage brakes, built by Ford and Vauxhall, are garaged in the Mews and used for official duties such as carrying the Queen's luggage between Buckingham Palace and Windsor Castle at weekends.

Whenever the Queen is being driven by road, her car flies the Royal Standard and a shield bearing the Royal Coat of Arms. She also has her own mascot which is transferred from car to car. It is of solid silver and shows a naked St George, poised over a slain dragon. A gift from Prince Philip, it is the only one in existence. It is transferred in seconds to whichever car Her Majesty is travelling in as its thread is identical – and unique – to all her cars. It travels abroad with her and when her aircraft lands at a foreign airport, the pilot opens his tiny side window and throws a small bag, containing the mascot, to a waiting attendant on the tarmac, so that by the time the Queen has disembarked, it has already been fixed to her car. When Prince Philip is being driven alone, his mascot, a heraldic lion wearing a crown, is mounted on his vehicle.

The Queen's head chauffeur, Joe Last, drives Her Majesty on all important journeys. He has a deputy and an assistant and these three are the only people allowed to drive the sovereign. In addition there are two first chauffeurs and three second chauffeurs, making a total of eight in all. Prince Philip has his own chauffeur who drives exclusively for him. He is based at the Mews but as he is on the strength of Prince Philip's personal staff, and paid by him, he is not part of the Crown Equerry's establishment.

The Queen likes to drive herself, but these days she does not venture onto the roads of central London, preferring to stick to the quieter, private roads of Windsor or the Sandringham Estate. She is a competent motorist, who can remember the basic mechanical skills she learnt as an officer in a motor unit of the Auxiliary Territorial Army towards the end of the Second World War. No one can actually recall ever having seen her change a wheel on a car but she says she could if the need arose. She has never passed her driving test; she's never had to, and she is the only person in Britain who is legally allowed to drive on public roads without holding a valid licence. And to the despair of the motoring organizations, she steadfastly refuses to wear a safety belt, either when she is driving herself or when she is being driven in one of the state limousines.

There is a healthy rivalry between the equestrian and garage sides of the Royal Mews. As the Head Coachman puts it, 'They don't like the smell of manure and we don't care for the smell of diesel;' and there is little fraternization between the Mews and the rest of the Palace, although the

Crown Equerry himself, as a senior member of the royal household, is, naturally, involved in many meetings and gatherings with his colleagues.

Continuity is considered very important among the Mews staff, and although in the stables some of the younger men do not remain for long periods, there is one coachman who has been in royal service for thirty-five years. All the staff in the garage tend to stick with the job. At the time of writing they had had no vacancies for over three years.

A young man starting as a liveried servant is paid £14,000 a year, rising to £20,000 if he becomes a senior coachman. This is before all stoppages. For example, a senior coachman living in would expect to pay over £3,000 a year rent for his accommodation, plus the local authority council tax on the property.

People who work in the Royal Mews tend to enjoy a special relationship with the royal family because of their mutual love of horses. There's an easy camaraderie that anyone who has been involved in the equestrian world will understand. In some ways, the Mews is a throwback to an earlier, more gracious age; a time when quality was considered to be more important than quantity and personal service meant just that. Nobody is ever going to get rich working in the royal stables, and nobody expects to. It is one of the few areas of employment left in the twenty-first century where satisfaction in a job well done is ample reward and cannot be measured in monetary terms.

Queen Victoria created the post of Crown Equerry in 1854 when she appointed Major John Groves to take charge of the Royal Mews. Since then, there have only been eight other Crown Equerries, and two of them served three monarchs. Sir Henry Ewart was appointed in 1894 during the reign of Queen Victoria, continued throughout the nine-year reign of King Edward VII and briefly into that of King George V. Sir Arthur Erskine held the post from 1924 until 1941, under George V, Edward VIII and George VI, while the present Crown Equerry's immediate predecessor, Lt Colonel Sir John Miller, was in office for twenty-six years, 1961–87. It was Sir John who taught both the Prince of Wales and the Princess Royal to ride and Her Royal Highness has often admitted that much of her success as a Three-Day eventer (she was European Champion in 1971) and as a jockey is due to his early encouragement. The Royal Mews is a showplace but it is also very much a working stables and garage, as smoothly efficient now as it was in the days when horses were accepted as an integral part of London life.

The titular head of the Royal Mews is the Master of the Horse, a post which has been in existence since the fourteenth century. He is the third most important of the Great Officers of the household, after the Lord Chamberlain and the Lord Steward, and the appointment is made personally by Her Majesty, though in previous centuries it was, like so many other Court positions, a political appointment. At one time the Master had direct responsibility for the stables. These days the post is purely ceremonial, and even though he makes occasional inspections of the Royal Mews, the only times the Master is seen attending the Queen in public are at the Sovereign's Birthday Parade on Horseguards or the State Opening of Parliament.

The Crown Equerry's job is without doubt one of the most important in the royal household, and the fact that he makes it seem so easy and relaxed is a tribute to his organizing skills and his considerable ability in delegating. He doesn't try to do everything himself but no decision regarding the work of the Mews is taken without his agreement, and even though many of the tasks have been performed hundreds of times before, his insistence on preparation and rehearsal for the most mundane routine duties, ensures that Britain's royal ceremonial is the envy of the world.

Despite his many responsibilities the Crown Equerry is a man who gives the impression of never being in a hurry. He is one of those 'old-school' cavalry officers who apparently without any effort manage to achieve a degree of perfection in all they attempt. Tall, impeccably groomed, with exquisite manners and courteous to everyone, he nevertheless maintains his own highest standards by demanding instant obedience to his every order. The secret is, he manages to make them all sound like the most reasonable request – just as the Queen does.

CHAPTER NINE

Pay Cheques

Of the 368 permanent, full-time staff who work in the royal household, more than two hundred earn considerably less than £30,000 a year and only three are paid over £100,000.

The fortunate three at the top are the Keeper of the Privy Purse (£170,000 plus), the Queen's private secretary (in recent years his salary has been equivalent to that of a Permanent Secretary in the Civil Service. At the time of writing this is £101,284–£173,808. Ten years ago it was half that amount), and her communications secretary, Simon Walker (£230,000), though Her Majesty pays only a small proportion of this amount (around £40,000), the remainder coming from British Airways from whom he is seconded for a two-year period.

Two of the most important posts in the royal household are the Director of Property Services and the Director of Finance, whose salaries reflect the value the Queen places on their expertise. The man in charge of Property Services is paid £85,048 a year, while the Director of Finance gets

£74,120. Five other members of the group responsible for administering the Grand-in-Aid (the money paid to the royal household by the Treasury) and the Property Section are in the salary bracket £40,000–£50,000. Nine people working in the Royal Collection earn over £40,000 a year, but only two are paid over £60,000 and one at the very top has a ceiling of £80,000.

Newcomers to the Palace – footmen and housemaids – all start on a basic wage of £10,329 a year, rising to £13,634. (Ten years ago it was £5,000 or £100 a week, with 80 per cent of the staff on less than £200 a week.) Senior footmen are paid within the scale of £11,123–£14,683. In the royal kitchens, the cooks are paid £12,313, which rises after ten years to £18,256, while the sous chefs begin at £19,862, with the top rate being £26,218.

There are three grades of housemaid. On promotion to the rank of senior housemaid, they can expect to start on a minimum of £10,725 and to eventually receive £14,157. Those right at the top, and there are only three head housemaids, are paid from £11,321 to £15,207. They also receive free uniforms, all meals and accommodation, for which they are charged up to 17 per cent of their wages. This scale applies to all the household, which means that Sir Michael Peat pays over £800 a week for his palatial apartments in Kensington Palace. Even this is unrealistic, as commercial rents for similar properties would be up to £5,000 a week.

It is harder for those at the bottom of the wage ladder, as a man on the scale between £15,889 to £20,974 a year, such as a senior footman or coachman, pays about £3,500 a year for his tied home. Seventy pounds a week out of a £400 wage packet is a considerable sum, particularly as most of the staff have to maintain private homes for the days when they retire from royal service.

At one time, the Queen provided rent-free accommodation for everyone she employed regardless of their circumstances. And most were granted lifetime tenancies in flats and cottages on the various royal estates when they retired. Widows were also taken care of, and even today a number of dependants of former royal household staff live in homes owned by Her Majesty.

Lady Maclean, widow of a former Lord Chamberlain, has been allowed to remain in Wilderness House, the magnificent home in the grounds of Hampton Court Palace, complete with its own ballroom, once occupied by the renowned eighteenth-century landscape architect Capability Brown. Lady Maclean's late husband was allocated the house when he retired, along with the part-time post of Constable of Hampton Court. Similarly, Lord Moore of Wolvercote, the former Sir Philip Moore, who was private secretary to the Queen from 1977–86, lives in a spacious apartment at Hampton Court Palace, even though he has his own house in Sussex.

Those tenants of the Queen – including other members of the royal family – who live in self-contained accommodation, pay their own council tax, except for chaplains who do not pay this tax under special arrangements for the clergy.

For generations royalty depended on aristocratic families to supply sons and daughters as private secretaries, equerries and ladies-in-waiting. They served simply for the honour and the question of money was never mentioned. Even today, the royal family like to regard it as a vulgar topic. For generations domestic staff were recruited from families who had worked in the kitchens and other areas below stairs. They didn't expect anything more than a living wage. But for the most part, life was comparatively comfortable, and for every vacancy in the royal household, a dozen or more applicants would have been easy to find.

Today things have changed. Temporary footmen, employed for evening receptions and banquets, are paid £4 an hour. A permanent footman with ten years' service who has not been promoted – which in itself is highly unlikely – would be paid £13,634 a year, rising to £14,683, if he makes it to the grade of senior footman; while lady clerks – yes, they do still employ such exotic creatures – average £21,000 a year no matter how long they have been in service.

The Palace Steward, a former personal footman to the Queen, is the senior domestic servant and his salary is said to be £25,000 a year. His right-hand man, the Sergeant Footman, who is the foreman of the footmen and under-butlers, makes just £21,000 a year.

The Travelling Yeoman, another senior domestic, is also paid up to £21,000, while Heather Colebrook, Her Majesty's Chief Housekeeper at Buckingham Palace, who occupies a splendid apartment overlooking the forecourt, is believed to be paid around £28,000.

The crème de la crème of the domestic staff, the personal valets of the male members of the royal family, are all paid just over £20,000 a year. Their female equivalents, the Queen's dressers, earn the same as a Head Housemaid.

The chefs and cooks in the royal kitchens earn slightly more than their colleagues among the liveried staff. The Queen's Chef is paid around £40,000 a year with his assistants earning £10,000 less. A married couple, such as the

Queen's head chauffeur, Joe Last, and his wife, Linda, a Head Housemaid, should have a combined income of around £34,000 a year, out of which they pay rent for their Royal Mews apartment and Westminster council tax.

Officials such as those in charge of State Invitations and the Central Chancery have a ceiling of £28,000 a year, while Senior Officials, middle management, accountants in the Privy Purse office, most of those who run the Royal Collection, the Personnel and Pensions managers and the Master of the Household's senior staff, are paid in the range of £27,000 a year to a maximum of £55,000. Nobody in the household is self-employed.

The vast discrepancies between those few at the top of the financial tree and the remainder languishing far below may be difficult to accept for the majority, but it has been a fact of life for some years and it is not likely to change in the foreseeable future. It is hard to understand, for example, why people such as the assistants to the Master of the Household, each supervising large staffs and responsible for budgets running into hundreds of thousands of pounds, should still require less than half the amount paid to the Director of Property Services. But there has never been any difficulty in recruiting excellent staff to these posts, and while that situation remains, there seems little prospect of more realistic salaries for these dedicated and highly skilled men and women.

The staff employed by the Prince of Wales all earn significantly more than their counterparts in Buckingham Palace. This is because they do not come under the jurisdiction of the Privy Purse office, but are paid out of Duchy of Cornwall funds, and Prince Charles recognizes that he has to pay realistic salaries to get the top people. His private secretary is paid more than the Queen's private secretary and his press secretary earns around £70,000 a year, an increase of more than £15,000 on her opposite number at Buckingham Palace. The differential is maintained throughout the Wales household. Even the footmen and maids are better off than if they worked for the Queen.

When the late Diana, Princess of Wales was alive and had her own household in Kensington Palace, they were paid by the Duchy of Cornwall, even after the separation and divorce. So none of the staff who opted to work for her after the break-up lost financially.

The gardens at Buckingham Palace cover thirty-nine acres and contain an herbaceous border nearly 150 metres long and a lake. Eleven gardeners work all year maintaining its immaculate lawns – a particularly difficult job after one of the three garden parties – and trying to keep at bay the foxes which invade at night. Apprentices start at £12,000 a year, with the senior gardeners earning £16,000.

From the figures quoted – which are all given as 'at the time of writing' – it is obvious that no one works for royalty for the money. It simply isn't there. And while a handful at the top earn respectable salaries, even their money compares unfavourably with what they could make in the outside world. If Sir Robin Janvrin decided to capitalize on the connections he has made since joining the royal household, and the reputation he has earned as 'Chief Executive' of 'Buckingham Palace Limited', he could name his own fees for joining any leading company in the country. An income of £500,000 would be his for the asking. Public quoted companies would be clamouring for his services and a clutch of lucrative non-executive directorships would be dangled before his eyes. The skills and loyalty which everyone, from middle-management to domestics, bring to their jobs at Buckingham Palace is not reflected in the money they are paid; nor can it ever be. Economics decide how much can be spent, and the only reason the royal household is viable is because of the dedication of those who run it and their willingness to subsume their own ambitions for the good of the monarchy. If the Queen had to pay the market rate for her staff, her annual Civil List allowance of £7.9 million would have to be doubled, or the size of the workforce greatly reduced. And if that happened, it would be impossible to maintain the dignity of the monarchy to the standard the country has come to take for granted.

In terms of sheer value for money, the royal household must be one of the most efficient organizations in the world. There is very little wastage and the extra hours many of the staff work for nothing would add tens of thousands of pounds to the wage bill if overtime were paid to all but a few domestics, as happens now. The members exercise a re-markable capacity for hard work, and in recent years com-placency has been replaced by total professionalism. The system is far from perfect; there is still too much privilege and, as some of the younger staff claim, the democratic process has some way to go. Modern business practices are being introduced in practically every area, although they do not always achieve the desired results.

Unfortunately, the bottom line seems to be to make departments profitable, when cost-consciousness is already part and parcel of everyday working life. So the danger is that accountants will take over the Palace and the conven-tional values of the Court will disappear. If that happens, the dignity of the Crown will also eventually evaporate.

There must be a happy compromise between the 'time and motion' men and the traditionalists, of whom there are not all that many left.

CHAPTER TEN

❦

The Royal Purse

When the Queen wants a ten-pound note for the collection at church – it used to be a fiver but inflation has caused the hundred per cent increase – she doesn't have to look inside her own handbag to find it. A brand new banknote, bearing her likeness, is handed to her by the equerry on duty who sits in the pew immediately behind her. But of course the money doesn't come out of his pocket: he gets it from the Keeper of the Privy Purse. Similarly, if Her Majesty wants to write a cheque – almost unheard of these days, as people insist on keeping those with her signature as souvenirs, and the fact that they do not cash them upsets the Palace accounting system – it is provided by the self-same Keeper, who until August 2002 was Sir Michael Peat.

His position in the royal household – and that of his successor Alan Reid – is unique in that the Keeper controls every single item of expenditure. If the Master of the Household needs to buy anything other than the smallest items, he has to get permission from Alan Reid. And not only does he control the Palace's finances, he also looks after those of the Queen herself, even her private bank account at Coutts in the Strand, now part of the giant National Westminster Group.

Apart from the Queen, the Keeper of the Privy Purse is the only person who knows the full extent of Her Majesty's wealth. Not even her bankers, stockbrokers or the Lord Chamberlain have any real idea of her true worth. Every item of the Queen's personal fortune is divided into segments and revealed on a 'need to know' basis individually. So, whereas Coutts know how much money is in her account and the value of the cheques that flow in and out, they do not know whether she has accounts elsewhere, or the extent of her holdings of stocks and shares. But the Keeper needs to know everything; this is the only way he can advise her properly and guide her in her financial dealings.

Admirably qualified to hold the post, Michael Peat joined the royal household in 1990, as Director of Finance and Property Services, originally on a two-year secondment from his firm, Peat, Marwick Mclintock. At that time, Sir Shane Blewitt was Keeper and Michael Peat (he had not received his knighthood then; it came in 1996) was brought in to try and sort out the financial problems besetting the occupied royal palaces and to reduce the annual running costs of £25.6 million.

He proved to be so effective that when Sir Shane Blewitt retired in 1996, Sir Michael was offered the post of Keeper, becoming the first fully qualified accountant to hold this prestigious position. At the time of writing, Sir Michael has just moved to St James's Palace as private secretary to the Prince of Wales. His home is an elegant apartment in Kensington Palace, which was decorated and furnished at great expense – said to be around £200,000 – before he moved in. The Queen raised no objection to the cost as Sir Michael was saving millions on her behalf in other areas.

In travel expenses alone, he was responsible for stream-lining what had previously been antiquated systems. Members of the royal household, as well as the Queen's family, travel extensively abroad, and Sir Michael, with his knowledge of world currencies, was able to ensure that money was moved around at the right time, thereby saving considerable amounts, even on occasion showing a healthy profit on the transactions.

Of course, the Keeper has a large staff to assist him, many of whom have years of experience, and the office is fully automated with the latest technological equipment. At the beginning of the Queen's reign they didn't even have adding machines and nearly all the accounts were kept in handwritten ledgers. Today forty-six men and women work in the office of the Keeper of the Privy Purse and a further seventy-three in the adjoining Finance and Property Branch. They look after the pensions of the house-hold, the personnel office and even have a small staff to control the supply of stationery throughout the Palace. This office maintains a standby supply of black-edged writing paper and envelopes which everyone uses when there is a royal death.

The Queen is registered for Value Added Tax, which means she pays 17.5% on nearly everything she buys and is then able to claim it back, as do all businesses with a substantial turnover.

The accounts are kept in immaculate order. Bills are paid promptly and discounts negotiated ruthlessly. Food and drink are bought in bulk and items such as fruit and vegetables grown in the grounds of Windsor Castle are sold through the Royal Gardens Enterprise, a profitable business, again operated by the office of the Keeper of the Privy Purse. The Windsor Farm shop has recently opened in some converted Victorian potting sheds, on the edge of the Castle's Home Park. Among other items, it sells milk, yoghurt, cream and ice-cream from the Royal Dairy and apples and apple-juice from Sandringham.

The Privy Purse Office also looks after the sale of game and fowl from Sandringham and Balmoral. When Prince Philip organizes one of his weekend parties, all the surplus pheasant and grouse that is shot is sold at market prices. The Queen likes to give Christmas trees she grows herself to the churches at Sandringham and Balmoral, as well as to Westminster Abbey and St Paul's Cathedral, but she also sells hundreds of trees all over the country at Christmas time. Her racing pigeons have been very successful and in a competitive market she is able to command prices running to thousands of pounds for one of her winning birds. Similarly, any puppy born to one of her gun-dogs at Sandringham finds an immediate buyer at practically any price she cares to name. No avenue that might produce a profit is left unexplored, and equally, as a customer, Her Majesty is just as businesslike. Suppliers are quickly made aware that just because their client is royal it does not follow that she has an open cheque book. No one bargains better than the Keeper of the Privy Purse on his employer's behalf.

The Queen has her own Royal Box at the Royal Albert Hall, which she uses only for the Remembrance Day ceremony in November. For the rest of the year it is made available to other members of the royal family or to the household. The allocation of seats is controlled by the Privy

Purse office and there is considerable lobbying when a particular event or star is scheduled to appear. Those permitted to use the box do not have to pay, but if they want the facilities of the private dining room which adjoins the Royal Box they must provide their own food and drink.

The Royal Box at the Royal Opera House in Covent Garden is reserved exclusively for the royal family with a strict pecking order for those who use it. After the Queen, who never goes privately, Prince Charles has first choice and everyone has to defer to him when making a reservation. He loves opera and when he attends there is as much of a performance behind the Royal Box as on the stage. He invariably takes a party with him, and hours before footmen from the Palace will arrive to set up supper in the private dining room that adjoins the box. Sparkling glassware, silverware and china are laid out on the finest linen tablecloths and food and wine are brought from the royal kitchens. At the first interval the Prince and his guests eat the first two courses, then pudding and coffee is served during the second. If other members of the audience sometimes wonder why the curtain hasn't risen precisely when it should have, it is usually because the Prince and his guests haven't quite finished eating.

If one of the other royals wants to attend on the same night as Charles they have to ask, and if he has room to spare he usually invites them to join his party. But if they have reserved the box before and he decides to go at the last minute, they are told their evening is off. He never puts off his own plans to accommodate others, even within his own family.

Another unusual aspect of the Privy Purse's responsibilities is in the naming of flowers after a member of the royal family. If someone wants to name a rose after the Queen or the late Princess Margaret, it is not simply a question of doing just that. They have to negotiate with the Keeper of the Privy Purse and he investigates to see if the person – and the intended flower – are suitable. Flowers which have unfortunate nicknames such as Sweet Williams, which in parts of Ireland are known as Stinking Billys after William of Orange, are immediately barred.

As well as overseeing all the financial affairs of the Queen, the Keeper of the Privy Purse has the task of supervising the royal burial ground at Frogmore. This is situated near Frogmore House, where Earl Mountbatten of Burma was born in 1900, and is where various members of the royal family have been buried since the ground was consecrated in 1928. The only British sovereign to have been interred there was King Edward VIII, who was, of course, Duke of Windsor when he died in 1972. His wife, the Duchess, lies alongside him following her death in 1986. The burial ground is never opened to the public, which is a pity as the grave stones record a fascinating history of those royals who do not warrant a more prestigious resting place.

As Receiver General, the Keeper of the Privy Purse is a member of the council that administers the accounts of the Duchy of Lancaster, the source of a major part of the sovereign's private income. The Duchy, as a corporate body, dates back to 1461, but its origins lie in the grant of lands to Edmund, first Earl of Lancaster, in 1265. Apart from its landed estates of approximately 19,268 hectares, it also owns some 27 miles of foreshore in Wales, Yorkshire and Lincolnshire. An unusual source of money comes from the estates of people in Lancashire who die intestate and where no legal ownership can be established. This is known as *Bona Vacantia*. In such cases the estate passes to the Duchy, which, after deducting expenses, distributes the remainder to various charities. In the financial year ending 31 March 2001, the Duchy of Lancaster Jubilee Trust received £695,000 in this way.

For the same period, the Queen received £7,306,741 from the Duchy for her personal use, which included net income from property of £4,629,737 and £2,787,474 investment income. This was an increase over the previous year of nearly £2 million (£5,777,767 March 2000). The total value of the Duchy of Lancaster is £205,892,807, but the Queen, who holds these benefits only for the duration of her reign, is not entitled to any part of its capital.

The Queen is not an extravagant woman. Her tastes are simple in the extreme. Yet two of her private past-times have been described as like 'fitting a tap to your pocket'. They are racing, which was at one time a hobby, but which is now run very much as a business by her racing manager, and the Balmoral Estate. A woman who relates passionately to animals, the Queen may well love her horses even more than she loves her dogs. The late Earl of Carnarvon, her racing manager for over thirty years, told the present author of the way in which Her Majesty used to show her excitement before and during a race if one of her horses was running. 'She would press her hands together so tightly that the blood would run out of them. She often had trouble in prising her hands apart and the funny thing was, she didn't even know she was doing it. It was the only time I ever saw her show any emotion – never about people, even her own family – just animals. I once asked her why she did it and she changed the subject.' Lord Carnarvon agreed that racing was an indulgence, and an expensive one, but as he said, 'She never let it get out of hand, she always watched the budget.' He died in September 2001.

Balmoral, in the Highlands of Scotland, is the personal property of the Queen, and she visits for around eight weeks every year, during August and September. For this privilege she pays out around £1 million annually. That is the total cost of running Balmoral. It loses money hand over fist, even though, with 80,000 visitors paying up to £4.50 each to see the gardens and the one room in the Castle they are allowed to see before being herded into the souvenir shop, the estate has an annual turnover of £1.75 million.

But Balmoral is a massive enterprise: a huge estate with 56 full-time employees, practically all living on the estate, some with their families, others as single men and women, and also a further thirty-two part-timers brought in to help during the season. Ten gamekeepers, who also act as stalkers, work on the hills and nine gardeners are employed in the immediate grounds, which are kept, like all royal gardens, in immaculate condition. The family love stalking and grouse shooting but the sport costs them some £200,000 a year, even though they manage to sell up to £60,000 worth of venison each season. The Duke of Edinburgh enjoys the farming aspect of life at Balmoral, even though he rarely gets his own hands dirty; so although the Home Farm, with its herd of twenty-nine Highland cows, costs around £300 a week, he thinks it's money well spent.

The Queen does not concern herself with the financial side of either her racing activities or the losses at Balmoral. That's a problem for her Keeper of the Privy Purse. He would desperately like to see costs coming down – how do you justify spending £3,000 a week, or £150,000 a year, on a garden simply because the family like their home-grown vegetables? The maintenance of the castle itself costs a similar amount, £150,000 a year, and there are other buildings, including Craigowan House, favoured by Prince Charles, which account for £200,000 a year.

The difficulty is that the Queen will not countenance reducing her lifestyle at Balmoral, which means the costs must remain as high as they currently are. The only alternative is to increase revenue. Here again there are problems. Her Majesty is not keen on opening up more of the castle to visitors, which would be an instant money-spinner. A possibility is to increase the number of trees grown commercially on the estate. The Queen is not too concerned about this, but there is a vast difference of opinion between the Duke of Edinburgh and his eldest son. Prince Philip believes in growing trees for profit; Prince Charles hates to see anything beautiful cut down. As Balmoral will one day be his property, to do with what he likes, he tries to employ delaying tactics when his father attempts to harvest yet another slice of forestry.

They could also let out some of the stalking, and with plenty of willing takers at £3,000 a stag, the profit would be substantial. But here the Queen and Prince Philip draw the line. They want to restrict the shooting on the estate to themselves, their family and friends, even if by doing so, they are depriving the estate of vast amounts of money. One million pounds is still considered by most people to be a lot of money. To be able to lose that much on a holiday property enjoyed for less than one-sixth of the year, without the slightest concern, shows an elegant disregard for the stuff. It also gives an indication that, however much her staff may protest, the Queen is a very wealthy woman.

A glance at the cost of maintaining the properties known as the 'Occupied Royal Palaces' or the 'Estate' – that is, those residences used by the Queen and her family for official purposes (as opposed to Balmoral and Sandringham, which are private) shows that a thousand men and women work in the various buildings. The numbers include household, police and armed services personnel, Post Office staff and building and maintenance contractors. The buildings they work in include Buckingham Palace, St James's Palace, Clarence House, Windsor Castle, parts of Kensington Palace, Marlborough House Mews, the Royal Mews, both at Buckingham Palace and Hampton Court Palace, and buildings in the Home and Great Parks at Windsor. The 'Estate' comprises some 360 individual properties, plus a further 286 houses and apartments available for residential use, mainly by staff and pensioners, and ten properties which are used as communal residential accommodation for staff.

The amount of money spent every year on maintaining and improving Crown properties is enormous. In the year ending March 2001, they spent some £15.290 million and seven projects alone each cost over £150,000: the kitchens at Buckingham Palace, cleaning the external fabric of Frogmore House, refurbishment of one apartment at Kensington Palace, upgrading the public address system at Buckingham Palace and redecorating the Throne Room at St James's Palace were included in these estimates.

Royal gardens are kept in excellent order and it is not cheap to maintain them in their pristine state. Last year

154

the 39 acres of Buckingham Palace accounted for £382,000 while those at Windsor, where there is a huge glasshouse covering one acre, in which they grow Christmas poinsettias for sale, ran up a bill of £66,000.

The Palace employs some thirty-two porters and non-domestic cleaners, whose duties include moving furniture, preparing rooms for various State and Official functions and doing the heavy lifting work when members of the Royal Collection want pictures moved and rehung. They cost £530,000 last year. In order to maintain the priceless works of art, carpets and furniture belonging to the Crown, skilled craftsmen are permanently employed. There are sixteen of them, including cabinet makers, gilders, upholsterers, French polishers and clockmakers. Their total expenses and salaries for the year amounted to £468,000.

The biggest single building project at Buckingham Palace is the redevelopment of the Queen's Gallery. This is estimated to cost £23 million including materials, labour, fees and Value Added Tax. Seventy-one per cent of the money is being found by the Royal Collection Trust out of the proceeds of opening the State Apartments at Buckingham Palace and Windsor Castle.

The occupied royal palaces require constant expenditure on maintaining and improving the fabric of the buildings. Frogmore House, in the grounds of Windsor Castle, is no longer used as a royal residence, though Prince Philip likes to hold informal dinner parties there, and it has been open to the public since 1990 for several days a year. Last year the Keeper of the Privy Purse authorized the spending of £618,000 on repairs. Altogether a total of £1.162 million is being spent on urgent repair work to the roofs, electrics and drainage system.

Until her death in 1997, the late Diana, Princess of Wales lived at Apartments 8/9 Kensington Palace. The Queen was determined that no one would occupy the apartments after her death and they were kept empty for four years, with all the furniture and pictures removed. It was eventually decided that the upper floors could be converted into staff flats and the ground floor used as office and storage space. The two apartments were divided – as they had been originally – and refurbished, the work taking five months to complete in 2000 at a cost of £371,000.

The Throne room at St James's Palace was designed by Christopher Wren in 1703 as a Council Chamber for Queen Anne. The State Apartments at St James's were used for royal entertaining until Queen Victoria's move to Buckingham Palace in 1837. But even today many functions are still held there and the Throne Room required major redecoration in 2000. A budget of £157,000 was set and the work, including gilding the throne and conservation of its canopy, and rewiring the wall lights and chandelier, was completed within this amount.

Every year the Queen invites approximately 80,000 guests to her different palaces. In addition, many more pay an entrance fee, and over the year visitors to the royal palaces bring in a vast revenue with Windsor Castle being the biggest attraction. In the financial year ending April 2001, 1,101,000 people provided a profit of £2,025,000 with the shops in the precincts adding a further £572,000. Buckingham Palace, which is open for only eight weeks in the summer, had 300,000 paying visitors and made a profit of £735,000, the souvenir shops adding a massive £618,000. The Royal Mews and Queen's Gallery, now refurbished and reopened in 2002, together admitted 84,000 people the previous year, providing a profit of £77,000 which was overshadowed by shop sales of £102,000. In Scotland, the Palace of Holyroodhouse in Edinburgh saw 250,000 visitors, with a profit of £527,000 and £10,000 in shop sales. Other guests come for nothing: to garden parties, State Banquets, diplomatic and business receptions. But each function has to be accounted for – and not all the money comes from the Queen. Large amounts are provided by various government departments. The Privy Purse Office makes sure nothing is wasted and, where possible, a profit returned.

As we enter the twenty-first century, the balance sheet shows that Queen Elizabeth II incorporated is in a pretty healthy state. With the exception of Her Majesty's two rare self-indulgences, the accounts are firmly in the black.

❧

CHAPTER ELEVEN

Pomp and Circumstance

There is a small department of the royal household – just eleven personnel – located above a dungeon in St James's Palace, which twice a year becomes the focal point of attention for thousands of men and women throughout the country, though they may not know it. For it is this office that holds the secrets of who is to receive awards in the New Year's Honours List and The Queen's Birthday Honours List. Central Chancery of the Orders of Knighthood is part of the Lord Chamberlain's Office, and confidentiality is the watchword in this ancient department of the household. They are the first to know who is being given a knighthood or an OBE, and they arrange the order in which the recipients are invested with their honours by the Queen.

Heading the office is the Assistant Comptroller of the Lord Chamberlain's Office, who is given the title of Secretary to Central Chancery. As such he becomes an officer of each of the five Great Orders of Chivalry: the Garter, St Michael and St George, the Bath, the British Empire and the Royal Victorian Order, the sovereign's personal order of chivalry. The staff consists of an Assistant Secretary, an Insignia Clerk, a Clerk of the Records, a clerk for the Orders of St Michael and St George and the Royal Victorian Order, two clerks for the Orders of the Bath and the British Empire, two messengers and two clerks for Investitures.

Since up to twenty-two investitures are now held each year in London, with one in Edinburgh at the Palace of Holyroodhouse plus the occasional ceremony held at Cardiff Castle, at each of which as many as one hundred and fifty men and women are presented with their awards, the sheer logistics are mind-boggling: 3,300 medals and decorations, each one with its own distinctive ribbon and leather box.

When you realize that the senior Order, the Garter, was founded in 1348 by King Edward III, and that the name of every single member of the order since then is retained in the archives of Central Chancery, the numbers soon add up. They have the name and address of every person who has ever received any sort of honour in the past seven hundred years and they will be kept for ever.

The attention to detail is meticulous. The assistant secretary, who is a senior official, liaises with her opposite number in the Prime Minister's office, and together they organize the publication in the *London Gazette* of the names of those to be honoured; first on New Year's Day and again on the Sovereign's Official Birthday in June. The spelling of every name, correct title and previous decorations is checked several times – and since many unfamiliar names from Commonwealth countries are included, High Commissions in London are discreetly asked to ensure that everything is as it should be.

A vital cog in the honours system is the Insignia Clerk, who, in spite of his lowly-sounding title, is in fact a very senior and experienced official. He has sole responsibility for buying the medals and other insignia. But he is not given *carte blanche* to spend what he likes. A recently retired insignia clerk explained the procedure: 'When the list of recipients came in, I had to add up the numbers of knight-hoods, OBEs, MBEs and so on and then tell the Treasury, who are paying for it all, how much it was going to cost. They always complained and told me it's too much. So I had to get at least three estimates from the established suppliers: Garrard's; Spink & Son; Collingwood; Toye, Kenning & Spencer and finally the Royal Mint, who do not automatically get government contracts as one might expect, they have to compete.'

Even the lowest orders are quite expensive, with an MBE, made of cupro-nickel, costing £20 and a KBE (Knight of the British Empire) of silver gilt, up to £1,000. The insignia for Members of the Royal Victorian Order costs up to £500, while right at the top are the collars, the insignia of the Grand Crosses. These are individually numbered and worth tens of thousands of pounds and so they are only lent to the recipient. On their death the insignia has to be returned to Central Chancery. When President George Bush (senior) was awarded an Honorary Knighthood by the Queen he had to sign a document agreeing to the return of his collar, valued at $65,000, when he died. But he did, along with all other honorary recipients, receive a badge, with an intrinsic value of £500, which is his to keep. One or two of the holders of these chains are wary of keeping them in their own homes, so for added security, and to avoid paying expensive insurance premiums, they leave them in a safe at St James's Palace. They are taken out when needed to be worn and returned immediately afterwards.

The Honours system is curiously British in that if one has been given a lower order and subsequently promoted, for example: given an MBE and then, some years later, made an OBE, the lesser medal has to be returned to Central Chancery on receipt of the higher decoration. In this way, medals can be used over and over again. The exception is when someone has been awarded a decoration in the Military Division and later receives another award in the Civil Division. They are then allowed to keep, and wear, both medals.

Men and women awarded the British Empire Medal (BEM), which is now only given to citizens of Commonwealth countries, or the Imperial Service Medal (ISM) are not invited to Buckingham Palace for a personal presentation. Instead the medal is despatched by post, together with an accompanying letter and certificate, which are then presented by a High Commissioner – if the recipient lives in a Commonwealth country – or usually by a head of department or senior officer of the recipient's organization when the award is to go to someone in the United Kingdom.

An official in Central Chancery tells of two people who were to be honoured by the Queen and their reactions. One was an elderly, retired postman from rural Suffolk, who was being rewarded for a unique record in not having missed a delivery in forty-one years' service. Thinking the journey to London might be too tiring for him, Chancery offered to have the award delivered and presented locally. He was having none of it, writing back to say, 'I've waited over forty years for this, and if you think I'm going to miss this chance to meet the Queen and see inside Buckingham Palace, you are very mistaken.' He made the journey and thoroughly enjoyed his day out. The other recipient worked as a refuse collector in Windsor and when he approached the Queen, she remarked that his face seemed familiar. 'It ought to, Ma'am,' he replied, 'I've been emptying your bins for twenty years.' If Her Majesty was slightly bemused by this unlikely reason for her recognizing him, she gave no hint. Later at lunch the Queen told the story to Prince Philip. Laughing he explained the reason why she thought she knew him. Apparently, the man 'moonlighted' occasionally, helping in the gardens at Windsor, and was regarded as one of the best rabbit catchers around.

At ten o'clock on a cold, dull November morning, a fleet of vehicles is approaching Buckingham Palace. It is directed through the left centre gateway towards the inner quadrangle. Each car – some are hired stretch limousines – displays a windscreen sticker bearing the letter A.

A group of armed police officers equipped with mirrors on long-handled poles is waiting to inspect the underside of the cars to check that no explosive device has been attached. This is, after all, just two months after the 11 September terrorist outrage in New York.

Once the cars have passed the inspection, their occupants are directed towards the Grand Entrance where uniformed attendants in red tail coats are waiting to check invitation cards. For this is an Investiture, the beginning of a splendid ceremony in the finest State Room at the Palace.

At the rear of the Grand Entrance Hall the Bow Room has been converted into a temporary cloakroom where the guests leave their top coats and are politely but firmly

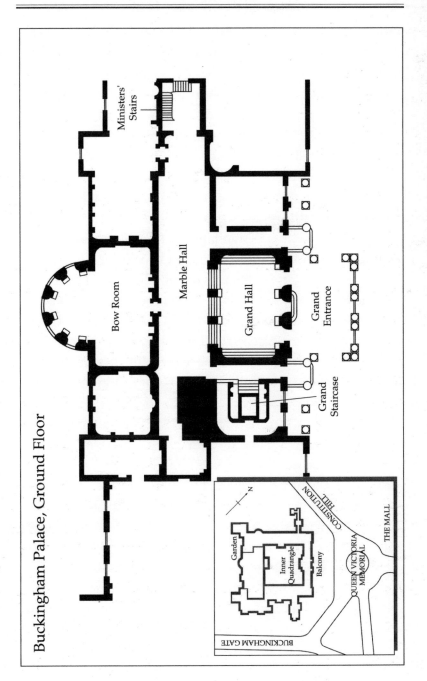

Buckingham Palace, Ground Floor

Ministers' Stairs

Marble Hall

Bow Room

Grand Hall

Grand Entrance

Grand Staircase

N

Garden

Inner Quadrangle

Balcony

CONSTITUTION HILL

QUEEN VICTORIA MEMORIAL

THE MALL

BUCKINGHAM GATE

relieved of any cameras. No private photography is permitted inside the Palace because a professional video production company, BCA Films, has been awarded an exclusive contract to film every Investiture. The recipients and their families are then invited to buy a copy to take home. Around 90 per cent take up this offer. The contract has been described as a licence to print money, for the whole package costs £139.90. This includes a 30-minute personalized recording, six prints and a booklet explaining how the Investiture is organized. As an alternative an official photographer is available to take pictures of everyone with their decorations at a cost of £25 for four prints.

As the guests make their way up the Grand Staircase, designed by Nash in the late 1820s, they are observed by dismounted troopers of the Life Guards, standing rigidly to attention in their scarlet tunics, gleaming breastplates and thigh-length boots. At the top recipients are guided towards the Picture Gallery and Green Drawing Room, while their supporters are led into the State Ball Room, where the Investiture is to take place. It is a magnificent room 123 feet long and 60 feet wide, and was built by Queen Victoria at a cost of £250,000.

Military, naval and RAF officers are on duty as ushers, directing those who are there to watch the proceedings to rows of gilt chairs in front of the two thrones which were originally used by King George V and Queen Mary in 1911 at the Delhi Durbar. (It was King George V, usually among the strictest observers of royal tradition, who in a dramatic and theatrical departure from Court protocol, knighted the actor George Benson on the stage of the Theatre Royal, Drury Lane, to mark the tercentenary of the death of William Shakespeare.) Three tiers of red plush banquettes line the walls of the room and these too are being used as vantage points. Almost every lady present has dressed for the occasion with large picture hats very much in evidence. In the Musicians' Gallery, the orchestra of the Grenadier Guards under the direction of Lt Col Philip Hills plays selections from *Funny Girl* and *Hello Dolly*. Every effort is made to select music appropriate to the person honoured. At a previous Investiture, an Australian was delighted and touched to hear the unofficial national anthem of his country, 'Waltzing Matilda', as he stepped up to receive his award. This was no mere coincidence. The director of music is given an advance copy of the order in which recipients will appear and works out the programme accordingly.

When the actress Julie Andrews was made a Dame of the British Empire, the orchestra played selections from *The Sound of Music*, her most famous film, as she approached the Queen. And when Shirley Bassey received the same honour, they played 'Big Spender', one of her many hit songs. Charlie Chaplin was visibly touched when he was knighted, and even more so when the orchestra played their own version of 'Limelight' as Her Majesty dubbed him Sir Charles.

In the Picture Gallery and Green Drawing Room, the recipients are prepared for their ordeal – at least that is what it looks like to judge from the apprehensive looks on some faces. Most could probably do with a stiff drink, but they won't get it here. No refreshments are offered; only plain water, if required. Tiny hooks are attached to lapels and dresses so that the Queen will have no difficulty hanging the decorations when the time comes.

When someone is to be knighted, officials from the Lord

Chamberlain's Office make preliminary enquiries to find out if the recipient is able to kneel. Anyone who cannot, either through disability or age, is allowed to receive the accolade standing or, if necessary, sitting in a wheelchair. But the usual procedure is that the person to be knighted is given a short rehearsal before the ceremony so that he knows which knee to bend and when to stand. The soon-to-be knights gather in the Green Drawing Room, the lesser orders in the Picture Gallery.

The Comptroller of the Lord Chamberlain's Office, Lt Col Sir Malcom Ross, a born impresario if ever there was one, resplendent in military frock coat, decorations and spurs, invites the assembly to come a little closer as he is about to explain what is going to happen. He says the first thing to remember is to relax. It's also the hardest part as for the majority this is a once in a lifetime occasion, so 'first-night' nerves are part of the ritual. But if they relax, as Colonel Ross tries to persuade them, they will enjoy the morning all the more and remember every detail. Not that this is entirely necessary as already the video cameras are zooming in on every face.

He then explains the order in which the awards will be made: Knights first – there are two today – followed by Companions of the Order of the Bath, then those joining the Order of St Michael and St George, then the senior awards for the Order of the British Empire. After that a single honour to Lady Nicholas Gordon Lennox, Princess Alexandra's lady-in-waiting. She is to be made a Lieutenant of the Royal Victorian Order, the sovereign's personal Order of Chivalry. Farther down the list, a face familiar to the Queen, Rosemarie Tart, her assistant housekeeper at Buckingham Palace, is being made a Member of the RVO and so too is Sergeant Paul Ridout, one of the royal body-guards. Within the royal household, a strict line of demarcation separates those who receive honours in the Royal Victorian Order. The grade depends on one's position. For example, royal chauffeurs can expect the Royal Victorian Medal (Silver), which is the same as that awarded to dressers such as the lady who attends the Princess Royal. One has to move up the ladder before being allowed into Membership of the Order with an MVO.

Once the bulk of the awards have been made, the final recipients will be those who are being given the Queen's Police Medal, the Queen's Fire Service Medal, the Queen's Volunteer Reserves Medal and an OBE in the Military Division for service in Northern Ireland.

Now comes the moment when things could go horribly wrong – but they never do. Those who are about to be honoured are lined up in order, twenty at a time. As there are 120 this morning there will be six groups and they are marshalled just outside the State Ball Room, at the opposite end to where the investiture is taking place. They walk across the lower end of the Ball Room to the corridor on the far side and wait until their names are called.

At eleven o'clock the Queen, dressed in a simple turquoise day dress, comes into the throne end of the Ball Room flanked by her Lord Chamberlain, Lord Luce – in a well-worn morning coat – the Master of the Household, Vice-Admiral Tom Blackburn, in naval uniform, the Secretary of Central Chancery, Lt Col Robert Cartwright, two Gurkha Orderly Officers and Her Majesty's Equerry-in-Waiting, Major James Duckworth-Chad of the Coldstream Guards.

Everybody stands while the national anthem is played

and then the Queen says, 'Ladies and gentlemen, please be seated.' A tableaux forms itself in front of the thrones, with the Lord Chamberlain to the Queen's left and the Master of the Household and the Secretary of Central Chancery on her right. Behind are the Gurkha officers and five members of the Yeomen of the Guard. All will remain standing for the duration of the ceremony.

The Lord Chamberlain calls out the first name, who is already standing in front of an officer a few feet away. He walks to a position directly in front of the Queen and gives a short neck bow. Two steps take him to the velvet investiture stool where he kneels to receive the accolade. The Queen uses the sword belonging to her late father, King George VI, when he was Colonel of the Scots Guards. She does not say 'Arise Sir Knight' – this is merely the stuff of royal legend. He then gets up, steps backwards, gives another bow and moves smartly away to the opposite doorway, where he will be relieved of his insignia for a few moments while it is placed in a small leather box. Once the two knights have been dubbed, the stool is removed and the investiture continues with Her Majesty hooking on the medals and hanging the decorations on ribbons around each neck. She speaks to each recipient for a few moments (a presentation lasts just twenty seconds) and then shakes hands. This is the signal that their moment of glory is over. Colonel Ross has warned them in his briefing that they should move away after bowing or curtsying. Or, as he put it: 'Now is not the time to start telling Her Majesty your war stories.'

At Investitures the ritual never changes, the whole thing runs like clockwork, as indeed it should. The Queen has performed the same duty around a thousand times in her

fifty-year reign with rarely a hitch, although on one
occasion a large lump of plaster fell from the ceiling, nar-
rowly missing her and slightly injuring one person. The
Queen didn't even flinch and he had a great story to tell
of his day at the Palace. On another occasion a mini-disaster
occurred, as a former Insignia Clerk recalled: 'We were
coming to the end of the ceremony with all the major
awards having been made. We always start at the top:
knighthoods, CBEs and then on down to OBEs and MBEs.
I laid out half a dozen medals on a cushion and handed
them to my boss. He chose this moment to faint and the
cushion and all the decorations fell to the ground in complete disarray, getting in an awful mess. I tried to gather
them up, without knowing the right order, and the Queen
said to me "Just put them any way you can. I'll give them
anything and you can sort it out afterwards.' So that's
what we did. Several people received awards they were
not entitled to and one or two were surprised – and disappointed – to see they didn't get what they were
expecting. When the Investiture ended, I took them back
into the ante-room where we managed to get the right
decoration onto the right person. You couldn't let them
walk away with any old medal. They had to have the right
one. What was fascinating was that throughout the entire
farce, for that was what it was, the Queen didn't turn a
hair, she kept a completely straight face and just carried
on as if nothing had happened. Though there were a few
words spoken after it was all over.'

Everyone who attends the Investiture, either as a recipient or spectator (each recipient is allowed three guests), is
given a small booklet with a potted history of the ceremony
and the names of all the recipients, the award they are

receiving and the reason. They range from services to Parliament, local government, political broadcasting and community care, to less common causes such as services to trampolining, women's rugby union football and, perhaps strangest of all to some eyes, services to Her Majesty's Board of Inland Revenue. Each receives the same courtesy and as they leave the State Ball Room at one end they are directed back into the Ball Room at the other end, where they wait until the ceremony is over. The moment the last person has been given his gong, the national anthem is played once more and the royal party leaves, walking through the centre aisle, with the Queen smiling as she passes. Strangely, no one bows or curtsies as she walks by apart from the members of the household. The custom appears to have died out in recent years together with other forms of good manners.

Outside the Grand Entrance the excited newly-honoured show their decorations to their families and friends, while the better-known among them are shepherded towards the press enclosure where photographers and reporters wait. The cars finally fill up and drive – somewhat reluctantly – back out through the Palace gates and it's all over. But not for the Queen. She has to go through it all again next week and the week after and the week after that.

Most honours are recommended by the Prime Minister of the day. His office writes to the prospective recipient some six weeks before the list is published, saying, 'The Prime Minister is considering submitting your name to Her Majesty to be included in the (for instance) New Year's Honours List. Would you please let us know by return if you are prepared to accept if such an offer is made.' There is no definite offer at this stage, so if the recipient indicates that they would not accept, it cannot be claimed that they have refused Her Majesty. And persons to be honoured are not told which grade or rank they are being offered, with the exception of knighthood. So it could be a modest BEM (British Empire Medal) or the much more prestigious CBE (Commander of the British Empire) just one step down from a knighthood; you don't find out until you have accepted the provisional offer.

These awards are usually made for political or some other form of public service and the selection of recipients has nothing to do with the Queen, although she does have a right of veto if she can prove that the proposed recipient is unsuitable. Her grandfather King George V once refused to dub a homosexual, saying 'I do not knight buggers.' The honours she gives herself, without any ministerial advice, are: the Garter, the Thistle, the Order of Merit, the Companions of Honour and membership of the Royal Victorian Order, the sovereign's personal Order of Chivalry, in which every decoration is individually numbered.

The senior Order is the Garter, founded by Edward III in 1348. The original members were the sovereign, the Prince of Wales and twenty-four companion knights. Their spiritual home has always been at Windsor Castle, today in St George's Chapel, which stood originally on the site of the present Albert Memorial Chapel, restored and dedicated to Prince Albert by Victoria in 1862. Throughout the centuries, various changes have been made to the constitution of the Order, and until 1901, reigning queens were the only females permitted to join. It was King Edward VII who made his Consort, Queen Alexandra, a Lady of the Garter, paving the way for other ladies to be admitted, including a number of foreign queens. Our present Queen was created a Lady of Garter as Princess Elizabeth, by her father, King George VI, in 1947, one week before her future husband, Philip, in order to preserve her seniority. The first Lady Companion was invested in 1990, when Lavinia, Duchess of Norfolk was installed.

When the Princess Royal was created a Lady of the Garter, she didn't want to be known as LG, so she asked the Queen if she could instead use the title KG, Knight of the Garter. Her Majesty agreed and so the Princess is the only woman who is a full Knight of the Garter. Edward III is probably turning in his grave.

Distinguished foreigners have been honoured with the Garter ever since its foundation. They are known as 'Stranger Knights' and are sometimes invited to join the Order to strengthen the ties between the House of Windsor and certain foreign monarchies. King Juan Carlos of Spain is currently a member, as is the Grand Duke of Luxembourg. Today there are twenty-five Companion Knights, Royal Knights and Stranger Knights.

Knights of the Garter wear a blue velvet mantle with the badge of the Order on the left shoulder and a black velvet hat garnished with white feathers. The emblem is a blue ribbon – or garter – worn by men below the left knee and by women on the left arm. Each knight is required to display his coat of arms on a banner in St George's Chapel. The banners are five feet square and made of silk with the arms emblazoned in gold leaf and oil paint. A wooden shield bearing each Knight's or Lady's name and date of entry is fixed to the ceiling in St George's Hall. Peter Gwynn Jones is Garter King of Arms – an office instituted by Henry V in 1415 – and it is his responsibility to oversee the production of the banners, stall plates and badges and also to arrange the details of the investiture ceremonies, the seating plan and the order of service. He also supervises, with the assistance of the Secretary of the Order, the printing of the official programmes and the allocation of tickets for the service to the families of the Knights and other guests.

There is a ritual for degrading a knight who is expelled, but the ceremonial has not been used since the eighteenth century. However, in 1915, King George V ordered that all banners relating to German Knights and their allies should be removed, and during the Second World War, those of the King of Italy and the Emperor of Japan were similarly removed. That belonging to the late Emperor Hirohito was reinstated shortly before his visit to Britain in 1969, and the present Emperor Akihito was created a Knight of the Garter on 26 May 1998.

Although membership of the Order of the Garter has been at the personal invitation of the sovereign since its inception, an element of political involvement crept in during the eighteenth century, when prospective members were nominated by the Prime Minister of the day. This practice continued well into the twentieth century and didn't end until 1946, when the Labour Prime Minister, Clement Attlee, renounced the privilege.

New appointments are usually announced on St George's Day, 23 April, with the ceremonial installation taking place in June, on the Monday of Royal Ascot Week. There is a colourful parade of the Knights, led by the Queen and the Duke of Edinburgh, from the Throne Room – where the installation has taken place privately – to St George's Chapel, for a religious service conducted by the Prelate, who is always the Bishop of Winchester.

In Scotland, the highest honour that can be awarded is The Most Ancient and Most Noble Order of the Thistle. Again this is solely in the gift of the sovereign and its members are known as Knights Brethren. In the United Kingdom, the Thistle is second only to the Garter in precedence and nobody knows the actual date of the Order's foundation. There are claims that James III of Scotland founded it in the fifteenth century, but realistically, it is generally accepted that the date of the revival of the Order, 1687, by James II (James VII of Scotland) is the true date of its foundation.

In terms of numbers, the Thistle is more exclusive than the Garter. Originally restricted to twelve Knights Brethren, their number was increased to sixteen in 1827. Ladies were included in 1987 and allowed to use the suffix KT after their names. The Queen is Sovereign Head of the Order and other royal Knights include the Duke of Edinburgh, Prince Charles (as Duke of Rothesay) and the most recent, the Princess Royal, who was created a Lady of the Thistle shortly after her fiftieth birthday, which she celebrated on 15 August 2000. Her installation took place in the Thistle Chapel at St Giles Cathedral in Edinburgh, on 5 July 2001. The chapel has been the spiritual home of the Order since 1911. Before that they had been without a permanent chapel as their original church, alongside the Palace of Holyroodhouse, had been destroyed by an angry mob in 1688, owing to political unrest in Edinburgh. The Princess Royal, a lady whose courage in the equestrian world has been demonstrated many times, and whose determination in other fields has occasionally been mistaken for arrogance, might easily say the Thistle's motto, 'No one harms me with impunity', was coined just for her.

Members of the Order wear a dark-green mantle lined with white, fastened at the neck by two gold and green cordons. A black velvet hat adorned with white feathers completes the outfit. The insignia, which is very expensive, consists of a gold and enamel collar chain representing sprigs of rue and a single thistle, a badge showing St Andrew carrying his cross of martyrdom, a green riband and a star made of silver saltire, with a gold medallion at its centre containing a thistle and the motto of the Order around the edge.

Attention to detail is taken for granted throughout the royal household. There is a file to cover every eventuality and the reason why there is a seamless transition whenever a new person takes over a particular job is because he or she always has an efficient back-up system to rely on.

A private secretary taking over with one of the royals (unless it is with the Queen, when the new man will have spent some time as assistant to get to know the ropes) is handed a complete set of files. When the late Lt Col Sir Peter Gibbs joined Princess Anne, with whom he was to remain for eighteen years, he said he found within weeks that he knew the details of every visit she had made since she was twenty, where she had been, the duration of the visit, who she had met and the gifts she had given and received. And when he checked with his opposite numbers in the offices of the other royals, it was exactly the same. They all had the same filing system – now on computers – and each could cross-check with the others to make sure there was no duplication of duties. And this applies to every department in the household.

Nowhere is this more apparent than in Central Chancery. They never accept anything as fact until it has been proved and checked over and over again.

⤬

CHAPTER TWELVE

Upstairs/Downstairs

There are four levels of servant within the royal household, and only on rare occasions has an employee managed to climb out of his or her designated level to the one higher up the ladder. The most recent was this year, when an official in the Lord Chamberlain's Office, was promoted to member. It meant dramatic change in his status: dining facilities, which room he would be allocated when he stayed at one of the royal residences and a better seat on the aircraft when he travelled with the Queen.

The four categories are: Member, Senior Official, Official and Staff. A member of the royal household is either head of one of the six departments, or occupies one of the top positions. For instance, the Queen's private secretary, his deputy and assistant are all members. So too is the Keeper of the Privy Purse, the Crown Equerry, the Master of the Household, the Comptroller of the Lord Chamberlain's Office and his assistant, and the Surveyor of the Queen's Works of Art in the Royal Collection. Altogether out of the grand total of nearly four hundred the Palace employs, thirty-four are members of the royal household, plus the ladies-in-waiting, full and part-time, who are accorded the same status. The private secretaries of the Princess Royal and other members of the family are also granted member status, which means they can eat in the 1855 Room and be waited on by liveried servants.

Members enjoy an informal relationship with one another, regardless of seniority or length of service. They all use Christian names and newcomers are encouraged to adopt this style. So assistant press secretaries, who only just make it into the 'member' category and who may have worked at the Palace for just a few months, will still address Sir Robin Janvrin, the Queen's private secretary, and by far the most influential figure in the household hierarchy, as Robin. The only exception to this unwritten rule is the Lord Chamberlain, who is always referred to and addressed as Lord Chamberlain. So far, the only Lord Chamberlain who relaxed this rule was the late Lord Maclean known as 'Chips' to the Queen. During his tenure, 1971–84, he urged his colleagues to call him Chips, which some did while others still used his formal title.

Visitors to Buckingham Palace enter by the Privy Purse door, which is on the extreme right as you look at the building from the front. The three steps leading up to the door are covered in red carpet, worn practically threadbare through daily use. You never have to knock or press the bell, because the police officer on duty at the North Centre Gate, who has admitted you to the forecourt, has telephoned to let the footman know you are approaching. Inside the hall is a table on which are laid a number of furled umbrellas. These belong to the members and tell you that the Court is sitting. The umbrellas are like the old-time standards of knights of the realm. They are never unfurled, or used to guard against the elements. They are badges of office, to be carried by their owners when attending the Queen outside the Palace, or in the grounds if a garden party is taking place. Only the members carry these umbrellas. If anyone below their rank should do so, it would be seen as an attempt to climb above their normal station. Not that it would ever happen; people in royal service know their place, and stick to it. And the members jealously guard the exclusivity of their privileged positions. Prince Michael of Kent once appointed a very able man to be his private secretary. However, it was pointed out to him that this was not possible because the man concerned had not held a commission in one of the services. In fact, he had been a non-commissioned officer in the Royal Navy. Prince Michael stuck by his original choice and kept him in his job, but his aide never received the title of private secretary, even though that is precisely what he was. And he was not allowed to eat in the Members' Dining Room or take tea in the Equerries Withdrawing Room with the other private secretaries. The 'Officer's Mess' was strictly off-limits to him.

The officials are equally aware of their status, and of the division between senior and simply official. There are forty-one senior officials and one hundred and seventy-six officials. These are the people who man the Palace engine room, performing tasks delegated by the members and relaying instructions to those farther down the scale. On a day-to-day basis, the Palace could not function without the officials. They look after the books, order the food, wine and all other equipment needed to keep the organization running. If the Master of the Household has been asked to supervise the arrangements for an evening reception, one of his assistants will check that a suitable room is available and ensure that the Yeoman of the Wine Cellar is told how much drink to provide. Another assistant will arrange for the guest list to be typed and the invitations posted, while a third looks after the accounts, making sure the budget is not exceeded and the bills are paid on time – with any discount deducted. Generally officials address those above them by their rank or title, though within the Royal Collection everyone seems to be on first name terms.

The senior official with one of the most important positions in the household, and one which could be the most lucrative if he so chose, is a gentleman by the name of John Hope. Major Hope is the State Invitations Assistant in the Lord Chamberlain's office, and it his responsibility to issue invitations to various royal functions including the garden parties. John Hope has nine ladies working with him who are called 'Temporary Lady Clerks' even though most of them work throughout the year and some have been doing the same job for over twenty years. Under his supervision, their task is to write out, in longhand, every one of the forty thousand invitations to the four garden parties the Queen gives every year (three at Buckingham Palace, one at Holyroodhouse). Thousands of people long to be invited, but you cannot apply. If you do your name is immediately added to the 'Black List' – the file that records those men and women who must not be invited to a royal function – and once on the list, a name is rarely removed.

Applying for an invitation is not the only reason for someone to be banned; you may have lobbied through a third party. If that happens both join the list. Or a guest might have claimed a title or honour to which they have no right. That's another reason. The ladies and their boss in the garden party office are meticulous about checking such details and also making sure the correct titles, decorations and professional qualifications are affixed to the name on the invitation. After all, they are sending them out on Her Majesty's behalf, so the only acceptable standard is perfection. If John Hope, or any of his lady clerks, wanted to make a lot of money, they could easily ask a small fortune for adding names to certain invitation lists. Ambitious social climbers with ample funds would shower them with cash. Fortunately, neither the State Invitations Assistant nor any of his clerks has ever been known to succumb to this temptation. Everyone who has held the post has been a model of propriety.

Within the garden party office there are six filing cabinets stuffed with details regarding false claims and records showing why such and such a person is 'unsuitable'. When the Queen first came to the throne, no divorced man or woman was permitted to be presented to her or even allowed inside the Palace. If that rule applied today, not only would it be impossible to hold a State function with those who have to be invited because of their official or government position, many of Her Majesty's own family would be on the 'Black List', as would several members of the household. And again in those early days, even minor brushes with the law, such as speeding offences or light-hearted clashes on Boat-Race night, would result in being refused an invitation to the Palace.

The most unpleasant aspect of this vetting is the secret file that contains the anonymous letters. Even today, so much jealousy surrounds the Court, that some men and women who find out that someone they hate or envy has been received, write to the Queen telling her of some dark secret in the past. Letters beginning 'I feel it is my duty to point out to Your Majesty . . .' followed by a string of allegations, usually without the slightest proof and invariably unsigned, arrive by the dozen every year. The lady clerks who write the invitations do not get to see any of these letters; they are passed to the Lord Chamberlain's office, where they are investigated thoroughly, not only to see if the allegations are correct, but also to protect any innocent victims of malicious accusations. Indeed during the Queen's reign, the parents of several of the clerks have been on the Black List for one reason or another, but it is a tribute to their integrity that there has never been a single occasion when one of them has tried to insert a member of their family onto a guest list.

These then are the workhorses of the household, the men and women who virtually run the place, unrecognized beyond the confines of the Palace. They rarely achieve distinction, or seek it, apart from the appreciation of their superiors, who know how valuable they are. They can expect, after many years' faithful service, to be made a member of the Royal Victorian Order, but usually only in one of the lower or middle ranks. Knighthoods are reserved for members. There was one occasion when the rule was broken, and it was welcomed by everyone. John Titman had worked in the Lord Chamberlain's office for over twenty years – always as an official – and on the day he was due to retire he was summoned to an audience of the Queen. This wasn't entirely unexpected; long-serving servants usually are granted a final meeting before they retire. What did come as a complete surprise was that when he entered Her Majesty's sitting room, he saw the kneeling stool standing there. The Queen then ordered him to kneel and dubbed him a Knight of the Royal Victorian Order (KCVO). It came as a delightful end to a royal career and was entirely the Queen's own idea. Nothing could have pleased him more.

The staff, who comprise the majority of those who work in the Palace, are usually addressed by their Christian names, and they in turn call those above them either Sir or Madam. But there are subtle ways in which one can gauge the standing of, say, a footman or maid by the way in which they address their superiors. The Palace Steward, Shaun Croasdale, who was once the Queen's personal page, and so enjoys a special place in the household, is technically still staff. But some members and officials, who have perhaps been at the Palace for only a short period, he manages to avoid calling anything, without giving any reason to take offence. The manner, despite the missing Sir or Madam, remains correct but with no servility.

Another full-time member of the household, but one who is there for only three years and who is paid by the Ministry of Defence during his time at the Palace, is the Defence Services Secretary. Always a senior serving officer, he is seconded to Buckingham Palace and retains his rank and pay during his attachment. This office has existed since 1964 and it rotates between the Army, Navy and Royal Air Force. So far no woman has held the position.

He works from an office on the first floor of the Palace, not far from Prince Philip's suite, and to get to his room, has to pass through what is easily the most fascinating dining room in the building, the Chinese Luncheon Room. The decor of this exotic apartment consists of displays of practically every knife, spear and bayonet ever used in warfare. Prince Philip likes to give private lunch parties here and there is never a shortage of topics of conversation.

In spite of the curtailment of Britain's armed forces in recent years, the royal family still retains strong links with every branch of all three services and the Defence Services Secretary acts as the conduit. If a regiment, ship or RAF unit with which the royal family has a particular association, is celebrating a special occasion, it is through him that they contact the Palace. He also accompanies Her Majesty on all visits to service establishments and his advice is sought on matters of protocol when it relates to military and naval matters. Another of his responsibilities is to keep the Queen and Prince Philip informed of any major promotions and appointments, both in Britain and throughout the Commonwealth. Prince Philip is Captain General of the Royal Marines, while the Queen is Commander-in-Chief of all the armed forces.

One major departure in recruitment and working policy in recent years has been the Court's attitude to divorced couples. In the early days of the Queen's reign, no one involved in a divorce case would even have been considered for employment at the Palace. Nowadays, it is a question that is not asked. This attitude to divorce has been forced upon the royal family by the divorces of the late Princess Margaret and three of the Queen's children. But as recently as 1967 Her Majesty's cousin, the Earl of Harewood, son of the Princess Royal, King George V's only daughter, was ostracized by the Court, and much of society, when he and his first wife, the former Marion Stein, divorced. And only comparatively recently has there been any thawing in formal relations between the Queen and her cousin, even though, privately, they have always remained on cordial terms. He is now fully accepted. It would have been hypocritical to act in any other way.

CHAPTER THIRTEEN

The Good Old Days

Although there are some 368 men and women working full-time in the royal household today, the number is practically half that of one hundred years ago, when well over six hundred were employed.

Many of the more picturesque job titles have disappeared. There are no lamplighters, pot scourers, rat catchers in ordinary, marshalmen and necessary women, and the need for thirteen coal porters vanished many years ago. Nor does the Queen any longer employ liveried Scottish attendants simply to ride on her State Coaches, as her great-grandfather and great-great-grandmother did. Neither does her Master of the Household have to 'pass' fifty members of her staff to attend compulsory morning service in the Chapel Royal, as in days gone by. This was an unpopular chore as it meant those chosen had to change out of their work clothes into formal suits at 10 o'clock and then back again once the service ended.

But there are still stalkers, pipers (the King's Piper was paid £70 a year in 1902), lodge-keepers, a Yeoman of the

Gilt and Silver Pantry and under-butlers working in the Glass and China Pantry. Plus Pages of the Presence, Backstairs and Chambers, a Lord Steward, Chief Clerk to the Master of the Household and a Royal Coroner.

In the Round Tower at Windsor Castle, the Royal Archives have records of nearly everyone who has worked at Buckingham Palace and in which capacity: their full names, their job description, the date they joined the household, if and when they were promoted. (Miss M. A. Jackson was second Necessary Woman to the Board of Green Cloth, which meant she was a cleaner. In 1902 she was paid £18 a year, plus 2/- (10p) a day lodging allowance and £6.10s (£6.50) a year washing allowance. The records also show that she had formerly been an assistant kitchen maid and that she was paid in the category of a third-class servant.)

The same pages in the Household Lists of a century ago reveal that the Lord Steward, the Earl of Pembroke, received a salary of £2,000 a year, his Treasurer, Victor Cavendish, was paid £904, as was the Comptroller of the Household, Viscount Valentia, whereas the Master of the Household, Lord Farquhar, received £1,000 a year – a very respectable sum in those days. The Office Keeper and First Messenger, a Mr Charles James Bentley, who had joined the household in 1885, had seen his salary rise to £100 a year, or just under £2 a week. But there were a few extras. He decided to 'live out' so he was paid an additional £25 a year in lieu of an apartment at St James's Palace, to which he was entitled, £10 a year for the 'porterage of venison' and a further £60 a year for working as an extra State Porter. So all in all he didn't do too badly.

A glance at the complement of the Lord Steward's Department, the Board of Green Cloth, which today is referred to as the Master of the Household's Department, shows the extent and numbers of people employed. Eighteen men and women worked directly for the Lord Steward, including the Master and Deputy Master of the Household, a clerk accountant, first, second and third messengers and the two Necessary Women.

Practically all royal appointments were family affairs and this lasted well into the twentieth century. As sons and daughters grew up, their names were automatically added to the household waiting list until a vacancy occurred. There was no such thing as advertising. It was a 'closed shop' and it was quite common to find four or five members of the same family working in the kitchens, sculleries or gardens and as housemaids.

In the Pay Office there was the Paymaster to the Household, Colonel Sir Nigel Fitzharding Kingscote, who was paid £700 a year, while among five others working in the Wine and Beer Cellars was a Thomas Kingscote, who was called the Gentleman of the Cellars and received £500 a year for his labours, with an extra £14 a year for his electric light. As we have seen, working in the royal household has always been something of a family affair, and it is very likely that the two Kingscotes were related. The second Yeoman of the Cellars, William Skene, had joined the household in 1883 as a coal porter at Balmoral. He was obviously ambitious and was brought down to Buckingham Palace, promoted in 1900 and given £110 a year plus 4/- (20p) a day lodging allowance.

The senior domestic servant, then as now, was the Palace Steward. His name was James Warren and he received the princely salary of £300 a year plus 5/- (25p) a day board and lodging. But he wasn't the highest paid of the royal servants. That distinction went then – and it still does – to the sovereign's chef. In 1902, Just Alphonse Menager was paid £400 a year, a little under £8 a week, with an extra 4/- (20p) added as a lodging allowance as he chose to live outside the Palace. At a time when the average wage for a working man in Britain was less than £2 a week, these two royal servants were the aristocrats of their class. The Royal Chef used to arrive at Buckingham Palace every morning just before eight o'clock, in a Hansom cab and wearing a formal frock coat and silk top hat. And he and the Palace Steward had all their meals and uniforms provided, so they were able to save most of their wages.

The Royal Chef had thirty-one cooks and apprentices working under him, apart from porters, dish washers and kitchen hands, plus Indian servants to prepare curry every day for lunch, a total of forty-five altogether. One of his apprentices was Gabriel Tschumi, who was paid £70 a year, and who went on to become one of the most famous of all royal chefs. Tschumi was the first Swiss national to be employed in the royal kitchens and he got the job, over the objections of the then Royal Chef, through the good offices of his cousin, Louise Tschumi, who was one of Queen Victoria's five dressers. In her fifteen-year stint in the royal household, Miss Tschumi would rise from dresser number five to be head dresser and one of the Queen's closest confidantes – mainly because she was the only one of the domestic servants who spoke fluent French, which the Queen liked to use frequently.

In the kitchen the duties of the six porters were allocated according to their status. They were numbered one to six with the senior, who had joined as a house porter in 1877, before being promoted to the more prestigious and highly sought after post of firelighter in 1892, being paid £52 a year, plus half a crown (12½p) a day board. The second kitchen maid, Lizzie Esson, had to manage on £22 a year and just 2/- (10p) a day, while Annie Mitchell, a Coffee Room Maid, earned £50 a year. But she had been in service for over thirty years, having joined in 1866.

Twelve men were employed in the Silver Pantry plus six under-butlers. The most important was the First Yeoman, on £3 a week with his deputy making only £2.10s (£2.50). But they were also provided with one suit of 'undress livery each year'. The under-butlers, apart from their £2 a week wages, were given £4 a year to find 'cotton stockings, gloves, shoes, hair powder and also to provide them with soap for washing'. They were supplied with livery and silk stockings.

The thirteen coal porters whose task was to keep the boilers and 200 open fires at the Palace supplied, were each paid £70 a year and received a 'Drab great coat every two years'. The seven night porters also received a coat, but their wages were slightly lower at £64 a year. The five lamplighters did not get a coat but the senior of them was paid £80 a year and he and his colleagues made a little extra by keeping the waste oil and selling it to local merchants. The eight Gentlemen Porters were among the highest paid of the lower orders. The first porter, W. J. Blane, had been in royal service for forty years by 1902 and his wages amounted to £180 a year.

Many of the domestic servants working in the royal household had no connection with the royal family at all but were employed to wait on other, more senior servants. There were three attendants working in the servants' hall and eight in the stewards' room. A Sergeant Yeoman supervised the five State Porters, three under-butlers and six marshalmen. The Sergeant, Richard Hutton, earned £200 a year, all found, and by 1902 he had been in service over thirty years. One of his Marshalmen, George Price, who like all the others was paid £2.10s (£2.50) a week, was noted in the household book as having been 'A Drill Sergeant in the Guards but was wounded in South Africa in 1900 and made to leave the Army. He was awarded the Medal for Distinguished Conduct in the Field.'

The Linen Room had two attendants, the junior of whom, Alice Cumbers, had been in the household for twenty years and still earned less than £1 a week. But even that was better than the official Coroner. His duties were not exactly onerous, having to attend only when a death occurred, but his honorarium was fixed at £24 a year, hardly guaranteed to make him a rich man.

King Edward VII employed eleven gamekeepers at Windsor Castle, some of whom had occasional duties at Buckingham Palace. Each was allocated a cottage and was paid £54.12s (£54.60) a year with the added bonus of '£2 per annum for killing vermin'.

Archibald Mackellan, the Head Gardener at Windsor, had a splendid house at Frogmore and £300 a year. He also managed to live practically free as all his vegetables, fruit and milk came from the Home Farm. Pay for the gardeners at Buckingham Palace did not come out of the household accounts as on 1 October 1901, His Majesty's Department of Works accepted total responsibility on payment of £1,000. The King did rather well out of the deal as his wage bill before that had been closer to £3,000 a year for the thirty-two gardeners employed.

Servants working on board the Royal Yacht *Victoria and*

Albert were particularly poorly paid. A hundred years ago, two assistant storemen, John Alexander and Edwin Webber, were lucky to get £12 a year – and they had to sleep in cramped conditions in hammocks which were slung close together in the seamen's mess where they ate, washed and lived.

The Ecclesiastical Household has never been very well off either. Even today its members are regarded as the Cinderellas of royal circles. In 1902, the only person who received anything like a living wage was the organist at St James's Palace, Walter Alcock. His salary of £250 a year enabled him to keep a comfortable if not luxurious standard. The four permanent priests each received £100 a year, or just under £2 a week, the same as the Sergeant of the Vestry, but he lived in a pleasant apartment in Ambassador's Court, St James's Palace, and he wasn't asked to pay part of his salary as rent, as the present holder of the post is required to do. They also employed an organ blower, a bell ringer and thirteen Gentlemen of the Chapel Royal, each paid respectively £26, £13 and £80 a year. The lowest paid was the man with the grandest title: Clerk of the Closet. He was the Bishop of Ripon, who received the grand total of £7 a year. Of course, being a bishop meant he lived in some style in his own palace with servants provided and paid for by the Church. But the Chapel Royal's Necessary Woman, Sarah Flett, probably needed every penny of the £13 a year she was paid for cleaning the chapel every morning. One figure stands out in the ecclesiastical section of the Lists. It is a salary of £700 a year for Mr C. R. Phellp. However, a note alongside records it is for 'Keeping and Teaching the Children of the Chapel'. So his £700 had to go a long way.

The second largest department in those far off days was that of the Lord Chamberlain. In the latter days of Queen Victoria's reign there was a Lord Chamberlain, the Earl of Clarendon, supported by a Vice-Chamberlain, eight Lords in Waiting, eight Ladies of the Bedchamber, eight Maids of Honour, eight Women of the Bedchamber, two Extra Women of the Bedchamber, a Master of Ceremonies, four Gentlemen Ushers, one Black Rod, five Sergeants at Arms, four Pages of the Back Stairs, a Page of the Chambers and a Page of the Presence. There were ten Grooms of the Great Chamber, one Governor of Windsor Castle, a Garter King of Arms who was paid £49 1s 4d (£49.7) a year, a sum fixed during the reign of William IV, and which remains the same today. There were ten other Heralds, two of them, Clarenceaux and Norroy & Ulster, receiving £20.5s (£20.25) a year, while the rest managed on £17.16s (£17.80). There was a resident Chaplain at Windsor (the equivalent of the present Dean), who was well recompensed at £600 a year, a huge salary at the start of the twentieth century, as was the Librarian, who received the same amount and lived in the magnificent house just inside the gates of the Castle occupied by the subsequent holders of the post. Also included in the Lord Chamberlain's department were three members of the medical household: the Physician to the household, who was paid £200 a year, the Dentist, who was a long way behind on a mere £100 and the Apothecary, who for some reason was paid more than any of his colleagues, earning £414 a year, plus £800 for supplying medicines.

Until 1968, the Lord Chamberlain's office was responsible for licensing all dramatic works performed publicly in Britain, hence the saying the 'legitimate theatre'. So a hundred years ago an Examiner of Plays was paid £300 a year to ensure that nothing 'unsuitable' was passed for public viewing. But the State Invitations Assistant, then as now one of the most discreet and trustworthy officials, earned only £60 a year. The surprising fact was that there was no corruption. Even then, affluent men and women would have paid handsomely for the privilege of receiving one of the stiff white cards bearing the words 'The Lord Chamberlain is commanded by His Majesty to invite . . .' But the men who held this post remained in royal service for many years; in most cases until they retired.

The same department employed the twenty-four musicians, at £46 a year each, who entertained royalty and their guests. In addition, a young man by the name of John Day, is entered in the accounts as a Kettle Drummer, on a yearly salary of £30.

Every royal residence had its own housekeeper. The one at Buckingham Palace was paid £112 a year plus a very elegant apartment on the ground floor and a maid to wait on her. At St James's Palace there was a housekeeper to look after the State Apartments. This was obviously a step up from the other housekeepers as the person doing the job in 1902 was the Hon. Lady Inglis, who was paid £250 a year. The State Apartments were used for entertaining on the grand scale and the duties of the housekeeper involved making sure the Throne Room and other magnificent apartments were kept in pristine condition. She didn't wield a carpet sweeper herself, of course, or soil her hands with a duster or scrubbing brush; there were legions of maids and cleaners to do that sort of menial work.

Once a year the Lord Chamberlain would carry out a duty that stretched back hundreds of years, and one which survives to this day. He would join the sovereign's watermen on the River Thames to mark the new swans which had hatched out during the year. All swans on the Thames are the property of the sovereign. The Keeper of the Swans, an ancient title, was paid £28 a year for his annual outing while the thirty-six watermen who both rowed him and the Lord Chamberlain, and caught the swans, received £3.10s (£3.50). An interesting name in the list of watermen for 1902 was one Richard Turk, who had been appointed in 1877. The Turk family has lived on the Thames almost as long as the British monarchy has been in existence and today the head of the family is Keeper of the Queen's Swans.

The office of Keeper of the Privy Purse has always been one of the key appointments in the royal household. The present Keeper is the eighteenth person to hold the post since Queen Victoria came to the throne in 1837. When her son succeeded her as King Edward VII, his Keeper was General Sir Dighton Probyn, a brave and distinguished soldier who had been awarded the Victoria Cross. He was given the use of residences at Buckingham Palace, Windsor Castle and Sandringham, as well as £1,500 a year – a small fortune in those days. His Majesty's private secretary, Lord Knollys, received the same salary, but had only two houses, at St James's Palace and Windsor Castle. The Senior Equerry to the King was paid £8 a week, with a flat thrown in, while his head valet, his senior personal servant, received £200 a year, and had the services of an assistant valet on £150 and a brusher at £80 a year.

Edward VII was a regular visitor to France and Germany and he employed a 'Manager of Continental Journies' whose name was Jaques Ferh. M. Ferh had responsibility for all the King's travel arrangements, in the same way that the Director of Royal Travel operates today, but without certain of the logistical problems of modern long-haul travel.

Today's Household boasts a Deputy Ranger at Windsor (the Ranger is Prince Philip), who lives in a splendid house, Ranger's Lodge, in the Great Park. A hundred years ago, he would have been called Land Steward and paid an annual salary of £370 but he lived in the same house. He also had free coal for the twelve open fires and a daily supply of dairy products from the Home Farm. There was also at Windsor an aviary keeper who, together with his wife, was paid £78 a year.

The Round Tower at Windsor Castle is repository for an extensive collection of Royal Archives, said to be among the finest in the world. A century ago the Keeper of the Tower, not to be confused with the Governor of the Castle, was a serving soldier, Gunner Sam Parsons, who was paid £20 a year. His duties were the equivalent of a modern day caretaker, making sure everything was locked up at night and opened the following morning. He lived on the premises, at the base of the one hundred stone steps that today have to be climbed by everyone, staff and visitors alike, before they reach the working part of the Tower, though in his day, the Royal Archives, as they are called now, were not in their present form.

The titular head of the Royal Mews was the Master of the Horse, the Earl of Sefton. His duties included attending the monarch on all occasions when His Majesty either rode on horseback or in a carriage. His annual payment was £2,000, but then, as now, the bulk of the responsibilities for all royal travel by road – either by horse or motor car – fell to the Crown Equerry. At that time it was Sir Henry

The Queen likes to open personal mail herself. Letters from family and friends
can be easily identified by coded initials in a corner of the envelope.

Throughout her fifty-year reign the Queen has posed for scores of portraits. So it is not unusual to see her dressed in full ceremonial regalia first thing in the morning as she fits a sitting for an artist into her busy daily schedule.

The Royal Collection employs experts in a variety of skills including picture restorers, gilders, engravers, armourers, binders, paper conservators and librarians. Here work is underway cleaning and restoring several masterpieces from the Collection.

Students from Camberwell College of Art volunteer to help with the restoration and conservation of drawings in the Royal Collection.

Working on part of the Riesener Jewel cabinet at the Marlborough House Conservation workshop.

The horses are kept in some of the finest stables in existence and were designed by John Nash, who completed the building in 1825. The Mews is open to the public all year round and attracts over 100, 000 visitors every year.

The Royal Mews at Buckingham Palace no longer employs its own farrier. They now use the services of an outside contractor who comes in regularly to check the horses and their shoes.

The lawns at Buckingham Palace require constant attention, particularly after a garden party when 9,000 pairs of feet have walked over them.

Arranging all the flowers at Buckingham Palace and Windsor Castle is a continuous operation and one that attracts the admiration of many of the Queen's guests. Here the famous Tulip Vase is being decorated.

Above: The Grand Vestibule at Windsor Castle and the fire systems are checked thoroughly every week. After the great fire in 1996 nothing is left to chance.

Right: There are surgeries at Buckingham Palace and Windsor Castle, and here Sister Gillian Frampton treats a patient at Windsor.

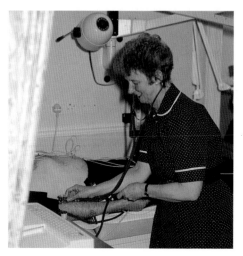

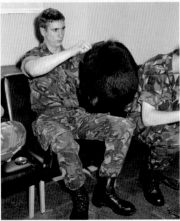

The Lord Chamberlain's Office is responsible for the twenty-two Investitures that take place every year at which up to one hundred and fifty people receive Honours. Before each ceremony every single decoration is checked to make sure all is as it should be.

The Guardsmen of the Household Division maintain their own uniforms which have to be in pristine condition at all times. The cleaning of the bearskin can take hours but it has to be done every day ready for inspection.

Footmen waiting at the entrance to the Royal Mews prior to acting as attendants on one of the royal carriages.

Two of the Queen Mother's most devoted servants: William Tallon, her Page of the Backstairs, and the late Reginald Wilcock, Page of the Presence.

The opening of the Queen's New Gallery at Buckingham Palace is by far the most exciting and ambitious programme ever undertaken by the Royal Collection. Here the giant Van Dyck painting of Charles I is being installed with great care.

Ewart, who lived 'over the shop' in the Crown Equerry's House, with cook, chauffeur, valet, under-butler and housemaids, all provided by a generous sovereign. He also received £800 a year. He had the services of eight further Equerries who were paid £600 a year and seven Pages of Honour, whose salaries were £230 a year. Today, the Crown Equerry is a full-time paid member of the royal household, as are all his staff, but the only paid equerries are those seconded from their service units for three years and who remain on the establishment of their original regiment, squadron or ship. The twenty-seven Extras and four Pages of Honour are purely honorary appointments.

In 1902, the Head Coachman was in charge of seven other coachmen, a head groom, postillions and outriders, all of whom received their living accommodation in the Mews and their meals. Their uniforms were provided and each was fitted with a white wig to wear on ceremonial occasions. The pecking order in their ranks was reflected in the wages they were paid, with the Head Coachman receiving £200 a year, equal to around £20,000 today, while ordinary coachmen earned £120 a year, postillions, £100 and outriders £80. Right at the bottom of the heap were the gate porters and motor drivers. This was a time when the motor car was still in its infancy, and the 'Red Flag' law, which required all motor vehicles to be preceded by a pedestrian carrying a red flag, and the speed limit of two miles per hour in town and four miles an hour outside, had been repealed only six years earlier. By the time King Edward VII came to the throne in 1901, the speed limit had been increased to ten miles an hour in town and a staggering fourteen in the country. Even so, cars gave way to horses and royal chauffeurs were paid only £78 a year, the same as the gate porters and the head stalker at Balmoral. The assistant stalkers, of whom there were four, were paid £47.10s (£47.50) a year, while the single shepherd on His Majesty's Scottish estate earned a meagre £34. Three upholsterers at Balmoral did much better, being paid £100, £90 and £52 respectively, but the housekeeper at Birkhall, a very large house on the Balmoral estate, had to manage on £20 a year.

Various other allowances were paid to the staff according to their rank. The Librarian at Windsor, who did not take his meals with his colleagues at the Castle but ate at home, was paid £50 a year 'in Lieu of Table'. A little farther down the scale the servant to the Librarian received 2/6d (12½p) a day as board wages while the charwoman in charge of the footman's room at Buckingham Palace had 2/- (10p) a day. If housemaids did not receive Board Wages, they were paid 3d (just over 1p) a day as 'Tea and Sugar Allowances'.

As has been previously mentioned, when men and women joined the royal household they expected to have a job for life. The 'cradle to grave' philosophy was similar to that in most aristocratic families. The employers demanded total loyalty, and their servants expected to be looked after until they died. Unlike the men and women who worked in factories or coal mines all their lives and were then thrown on the scrap heap without a penny when they were too old to continue, those lucky enough to be in service at one of the great houses were regarded as part of the family, and as such, their welfare was of concern to the master and mistress long after retirement.

A search of the Royal Household Lists of one hundred years ago confirms the fact that it was not uncommon for staff to serve the sovereign all their working lives. John

Blackburn, who retired as Palace Steward after forty years, working his way up from junior footman, received a pension for life of £300 a year. In 1902, this was more than sufficient to see him comfortably into old age. Joseph Bailey, First Yeoman of the Silver Pantry, had a salary of £327.15 (£327.75p) at the time of his retirement after forty-four years' service. He was given a pension of £206, or £4 a week. White collar officials, whose salaries were higher than their domestic colleagues', received pensions structured accordingly. George Courmont, Secretary of the Board of Green Cloth, retired after thirty years at the Palace. He was earning £1,200 a year and given a lifetime pension of £750. The Clerk Comptroller to the Master of the Household, A. W. Lloyd, was one of the longest-serving members, having completed forty-six years when he retired in 1902. He received a generous pension of £480 a year compared with his working salary of £741.

Even those at the bottom of the household ladder were compensated for years of loyal service. John Cooper, a labourer in Windsor Castle gardens for twenty years, earned only £46.16 (£46.80p) a year, yet he was given a pension of £15.10 (£15.50p). Perhaps not enough to live on, but it helped to supplement anything else he managed to make after he left. Fred Ralph, an usher in the servants' hall at Marlborough House, the home of the then Prince of Wales, later King George V, had worked in the household for thirty-nine years and his final salary was £113 a year. His pension amounted to £65, but he was allocated accommodation in the servants' quarters for the rest of his days. One Samuel Edwards, who was described as a 'Hunt Helper', a job he had held for forty-six years, was pensioned off on £17 a year. The largesse of the royal family even extended in some cases to the families of their old retainers. The children of Charles Perry, a former footman, were given a pension of £15 a year in recognition of his loyalty and their impoverished state.

But pensions were not automatically awarded to every member of staff and when there might be a problem for someone who was considered worthy by his superior, an exchange of correspondence at the highest level took place on his behalf. The following letter, written by the Crown Equerry, Major General Sir Henry Ewart, to the Keeper of the Privy Purse, is a perfect example of the lengths to which a head of department would go to obtain the best possible pension for a loyal member of staff.

The pension was granted, and the handwritten note reads: 'Pension papers returned to Sir H Ewart 2/I/05. Dr Jackson's letter also returned.' It is initialled 'DMP'.

Master of the Horse's Office,
Royal Mews,
Buckingham Palace, S.W.

31st December, 1904.

My dear Probyn,

Herewith application for pension on behalf of out livery helper, Martin Senter, (Sandringham Establishment), for favourable consideration and sanction of His Majesty The King.

This man has been in failing health for some considerable time, and quite unable to do any light work allotted to him.

Attached is Dr. Jackson's report, who thinks the poor old man quite past any sort of labour.

Service ... ... 28$\frac{7}{12}$ years.

Proposed pension . ... £24 per annum.

Yours very truly,

Henry Ewart

MAJOR GENERAL
& CROWN EQUERRY.

General Right Hon. Sir D. M. Probyn,
G.C.B., G.C.V.O., K.C.S.I., I.S.O., V.C.,
S A N D R I N G H A M.

CHAPTER FOURTEEN

By Royal Appointment

Throughout the royal household, one department is known by its initials, LCO. They stand for the Lord Chamberlain's Office, but although the Lord Chamberlain has titular responsibility, he has practically nothing to do with the everyday running of this large and far-reaching organization. This is left in the capable hands of the Comptroller, always a former senior service officer, usually from the Brigade of Guards, where knowledge of royal ceremonial is part and parcel of the job.

The Queen has been served by seven Lord Chamberlains since she came to the throne in 1952, the first, the Earl of Clarendon, being inherited from her father's reign. Lord Clarendon had held the post since 1938 and, as is the custom in the royal household, he tendered his resignation on the death of the sovereign. The Queen asked him to remain for several months before she could make her own appointment, the Earl of Scarbrough. Since then the Lord Chamberlains have been a mixed bunch. Lord Maclean, a former Chief Scout who had to be made a peer before he could take up his post, was sandwiched between two bankers: Lord Cobbold (1963–71) and the Earl of Airlie (1984–97). The Queen likes her Lord Chamberlains to stay for some time and most have been in office for five years or more. The exception was Lord Camoys (1998–2000), who departed after only two years due to ill health. The present Lord Chamberlain is Lord Luce, a former Conservative Member of Parliament for Arundel and Shoreham. Like most of his predecessors, he recognizes that his is essentially a part-time appointment, so he turns up at the Palace only two or three times a week.

His responsibilities sound awesome. They include all aspects of Court ceremonial and Court Mourning, all appointments to the royal household, looking after visiting Heads of State (two a year), calling out the names of those about to be honoured by the Queen at the twenty-two investitures held every year, making sure the right flags are flying at all Her Majesty's residences and ensuring that the Crown Jewels in the Tower of London are well maintained.

The Lord Chamberlain coordinates the activities of all the other departments in the household by presiding at the monthly meetings between the heads of those offices. He also acts as the channel of communication between the Queen and the House of Lords and attends Her Majesty on all ceremonial occasions, with the exception of the State Opening of Parliament, when he remains behind at Buckingham Palace until the 'safe return' of the sovereign from the Palace of Westminster.

Most modern Lord Chamberlains have preferred to remain in the background, giving encouragement and advice where necessary, but not interfering in the day-today running of the household. The rest of them like to see him around occasionally but the Comptroller is the person with the power, and the man with de facto responsibility for practically all ceremonial duties involving royalty, including the diplomatic precedence at Court and the dress to be worn at various royal functions.

The Lord Chamberlain's Office is responsible for royal weddings and funerals, and as always meticulous attention to detail is considered the most important part of arranging these. When rehearsals for the funeral of Earl Mountbatten of Burma in 1979 were being held, it was discovered that the advance division of the Foot Guard had drawn too far in front of the Gun Carriage which would carry the coffin, and was pulled by naval ratings. The reason was that the length of the Guards' pace for the slow-march is thirty inches while that of the Royal Navy is eighteen. Adjustments were made and on the day the procession passed with impeccable precision. Royal funerals have code words which are used internally at the regular meetings held to update the arrangements: the Queen is London Bridge, Prince Philip is Forth Bridge, while Prince Charles is Menai Bridge.

The office also looks after State visits, garden parties, investitures, the administration of the royal palaces, the awarding of Royal Warrants and even the Queen's swans on the River Thames. All come under the jurisdiction of the LCO and its Comptroller. They even have a committee which is already preparing for the next coronation. In January 2002, it met for the first time when among those present were the Earl of Arundel (representing his father the Duke of Norfolk, who will have overall responsibility for the arrangements when the time comes), the Lord Chamberlain and the Comptroller of the Lord Chamberlain's Office, who will look after the details of the ceremonial side. They came up with a revolutionary plan to scale down the ceremony (which they believe will take place some time between 2010–20) and, working on the assumption that Prince Charles will be the next sovereign, agreed that he will not be asked to wear the elaborate robes of previous kings and queens. Instead, as an Admiral of the Fleet, he will wear his full dress uniform, though he will be crowned with St Edward's Crown. And by the time of the coronation it is highly unlikely that the Gold State Coach will still be fit for use so one of the other carriages will carry the new king in the processions between Buckingham Palace and Westminster Abbey. There will be fewer peers and peeresses in their robes, and a wider ethnic representation will be invited. After the initial meeting of this committee, the plans were submitted to the Queen and to Prince Charles for their comments and decisions, but no details are to be released for many years. It is simply another example of the forward planning and attention to detail for which the Palace is renowned.

Since 1968, one of the office's more colourful, and unwanted, tasks has ended. The Lord Chamberlain – or his representative – no longer has to read all plays intended for public performance in Britain, in order to license them. It is extraordinary that until only a little over thirty years ago no representation of any member of the royal family, alive or dead, or of any other living person could be staged. Nor was homosexuality a suitable subject for entertainment, and no man and woman, even if married in real life, could appear in bed together under a blanket on any stage in London.

Sir John Johnston, who retired as Comptroller of the Lord

Chamberlain's Office in 1987, disclosed in his book: *The Lord Chamberlain's Blue Pencil*, the feelings of King George V in 1924, when a play about Queen Victoria by Louis Parker was submitted to the then Lord Chamberlain, Lord Cromer. Cromer sent it to the King, who instructed his private secretary, Lord Stamfordham, to write the following memorandum: 'The King has read Mr Louis Parker's play *Queen Victoria* and considers it is vulgar and in many instances historically incorrect: and permission for its performance ought never to be given in HM's lifetime.'

Although censorship accounted for less than twenty per cent of the time of the Lord Chamberlain's office, it was the subject that attracted the most attention. So when the Theatres Act of 1968 ended a tradition that had existed in some form or another since the fifteenth century, it was welcomed by his office as much as by the playwrights and theatre managers who had suffered from the decisions forced upon them. Many people in the theatre believed that the Examiners – the men and women who read the plays on behalf of the Lord Chamberlain – were actively seeking ways to prevent their work being performed. The truth was that most of them were ardent lovers of the theatre and went out of their way to reduce the number of changes they felt were needed before a licence could be granted. During the time of Lord Cobbold, the last Lord Chamberlain to act as Official Censor (1963–68), of 4,405 plays submitted, some 4,347 were licensed with a further 47 waiting for a decision and only 11 refused altogether. Not a bad record for an organization thought to be among the stuffiest in the land.

The Lord Chamberlain's Office also has responsibility for one of the oldest of the sovereign's corps of personal bodyguards. It was in the twelfth century that King Richard I (the Lionheart) formed his bodyguard of Serjeants at Arms. There were twenty-four of them and all were knights or gentlemen of high birth. Throughout the centuries succeeding monarchs maintained the custom, and even the Great Officers of State appointed their own Serjeants at Arms. The tradition survives to this day in both Houses of Parliament.

In the royal household, their numbers have been reduced to three and their duties are purely ceremonial. Two attend the Queen at the State Opening of Parliament, with the third held in reserve. Nowadays they are not knights but senior officials of the household (one had to relinquish his post recently when he was promoted from being a senior official to a member, as members are not permitted to be Serjeants at Arms) and the position is awarded in recognition of loyal and commendable years of service to the monarch. Jonathan Spenser had been secretary in the Lord Chamberlain's office and was promoted in 2001 to be Deputy Comptroller and a member. His place as Serjeant at Arms has been taken by Stuart Stacy, a senior clerk in the Master of the Household's department. Serjeants at Arms need to be reasonably fit as the mace they carry before the Queen at the State Opening of Parliament is very heavy – and they only get one rehearsal, the day before. They are rewarded with pay of £5.83 a month.

Another important post within the Lord Chamberlain's Office is that of Marshal of the Diplomatic Corps, invariably a retired senior service officer who is based at Ambassador's Court in St James's Palace. His post is normally held for ten years and during this period he is responsible, with the Crown Equerry, for collecting ambassadors and high commissioners from their residences and taking them to Buckingham Palace to present their credentials to the Queen, in a ceremony where they all wear full evening dress even though it takes place in the morning. He also arranges for diplomats to attend Royal Ascot, garden parties (where they eat in the royal tent), the State Opening of Parliament and, the highlight of the social year, the Diplomatic Reception for 1,800 guests. He is assisted by two deputies, both of whom are part-time and are based at the Foreign and Commonwealth Office, and at the reception, the Marshal escorts Her Majesty and presents various diplomats, while one of his assistants accompanies the Duke of Edinburgh. Newcomers to that job suffer near heart failure as the Duke likes to dawdle and chat and their task is to get him to the end of the State Rooms at the same time as the Queen, who is frequently yards ahead. But Prince Philip has many years' experience of this type of thing and he has some inbuilt sense of timing that always enables him to sense when to move on. So far he has never – in fifty years – kept Her Majesty waiting.

In addition to the 368 full-time staff already discussed, a further 215 part-timers who are either not paid at all or receive only a small honorarium, mostly come under the jurisdiction of the Lord Chamberlain. For example, thirty-two Gentlemen Ushers and Extra Ushers can be called upon to represent Her Majesty at funerals or marshal the guests at garden parties and investitures. These are often former service officers or retired members of the royal household invited to serve as reward for loyalty, such as John Haslam, a former assistant press secretary. The twenty-seven Extra Equerries include three of the Queen's former private secretaries: Sir William Heseltine, Lord [Robert] Fellowes and Lord [Philip] Moore, as well as four former Masters of the Household, former Crown Equerries and the last officer to command the Royal Yacht, *Britannia*. Four Pages of Honour are unpaid, as are fifteen part-time Lords-in-Waiting who greet visiting Heads of State. The Queen never goes to the airport no matter how exalted the visitor.

The Ecclesiastical Household under the supervision of the Clerk of the Closet, the Bishop of Derby, consists of nearly fifty clerics and lay workers. There is a Deputy Clerk of the Closet, a Dean of the Chapels Royal, Sub-Dean of the Chapels Royal, an Organist, Choirmaster and Composer, Domestic Chaplains at Buckingham Palace, Windsor Castle and Sandringham, and a further thirty to forty Chaplains and Extra Chaplains to the Queen. Easily recognizable by their scarlet cassocks, they are often seen mingling with the guests at Palace garden parties. All are paid by the Church and do not receive a royal stipend although the Chaplains do get a fee for preaching at royal services, which they do according to a Rota of Waits. One sermon a year at St James's Palace is the norm. They also get an unofficial briefing from their colleagues that sermons should be lively and not too long. The Duke of Edinburgh has been known to huff and puff if a sermon looks like lasting longer than twelve minutes. He once observed to the Dean of Windsor, 'The mind cannot absorb what the backside cannot endure.'

In January 2002, after a gap of five hundred years, a Roman Catholic priest, Cardinal Cormac Murphy O'Connor, Britain's senior Catholic cleric, was invited by the Queen to preach at Sandringham. It was a further move on her part to heal the breach between the Catholic Church and the Church of England in which she had been encouraged by Prince Charles, who attended the service. There is no record of Prince Philip's reaction to the sermon, but it lasted only about a quarter of an hour.

The royal family are not sympathetic towards the more modern forms of Christianity. One priest who was invited to preach at Sandringham at the time of the Gulf War explained how he was advised to proceed: 'I was told that under no circumstances was there to be any sort of "Happy-Clappy" service, and the idea of turning the other cheek did not extend to offering prayers for Saddam Hussein.' So, in more recent times, it is safe to surmise that the name of Osama bin Laden has not featured in the royal prayers.

The Clerk of the Closet still retains certain duties to the sovereign which have lasted for centuries. One is to thoroughly examine every book or article on theological matters that is offered to the Queen. In days gone by, it was a common practice to try and influence the sovereign by writing something sacred which also contained opinions the writer was attempting to convey. Although such reasons no longer exist, the Clerk of the Closet still has responsibility for ensuring that Her Majesty sees nothing 'unsuitable'.

Buckingham Palace does not have a Chapel Royal, neither does Windsor Castle. The only royal residences which do boast such establishments are St James's Palace, the original seat of sovereignty, Hampton Court Palace, which Henry VIII accepted as a 'gift' from Cardinal Wolsey and whose last royal resident was George II, and the Tower of London, where the Chapel Royal – or, to give it its correct title, the Chapel of St Peter ad Vincula – lies within the White Tower, and was the first permanent Chapel Royal in England. In fact, the whole concept of a Chapel Royal is usually misunderstood to mean the buildings where royalty worships, when in reality by origin, and still in principle, they are the establishments of priests and choristers that were formed to serve the spiritual needs of the sovereign, travelling with him wherever he went.

The Medical Household consists of twenty-two doctors, dentists, oculists, chemists and one coroner. Its nominal head is also Physician to the Queen. There is also a Sergeant Surgeon, but he no longer has to carry out such delicate tasks as cutting the toenails of the sovereign as was the case in centuries past. Selling the cuttings to gullible members of the public who believed they possessed sacred qualities was a profitable sideline. Medical household members are all leading professionals in their various fields with their own hospital appointments and consulting rooms. Other doctors hold the position of Apothecary to the Queen, and to the households at Windsor, Sandringham, Balmoral and Holyroodhouse, where they receive a fee for each consultation.

Then there are the officers of the Orders of the Garter and Thistle, such as Garter King of Arms, Peter Gwynn-Jones, who works from the College of Arms (see chapter 19) and who also has responsibility for introducing new peers into the House of Lords; and the Gentleman Usher of the Black Rod, who is seen at the State Opening of Parliament, knocking at the door of the House of Commons to summon MPs to the House of Lords to hear the Queen's Speech. In Scotland, Lord Lyon King of Arms performs the same tasks as Garter King of Arms for the Order of the Thistle, and the Gentleman Usher of the Green Rod is Black

Rod's opposite number. The officers of the Garter and Thistle all come under the jurisdiction of the Lord Chamberlain. So too do the Gentlemen at Arms, whose ranks include such colourful titles as Clerk of the Cheque and Adjutant and two Exons, the Yeomen of the Guard, and, in a tiny sub-department of his own, the gentleman bearing the unique title of Swan Warden.

The armed forces provide a number of part-timers to the royal household. There are two Gold Sticks in Waiting, a Vice-Admiral of the United Kingdom, a First and Principal Naval Aide-de-Camp and a Flag Aide-de-Camp. The Army furnishes Her Majesty with four Aides-de-Camp, who are all Generals, while the Royal Air Force supplies just two, both of whom are Air Chief Marshals.

The Queen's household in Scotland includes the Royal Company of Archers, headed by the Captain-General and Gold Stick. There is also an Hereditary Carver, who no longer has the task of cutting up the sovereign's meat, and an Hereditary Standard Bearer for Scotland, whose job is self-explanatory. The post of Hereditary Master of the Household in Scotland is always vested in the Duke of Argyll, while that of the Hereditary Lord High Constable belongs to the Earl of Erroll. Two Earls: Dundee and Lauderdale, hold the respective posts of Hereditary Banner-Bearer for Scotland and Hereditary Bearer of the National Flag of Scotland. The Duke of Hamilton and Brandon is Hereditary Keeper of the Palace of Holyroodhouse, while a Major-General is traditionally appointed Governor of Edinburgh Castle.

When the Queen takes up residence in Scotland she can also call on the services of a Historiographer, a Botanist, a Painter and Limner, a Sculptor in Ordinary and an Astronomer, as well as Medical and Ecclesiastical Households north of the border.

Included in the long list of part-timers are: the Lord High Almoner, the Master of the Queen's Music, the Poet Laureate, the Keeper of the Royal Philatelic Collection (said to be worth over £50 million – that's the collection not the Keeper), the Bargemaster and the Swan Marker. However these, along with Her Majesty's Representative at Ascot, her Racing Manager and the Clerk of the Royal Cellars, come under the wing of the Privy Purse and Treasury Office, not the Lord Chamberlain. So too does the Assistant Secretary of the Royal Almonry, who comes in just once a week, in the run-up to the annual Royal Maundy Service, for which he is paid around £30 for a day's work, while the Keeper of the Royal Philatelic Collection does it for love – and the honour.

There are six major political appointments to the Royal Household – all members of the Government – who change whenever a new Government comes into power. The Captain, The Honourable Corps of Gentlemen-at-Arms, is Chief whip in the House of Lords, while his Deputy Chief Whip holds the appointment of Captain, Queen's Bodyguard of the Yeomen of the Guard. The Treasurer of the Household is Deputy Chief Whip in the House of Commons and the Comptroller of the Household is a junior government whip, so his principal duties are undertaken in the Whips' Office of the House of Commons, but he can be called upon to act as an usher at royal garden parties. The Treasurer is the senior of the three political appointees from the Commons. He also works mainly in the Whips' Office, but together with his colleague, the Comptroller, he travels in the carriage procession from Buckingham Palace to the Palace of Westminster at the State Opening of Parliament, and he is included in the royal procession in the House of Lords.

The Vice-Chamberlain of the household is also a Commons Whip, and concerned mainly with party politics, but he fulfils an important role as a conduit between the Commons and the sovereign. As part of this duty he is required to write a report on the day's proceedings in Parliament before dinner every evening. Any important developments which occur after dinner are included in the next day's report. At one time, the report was hand-written and delivered by carriage to Buckingham Palace. Today, it is recorded on a word processor and electronically transferred. It is a completely confidential document and is read only by the Queen in the privacy of her sitting room. Another custom which dates back centuries is that during the State Opening of Parliament, when the sovereign is at the Palace of Westminster, the Vice-Chamberlain remains at Buckingham Palace as a 'hostage' until she returns. He usually sits in the Equerries Drawing Room, drinking coffee and watching the events on television.

Parliament also provides a number of part-time Lords-in-Waiting and Baronesses-in-Waiting who represent the Queen when meeting important visitors to Britain and can be asked to attend funerals and memorial services on her behalf. None of these political appointments to the royal household is paid by the Privy Purse. Their money all comes from Parliament, and the appointments, approved by the Queen, are made on the advice of the Prime Minister, which means they are in his gift, not Her Majesty's.

The Lord Great Chamberlain – not to be confused with the Lord Chamberlain, the full-time head of the royal household – is one of the Great Officers of State and has responsibility for the conduct of royal affairs in the Palace of Westminster. It is an hereditary office and lasts for the duration of each reign, when it is handed over to the house of Cholmondeley, that of Ancaster or of Carrington. When the Queen dies, the present Lord Carrington, or his heir, will become Lord Great Chamberlain. His first duty to the new sovereign will be to stand on his immediate left at the coronation in Westminster Abbey and fasten the clasp of the Imperial Mantle.

The present Lord Great Chamberlain, the 7th Marquess of Cholmondeley, has only one annual duty: as Keeper of the Palace of Westminster he helps organize the State Opening of Parliament, where he has an office in the House of Lords. He is unpaid but, as he is said to have inherited a fortune in excess of £60 million, the matter is academic.

Many of the part-timers and holders of honorary posts belong to families with a long tradition of royal service, their positions handed down from generation to generation. Others are more recent appointments. But even those holding an historic place in the royal household for the first time, and coming from a background with little or no royal connection, seem to adapt to the splendour and dignity of regal ritual. Nobody could have come from a more modest family than the late Viscount Tonypandy who, as George Thomas, became one of the most successful Speakers of the House of Commons in the past century, and a friend of several members of the royal family. He never tried to hide his humble beginnings as the son of a miner in the Rhondda Valley of South Wales. Yet he grew into the job and thoroughly enjoyed his place in the order of precedence when he was required to attend the

Sovereign at State Banquets. As he once told the present author just after escorting the Queen Mother into dinner, clad in his Speaker's ceremonial robes: 'My Mam would have been so proud.'

CHAPTER FIFTEEN

Ladies-in-Waiting

The Queen has fourteen, the Queen Mother had eleven, as does the Princess Royal; Princess Margaret had ten, the Duchesses of Gloucester and Kent have five, Princess Alexandra has six, while Princess Michael of Kent manages on just four. They are, of course, those indispensable companions to the female members of the royal family, the ladies-in-waiting, without whom no royal lady is ever seen in public. There are more than fifty altogether, and if they all decided to pop in to the Palace for lunch on the same day – which they are perfectly entitled to – it would cause a minor crisis in the 1855 Room where household members eat.

Their numbers include a duchess, two countesses, a marchioness, several 'Ladies', a sprinkling of honourables with the remainder plain Mrs or Miss. But even those in this last category could hardly be classed as ordinary. Each comes from the upper echelons of society, with no need of a paid job to supplement her income. Which is just as well, for none of these posts is salaried, although the ladies are reimbursed for all their travel and out-of-pocket expenses. Yet they can be on duty from seven in the morning until well past midnight.

Although most of the ladies-in-waiting have homes in London, within taxi distance of Buckingham Palace, the majority also have large houses, castles or estates in the country. The senior lady-in-waiting, the Duchess of Grafton, who is Mistress of the Robes, lives in Norfolk, while one of Princess Alexandra's has a house in London and a castle at Craven Arms in Shropshire.

It's not a job one can apply for, nor are they ever advertised, and the royal ladies themselves do not offer the posts. Instead an intermediary makes the first approach. Usually it is an existing lady, who will explain what is required, the hours and days involved and the fact that there is no salary. So, if the candidate does not wish to accept – it has been known but only on rare occasions – Her Majesty or one of her royal kinswomen does not receive an embarrassing rebuff, a diplomatic nicety appreciated by both sides.

Until the reign of Queen Victoria, ladies-in-waiting were always chosen on the 'advice' of the Prime Minister of the day, and consequently changed when the Government fell. In 1839, when the Whig Lord Melbourne was defeated by his Tory rival Sir Robert Peel, Queen Victoria resisted attempts to force her to get rid of her ladies, all of them Whig and chosen on her accession two years before. Her first Mistress of the Robes was the Duchess of Sutherland, who was not only one of the great beauties of her day, but also a woman with political acumen and a sense of social responsibility. The Duchess lived virtually on the doorstep at Stafford House in St James's, where the Stafford Hotel now stands.

The Queen, arguably the most autocratic British monarch of the last two hundred years, had a furious row with Sir Robert Peel when he insisted that he could not serve as her First Minister if she surrounded herself with Whig ladies-in-waiting. She dug her heels in and refused to change her household, whereupon Sir Robert declined to form a Government, believing, quite correctly, that he did not have the confidence of the Queen, and the royal favourite, Lord Melbourne, continued in office until 1841. There was one victory for the politicians, however. Throughout the remainder of Victoria's reign, the Mistress of the Robes changed with each Government, even if the rest of the ladies-in-waiting did not.

Today, there is no such pressure on Her Majesty. She chooses whom she likes and interference from any official source would soon receive short shrift. Not that any modern Prime Minister would have the slightest interest in trying to influence the Queen in this way. Nowadays the ladies-in-waiting carry no weight in political terms.

Only the Queen's ladies-in-waiting are divided into separate divisions. There is a strict pecking order and the various grades are rarely crossed. One can be a 'Woman' even if untitled. But one cannot become a 'Lady' unless one is the wife or daughter of a peer, and no one below the rank of 'Duchess' has ever been appointed 'Mistress'.

The Mistress of the Robes, whose only duty regarding clothes is when she supervises the robing of Her Majesty at the State Opening of Parliament, is fortunate today in that she no longer has to present the wives of foreign emissaries to the Queen. In former times the Mistress of the Robes sometimes had to practise for days to perfect the correct pronunciation of the more difficult names, but the custom ended in 1936 with the accession of Edward VIII who had no female consort at his side. The present Mistress of the Robes is assisted by the Countess of Airlie and the Lady Farnham, the two Ladies of the Bedchamber who, equally, have nothing to do with putting the Queen to bed. The wives of peers, they attend the Queen on more important public occasions, and one of them, along with a Woman of the Bedchamber – a lower rank – always accompanies the Queen on overseas visits. There is also one Extra Lady of the Bedchamber to help out when necessary.

The bulk of the day-to-day work falls on the Women of the Bedchamber, of whom there are five regulars and five extras. The regulars work a shift system of two weeks on and four weeks off. Technically, they are part-time members of the household, which means they are included in the White Book and not the Green Book, which lists all full-time members. But they work to such a regular pattern that, to all intents and purposes, they are staff – even if unpaid. Of the five Women of the Bedchamber, three are titled, one is an Honourable and only one is a plain Mrs.

During their periods of duty they stay wherever the Queen is in residence. At Buckingham Palace, they have a pleasant suite of rooms on the second floor of the north front; that's the side facing you as you look at the building from The Mall. Their suite is near what used to be the Palace schoolroom and they wait there to be summoned by Her Majesty's page. Any small item of personal shopping Her Majesty might require is done by the lady on call. The days when the Queen was able to go into stores herself, even if they closed specially for her, as Harrods used to do at Christmas time, have gone.

Unless the Queen invites them to join her for lunch or

afternoon tea, the ladies usually eat in the 1855 Room with the other members of the household. But at Windsor, Sandringham and Balmoral they become much closer to the royal family and eat in their private dining room, because the Queen likes comparative informality in her life outside the official London residence. The lady on duty at Christmas and New Year is always included in all the family's festivities.

Mornings are often taken up with writing replies on behalf of the Queen to young children or very elderly men and women. The Queen likes these letters to have a personal touch, and the golden rule is that all correspondence must be answered by return. The day following an official visit is particularly busy, for although the Queen always writes personally to her host, the lady-in-waiting writes to those who have arranged the visit. As this can involve up to three or four engagements in a single day, it can mean twenty letters, each a personal expression of gratitude.

A clerk handles the office routine, typing, filing and making sure the duty rota is circulated in good time. The system is fairly relaxed and if one of them is scheduled to be on duty when they have a private engagement (it used to be for school holidays for their own children; now it's more likely to be for their grandchildren) the office clerk arranges to change the dates. They are all flexible, but knowing the Queen's programme months in advance means they are able to make their own arrangements accordingly. Her Majesty never expresses an opinion about which lady she would like for a particular occasion.

The personal qualities of the ladies-in-waiting are of prime consideration when the Queen and the other members of the family are choosing them. They need to be easy-going, good conversationalists and with an ability to mix with people from all walks of life and many different stations. Many of the functions held at Buckingham Palace are now open to a variety of men and women, so it is important that the Queen's ladies are able to blend in with the crowd. Most are fluent in French and those with other linguistic abilities are particularly valuable when foreign guests are expected. The Queen always attaches one of her ladies to the visiting suite of a Head of State. This is one way to smooth the path for wives who may not be familiar with the ways of the Court and who may also need a little help in getting around London. It's a personal touch that is much appreciated by some foreign guests and friendships have lasted long after the official visit has ended. There have also been occasions when the ladies-in-waiting have needed all their diplomatic skills. One or two foreign wives – or companions – have tended to treat the lady on duty as a personal servant, not realizing, or perhaps not caring, that she is probably of higher birth and breeding than themselves. In one instance a Woman of the Bed-chamber – a member of an old aristocratic English family – found underwear thrown at her with the instruction to 'wash them carefully by hand before you bring them back'.

All the Queen's ladies are personally chosen by herself and are either friends she has known for years or former long-serving members of the household invited to become ladies-in-waiting as a reward when they retire. This is what happened to Mrs Michael Wall, who was assistant press secretary to Her Majesty for twenty-seven years. On her retirement she was created Dame Commander of the Royal Victorian Order and made an Extra Woman of the Bed-chamber.

The ladies-in-waiting have become adept at recognizing the moods of the Queen. They know how she is feeling at any particular moment and they all know instinctively when she is feeling nervous before an important event. It may come as a surprise to learn that Her Majesty suffers badly from nerves before making a major speech or attending functions such as the State Opening of Parliament. The worst time is just before she is about to make her annual Christmas broadcast. She has never conquered her fear of radio and television and one of her ladies told me that the way she shows it is in the tone of her voice. Normally the Queen has a pleasant, low voice to which anyone who has met her will testify. When she speaks in public her voices rises almost an octave and she speaks with a slightly strangulated 'Church of England' vowel sound that is quite unnatural.

All the women in the royal family who are Royal Highnesses have ladies-in-waiting. The Princess Royal has eleven, seven regulars and four extras, and they have some of the toughest jobs as she is one of the busiest members of the family. All her ladies have been personally chosen and most are roughly her age and share her interests. One, Rowenna Feilden, was with the Princess when an attempt was made to kidnap her in the Mall in 1974 when several people were shot. Mrs Feilden was made a Lieutenant of the Royal Victorian Order by the Queen in appreciation of her part in foiling the attempt.

The Princess's ladies require stamina as she undertakes journeys to some of the most inhospitable areas in the world, and she is known not to have much patience with those who cannot keep up. These women are arguably among her closest companions, but even they find there is a barrier between them. Some are married with children, one or two are single, with jobs or businesses outside the Palace, and none is permitted to address the Princess by her Christian name. She is Your Royal Highness or Ma'am at all times, even to Victoria Legge-Bourke who was a fellow student at Benenden (though they were in different forms); and the ladies curtsy when they first see her in the morning and when they are dismissed.

By the time of her death in February 2002 only one of Princess Margaret's ten ladies was a regular as she was no longer able to undertake any public duties after suffering several strokes. But Princess Alice, Duchess of Gloucester, who has also retired from public life, retains the services of four, while the present Duchess of Gloucester, who is very much involved in royal duties, has three part-time ladies and two extras.

The Duchess of Kent has five ladies; Princess Michael of Kent four, while Princess Alexandra has a permanent lady in the Lady Mary Mumford and five others, including Dame Mona Mitchell, who was her private secretary for many years until she retired.

Some ladies-in-waiting have been around for many years; Lady Susan Hussey has over thirty years' service as a Woman of the Bedchamber and she sees the Queen every day when she is on duty. Others, particularly those living far distant from London, may be in attendance only on rare occasions. But they don't retire, no matter how old they are. If they become unable to perform their duties, they are usually appointed to be Extras, so that they keep the title but are not called upon. In the days when Queen Victoria had a vast retinue of ladies-in-waiting, every one was of noble birth, and all her household were required to stand in her presence. No one who was not royal was permitted to sit down.

Some of the longer-serving ladies have known the younger members of the royal family since they were born, and on occasion the behaviour of one or two of the Queen's children has stretched their patience. Not long after she had passed her test Princess Anne was driving one of the Queen's ladies-in-waiting. At that time Anne thought it was smart to use bad language, and during the drive it became so ripe – aimed at other drivers – that the lady threatened to get out of the car in the middle of London if she didn't stop. Anne realized the story would be bound to get back to her mother, so she obeyed – reluctantly.

All ladies-in-waiting play an important part in royal work. One of the Queen's sits alongside her in the limousine when they are travelling to official functions, explaining details of the programme, and when they arrive remains close at hand. As a result most have amusing stories to tell about the way they are treated by the Queen's hosts, for many of whom, of course, this may be the one and only time that royalty comes to visit. Many ladies have been curtsied to by overwhelmed mayoresses and consorts, and more than one has received a curtsy from a male host who has become confused. Others have been received with contemptuous indifference by the wife of the local mayor, who hasn't quite worked out the difference between a lady-in-waiting and a housemaid. But however they are treated the ladies react in exactly the same way – with perfect manners and good humoured tolerance.

Perhaps the most unusual situation that any lady-in-waiting has found herself in was when the Duchess of Grafton and Lady Susan Hussey accompanied the Queen on a State Visit to Saudi Arabia in 1979. Islamic religious traditions preclude women from taking an active role in public life, so Her Majesty, as one Head of State visiting another of equal rank, was accorded the style of 'Honorary Gentleman' for the duration. Her ladies-in-waiting were not given the same privilege, but as they were required to attend her at public functions, a blind eye was turned. In other words, they were totally ignored, but in the politest fashion.

At home Buckingham Palace is the venue for more than eighty functions every year, at each of which at least two ladies-in-waiting will be on duty. Essential qualities needed are cheerfulness, diplomacy, the patience of Job, a tolerance level that has no limits, a sense of humour bordering on the ridiculous and the ability to get on with people from all walks of life. And, as one of them told the present author, a bladder with the strength of a cast-iron tank comes in handy as well.

CHAPTER SIXTEEN

~~~

The Royal Bodyguards

Princess Anne once got rid of a police protection officer because she didn't like his aftershave. That wasn't the reason she gave, of course, in fact she didn't have to give a reason. She simply wanted him removed. He didn't mind a bit, because he knew they were not getting on and she irritated him as much as he did her. In fact, he let it be known to another of his colleagues that the prospect of accompanying her on a twenty-six hour flight to Australia was pretty daunting. He was moved to guard another royal, with whom he gets on very well – and who, apparently, is not offended by his aftershave. Another royal police officer asked to be moved to other duties because his principal kept on making jokes about his receding hairline. His request was granted but not as he would have preferred – and he found himself back on ordinary duties behind a desk in a police station in outer London.

One of the most highly sought after positions in the Metropolitan Police is to be attached to the Royalty and Diplomatic Department. This is the full title of what is commonly known as the Royal Protection Squad. The men and women who join the department, particularly those who work for the royal family, as opposed to the London-based Diplomatic Corps, can expect a complete break from the mundane routine of everyday police work; and a select few even go on to become famous as bodyguards to royalty.

The department is based in a special station in the grounds of Buckingham Palace. It was built at a cost of £1.6 million shortly after the Michael Fagan break-in incident in 1982, the funds coming from the police budget with the approval of the Home Office. The man in charge is a Commander of 'A' Division whose headquarters is at Cannon Row police station, but who is based at the Palace where he is given 'royal household status, but he is not a member of the household.' This means that he can eat in the Members' Dining Room if he chooses but, fortunately for him, he is not paid household rates. His salary of £61,428–£74,040, places him well above all but a handful of those paid directly by the Queen.

The Palace police post is located behind the Queen's Gallery and the only entrance is via the side door in Buckingham Palace Road. The building is completely covered by a large mound of earth and grass and shielded from the gardens by a screen of trees. It is invisible from outside; you cannot see it even from Buckingham Palace itself.

It is self-contained with nearly, but not quite all, the functions of a normal police station. There is a canteen, briefing rooms, changing rooms for the men and women who work on Palace security, a very high-tech radio communications centre and a large underground garage, for the police vehicles do not form part of the Royal Mews.

But there is no charge room or cells. This is not what in police terms is described as a 'custody station'.

They are linked to Cannon Row station at the west end of Westminster Bridge and also to a control room which is just inside the side gate of the Palace. A uniformed Chief Inspector runs the control room, with a Chief Superintendent commanding the Royalty, Special Patrol and Special Escort Motorcycle Group. He answers to the Commander who has the 1,000 men and women of the entire Royalty and Diplomatic Department under his command. This group is responsible for all embassy and high commission security in London. The royal palaces account for between seventy and one hundred officers.

The sophisticated network of electronic equipment housed in the police post provides instant communication with every royal residence, not just Buckingham Palace. So if an incident occurs at Highgrove House, the Prince of Wales's home in Gloucestershire, Gatcombe Park, where the Princess Royal lives, or any other royal home, the Palace police are immediately aware. They do not have to rely on normal lines of communication either. They have their own back-up systems should a bomb or other explosion cause the everyday lines to fail.

The police are also responsible for tracking royal vehicles wherever they may be. Special homing devices are fitted to all cars carrying the royal family, which means they can be located at all times. When a member of the family is leaving on a journey, the proposed route is notified to the police post and any deviation registers immediately on the monitor screens back at Buckingham Palace.

They also keep detailed plans of every room in every building occupied by royalty, and these are duplicated at

SAS Headquarters in Hereford. So in the event of a terrorist attack, rescuers know the lay-out before they go in. Because of this, the police and the SAS must be informed when any furniture is moved around.

The officers one sees escorting the Queen and other members of the royal family are not detectives, but uniformed policemen working in plain clothes. But there are uniformed policemen and women in the department, and these are easily visible as they man the gates at Buckingham Palace, Windsor Castle, St James's Palace and Clarence House. They are all volunteers and, as there is usually a shortage of men and women prepared to spend their days standing at the gates, there are often vacancies. Even those who stand guard admit the job can be 'as boring as Hell', but it can appeal to young constables who want a comparatively easy time so that perhaps they can study for promotion exams. If there are not enough volunteers, various police stations will order officers to work at the Palace, promising that if they stay for two years they will then be posted somewhere near their homes.

Everyone who joins the Royalty Protection Group is specially trained, even those who man the gates and check visitors in and out. These days these too are armed, with their guns carefully hidden from public gaze.

A uniformed sergeant – also armed – has the task of sitting outside the Queen's bedroom all night, wearing slippers instead of regulation boots, to avoid waking her when he walks up and down the corridor. His shift starts at eleven and lasts until 7.30 the next morning. The sergeant is an experienced police officer who has served his time on the North Centre Gate – that's the one on the right as you face the Palace from the Mall – and his instructions are to 'shoot anything that moves, that shouldn't move'.

The officers chosen to act as bodyguards have all reached the rank of at least sergeant, and they undergo a rigorous selection process. Vacancies are advertised in the twice-weekly Police Orders circulated to all officers. Applications are invited, but all would-be bodyguards have to be recommended by their own senior officer before they go any farther. Their records are examined for anything that might militate against their being appointed to a position close to royalty. Then a series of interviews is carried out before they are finally seen by the Commander in charge. He has the last word and if he decides against the applicant there is no appeal.

Once chosen to join, the new recruits are sent on various intensive courses before being posted to the Palace. At Hendon Police College they undergo special training in high-speed driving; most have only had experience in handling Panda cars. Now the need is to be able to control large, powerful vehicles in all conditions. If they are going to be driving one of the private cars belonging to Prince Charles, the Princess Royal or Prince Michael of Kent, all of whom have top of the range Bentleys, they have to be able to handle such vehicles with confidence.

As well as being expert in small arms fire (they are armed at all times), communications and elementary medical care, the chosen officers also have to be able to mix socially with people of all kinds. The Queen and Prince Philip accept as inevitable that they must have bodyguards with them wherever they go, but like them to be as unobtrusive as possible.

The instructors on the courses take particular care in watching the demeanour and dress of the trainees. They want maximum confidence and efficiency but aggressive behaviour is not acceptable. Good manners are important and while they are not too concerned about the details of etiquette it is not good if the officer is too shy or retiring. The royals like people around them who do not irritate or make them feel uneasy.

There is a small clothes allowance, which is taxable, and suits have to be conservative and loosely cut to enable a shoulder holster to be worn. Men have to be comfortable in a dinner jacket and morning clothes, for formal occasions such as Royal Ascot, while females – the Queen appointed her first woman bodyguard when Inspector Carol Quirk joined her four-man team – need clothes which, again, have to be constructed to hide the ever-present firearm.

A rather unusual accomplishment that officers are expected to acquire is the correct way to furl an umbrella. They are instructed that the proper way is to hold the handle in the right hand, then with the left hand tightly grasp the point of the instrument and slowly drag the hand down the spine while turning the handle in a clockwise direction, making sure the pleats are securely fastened in place. When opening an umbrella alongside one of the royals, one must always ensure that it is fully open and facing away, before moving in to shelter the royal concerned. Police officers are also told to make sure they have at least two umbrellas in the royal car, so that if one gets wet, another is available at the next stop.

The Princess Royal was the first to have a female bodyguard but they are in the minority, and men occupy all the senior posts. The Queen insists on choosing her police officers herself and until recently all have been men. Her female bodyguard, Carol Quirk, has been with the Royalty

Protection Department for just over twelve years. She began as a 'backup' officer, then was appointed to the team of the Princess of Wales before joining the Queen. She is in her late thirties, unmarried and is said to be quiet and fairly reserved. Another female officer, recently retired from the Royalty Protection Department, has been recruited privately by Prince Charles to protect his long-time companion Camilla Parker Bowles.

Overall appearance is very important and, unfair as it may seem, a number of otherwise excellent people have been rejected simply because of facial blemishes. One man, who had a brilliant record and had passed all the preliminary tests with flying colours, was turned down because of an unsightly birthmark on his face. It wasn't that the royal family would object; it was because he would have stood out and Royalty Protection officers need to remain unobtrusive.

The men and women chosen to guard the Queen and her family say the process is comparable to an officer's selection board in the Royal Marines or for one of the toughest regiments in the Army. They also like to claim their training courses are more rigorous and make them more efficient than the Special Branch policemen who guard the Prime Minister and his Government colleagues. And failure in any one segment of the course means an instant return to their original unit.

Having passed all the tests and been accepted, the new recruits arrive at Buckingham Palace where they can expect to spend six months to a year as back-up to one of the royal bodyguards. They shadow them wherever they go, learning the ropes and gradually becoming used to the ways of the household, and also allowing their faces to become familiar to members of the royal family. Only then are they placed on regular duty with a particular member. As one former police bodyguard explained: 'You are moved around quite a bit in the early days to see if the chemistry works, and then when you hit it off with one, you quickly learn how to mix their favourite drinks. If you do it the right way, they keep you on.'

Contrary to popular belief, the family often ask for particular policemen to be allocated to them. It's not just a case of taking whoever is next on the list. They would never ask directly, but the private secretary will chat to the chief superintendent and mention that 'Inspector so-and-so seems a good chap.' Shortly afterwards that inspector will find himself attached to that royal person. A much more common occurrence is the use of the royal veto to get rid of someone. They all have their peculiar likes and dislikes. The Princess Royal had one bodyguard for over twenty years but other members of her team have been moved with great frequency, and nearly always at her request.

Different members of the royal family have different requirements. The Duchess of Kent is very popular with her policemen and prefers people around her who are quiet. Only once has she asked for someone to be moved because she considered his manner a 'little too fast'. Both the Kents and Gloucesters are easy to work for, but there is not much glamour. Placement with them suits the people who like to keep out of the limelight and have an easy-going working life. Surprisingly, Princess Alexandra is not high on the list of popular royals. The police officers say she is a 'ditherer'.

Prince Charles is popular, partly because of the glamour attached to being with the heir to the throne, and partly because he likes to travel and take his team with him. When the Queen Mother took her annual holiday at Birkhall on the Balmoral Estate, she liked to have a Scottish policeman at her side.

Prince Philip's two-man team are among the most loyal at the Palace. They enjoy working for a man who is decisive in all things and who will back them up against anyone if he believes they are right.

By the time the officers graduate to the status of personal bodyguard they can expect to have risen to the rank of inspector, but volunteering for the Royalty and Diplomatic Protection Department can mean having to forego the usual run up the promotion ladder. Several senior officers have found when applying for posts outside the Palace that they have been turned down on grounds of being 'too specialized': in other words, staying in the same job too long. The attractions to compensate are free, first-class travel all over the world, meeting some of the most important and glamorous figures in politics, the media and the arts and the chance of becoming highly visible and well-known personalities in their own right. Ken Wharf was immediately identified as Princess Diana's strong right arm when he accompanied her everywhere during her most famous period. Jim Beaton achieved fame of a different sort when he was shot five times protecting Princess Anne during a kidnapping attempt in the Mall in 1974 and again some years later when he spent nine years as the Queen's personal bodyguard.

Inspector Philip Robinson, now retired, was anonymous but became instantly recognizable as Princess Anne's police officer, a job he held for eighteen years, when he was seen with either Peter Phillips or his sister Zara on his shoulders walking around Gatcombe Park. Many people assumed Philip Robinson was a sort of 'Uncle Phil' figure to the children as they were seen together so often. He denied this, saying that nothing could be farther from the truth and that he was no more than anyone else on her staff who would be replaced instantly when he left.

Because the policemen spend so much time with their royal charges, it is a common assumption that they are friends and close companions. What few outside the royal circle realize is that no one who is not royal ever becomes close, and there is not the slightest chance of any familiarity. The Queen always addresses her bodyguard by his surname – without even using his rank – and she considers him to be just like any other of her servants. But in this she is wrong. As we have seen, the policemen and women remain on the strength of the Metropolitan Police Force throughout their service even if they spend their entire working life at Buckingham Palace. And the fact that they are paid by the Met is a bone of contention, as they earn far more than their counterparts who are genuine members of the household. The constables who man the gates at Buckingham Palace start on a minimum salary of £16,635 a year, rising to £26,325 even without promotion. The sergeant who guards the Queen's room at night earns £29,634, while the inspectors who are personal royal bodyguards have a salary scale between £32,862 and £37,261. Chief inspectors in the Royalty Protection Department are paid £41,190, while the Queen's leading protection officer, with the rank of superintendent, earns £53,556. All their expenses are also paid out of police funds. So when they travel abroad, the first-class fares and five-star hotel bills are all met out of the budget of the department. The Queen and her family pay nothing for the protection they receive. Indeed the Keeper of the Privy Purse keeps such a tight rein on royal spending that when policemen travel on aircraft of No. 32 The Royal Squadron, they are even charged for a cup of coffee and any food they may eat.

The animosity that is generated because of the difference in pay between that earned by the police and the wages and salaries of the household occurs not so much at the higher levels, but among the domestic staff. A man earning £18,000 a year after fifteen years' service in the Queen's household, can feel very hard done by when he sees a constable on the gate topping his wages by up to £8,000. Several footmen have let it be known that they think the police have it easy compared with their long hours and duties. They also see some of the police officers turning up for work driving expensive cars, when the best most servants can hope for is a second-hand model several years old. So it's quite natural for there to be a certain amount of jealousy. Not that it bothers the police too much. They rarely mix with the household anyway, apart from the inspectors who are personal bodyguards and who spend a lot of time in the company of private secretaries on overseas visits.

There have been two major reviews of royal security during the Queen's reign. The first was in 1974 after the attempted kidnapping of Princess Anne. Prior to that Inspector Jim Beaton was her sole bodyguard and most of the senior members of the royal family had only one, or at most two, policemen to call upon. After 1974, Parliament voted an increase in the security budget and the Royal Protection Department was expanded. Then, in 1982, after Michael Fagan managed to get into the Queen's bedroom, the whole system was upgraded to its present size and efficiency.

When the Queen pays a visit to an area, the Chief Constable attaches up to 150 of his local force to augment the Palace team. There are also occasions when special precautions are taken. If a suspected terrorist is arrested and a piece of paper with Her Majesty's name on it is found in his possession, security is immediately increased. But the Queen refuses to live in a cage, no matter how gilded. She dislikes the presence of secret service agents like those who surround the President of the United States, and even after a man fired blank shots at her while she was riding to the Trooping the Colour Parade in 1981, she refused to change her programme.

The royal family are aware of the disruptive effects on normal family life that working for them can mean. There has been a number of divorces among royal police officers which some say are caused by the long hours and absences from home. The Queen tries to involve the families of her bodyguards in some Palace functions; they always receive an invitation to one of the garden parties. But, as more than one wife has admitted: 'Even mixing with royalty palls after a while, especially when your husband is pictured apparently enjoying himself on the other side of the world, while you are stuck at home bringing up the kids on your own.' And it is certainly true that some bodyguards spend more time with their royal charges than with their own families.

But there are compensations. Police officers generally retire at an early age, and those who have served in high-profile positions often then take on remunerative jobs outside. Former royal bodyguards have become heads of security for the oil industry, at leading hotels throughout the world and occasionally guarding controversial, entrepreneurial figures in business. High finance means top security, and the recommendation doesn't come any higher than when it is written on paper headed by a Buckingham Palace address.

CHAPTER SEVENTEEN

❧

Protecting the Image

The Queen's press secretary is at her desk before eight o'clock every morning together with one of her assistants. Their first task is to read every national newspaper, looking for items which mention the royal family or which may be of interest to the Queen. A selection is marked and sent upstairs to Her Majesty's dining room so that she and Prince Philip can peruse them over breakfast. Of particular interest will be the regional press if the Queen has made a visit to one of the provinces the previous day. Every member of the royal family takes an intense interest in their own press coverage, even if they like to give the impression that they couldn't care less. Press secretaries are often grilled when a particular event has not been given what the royals consider adequate coverage.

The digest that the press office also prepares each day is typed up in columns, each story marked with the name of the paper in which it appeared, the page number and whether a picture accompanied the article. It is circulated to every department in the royal household as well as the royal family themselves, and there is usually a feedback if something has been particularly well reported (this means favourably) or if the Palace thinks something is inaccurate. The press office rarely complains to newspaper editors if a story appears that annoys the Palace, although the press secretary, who lunches with royal reporters regularly, may mention the point months after the event.

The Queen has a relaxed attitude to the media, in spite of the fact that in the early days of her reign she was terrified of radio and even more so of television. It was many years before she was able to appear relaxed in front of the cameras when she taped her annual Christmas message. Some of her household, though, remain in the dark ages where press relations are concerned. They loathe the media and would prefer royal reporting to be confined to the daily Court Circular, listing the movements of the royal family without any further details. It is only because the Queen and Prince Charles realize that to do their jobs effectively they need the media, that the press office is able to cooperate to the extent they do. The family often agree to carefully choreographed photo-calls when on holiday, on the understanding that they will be left alone afterwards. It doesn't always work; usually one freelance paparazzo will break the embargo.

The daily news items the press office selects are not necessarily about the Queen or her family, but inevitably few days pass without a reference to some member. Royal stories still sell newspapers and magazines, even if the golden days of Diana have gone for ever. These days it is much more likely that the latest details of Prince Edward and his wife's business dealings will make the headlines, rather than stories about the Queen and Prince Philip. Their comings and goings rarely warrant coverage in anything other than regional newspapers. The Duke of York is still good for a few pages in the tabloids, especially if he is seen with a new blonde in tow, but Prince Charles has virtually disappeared from the papers, now that his romance with Camilla Parker Bowles is openly acknowledged. There's nothing particularly newsworthy in seeing them together any more. But if they do decide to marry, then of course, it will be reported all over the world, with countless columns devoted to their love story and the break-up of Charles's marriage to Diana regurgitated once again.

Stories about royal marital discord are always popular, even if they are untrue. Princess Anne, the Princess Royal, rarely makes the headlines these days, unlike twenty years ago when she was hardly ever out of them. In the past year, the only time she figured prominently in the press was when stories of a possible divorce from her second husband, Tim Laurence, appeared. The story was totally fabricated, but it was a bad news day and most of the newspapers jumped on the bandwagon until something better came along.

The Queen reads the press reports that are prepared for her, but she does not take too much notice of them. She is completely uninterested in stories about herself, unless they are accompanied by cartoons, which she loves. It doesn't matter if they are cruel and malicious, she appreciates them all, as long as they are well done and clever. Cartoonists have lampooned the monarchy for centuries; it's healthy and to be welcomed even by the family themselves. At least it shows the people are still interested. Prince Charles once remarked to a gathering of journalists, 'It's when you chaps stop taking our pictures and writing about us that we have to worry.' He also wrote that a free press is essential to a democratic society.

The Queen does not, however, apply the same sang-froid attitude to photographs. If one appears that she believes does not show her in a flattering light, her press secretary is made aware of her displeasure. It's not that the Queen is a vain woman; if she was she wouldn't wear glasses in public of a design that went out of style twenty years ago. It's just that she thinks it is important for the image of monarchy, as personified by herself, always to be seen in the best possible light. Newspapers defend their use of such pictures by captioning them as showing the Queen 'off guard'. Prince Philip does take notice of adverse press reports, but usually it is when they are about the Queen rather than himself. He is a fierce protector of her image and many of his inflammatory comments in the press are the result of some real or imagined slight against his wife. And all the royals hate to appear in gossip columns, although they love reading them.

The press office at Buckingham Palace is tiny, with fewer than a dozen people working there. They are divided into sections dealing with different members of the family. Penny Russell-Smith is the Queen's press secretary – and the only woman to have held the post. She was suddenly promoted after serving as assistant to Geoffrey Crawford, an Australian who left the press office to return to his native country and the more lucrative pastures of commercial public relations. The Queen was expecting him to remain with her until the end of her Golden Jubilee year, but he received an offer he couldn't refuse – it is said that he quadrupled his Palace salary – and the parting was amicable in the end. Her Majesty's private secretary, Sir

Robin Janvrin, gave a farewell party for Geoff in the Bow Room at the Palace and practically the whole of Fleet Street turned up to wish him well. After his departure new personnel were recruited as Penny Russell-Smith reorganized the staffing.

As well as handling the Queen's media affairs, she looks after those of the Duke of Edinburgh and until early in 2002 also those of the late Princess Margaret. She has three assistant press secretaries: Samantha Cohen, who likes to be known as Ms, Ailsa Anderson, who joined the Palace from the Cabinet Office and in doing so took a substantial drop in salary, and Stuart Neil, whose responsibilities include all ceremonial events. These assistant press secretary posts were all advertised. Previously, applications would be invited from a handpicked list of candidates, from either government departments or semi-official organizations like the BBC. The press office also has six information officers, including one with responsibility for the daily Court Circular, and a Web Editor, as Buckingham Palace now has its own website giving information on various aspects of the royal family and their activities.

Among the information officers one each looks after the Duke of York, the Princess Royal, the Earl and Countess of Wessex, the Duke and Duchess of Kent, the Duke and Duchess of Gloucester and Princess Alexandra. The Palace press office does not handle the media affairs of Prince and Princess Michael of Kent.

There is also a Communications Secretary, who works in the private secretary's office, and who is nominally higher than the press secretary in the household hierarchy, but the men who have held this post – and they are always seconded from industry for several years – have made little impact on the press office. In terms of sheer prestige, the press secretary to the Queen far exceeds her communications secretary. But unfortunately for her, the press secretary earns around a quarter of his salary as the bulk of his money comes from his parent company and not the Keeper of the Privy Purse.

One of the biggest problems facing the press office is not the intrusive nature of tabloid journalism or the leaking of stories by poorly paid members of the staff, or the way in which members of the royal family refuse to cooperate even when favourable articles and television programmes are proposed. The problem is the lack of influence they have. Nowhere in the modern world of big business is there such a disregard for public and press relations as there is at Buckingham Palace. The very phrase 'Public Relations' is anathema to those working in the press office. As they are anxious to emphasize at all times, the Queen does not employ a public relations officer and never has although, strangely, most of the press secretaries in recent years have left to take up highly paid posts in this very field. They see their role as supplying information, strictly controlled, to the media on those occasions when such information is beneficial to the royal family. In other words, good public relations, but by another name.

If a reporter asks for details on a subject which they regard as being on dangerous ground, the answer is invariably, 'That is a private matter and we never comment on the royal family's private affairs.' When Princess Anne, Prince Charles and Prince Andrew all separated from their spouses, the Palace press office stated on each occasion that there were no plans for divorce, when everyone else in the country knew it was only a matter of time. There is an endless battle between the press and the Palace over privacy. It is a row that will never end as long as the world's media regard the royals as 'fair game', and although there are periods of truce they never last very long.

The two most successful manipulators of the media have been without doubt the Queen Mother and Diana, Princess of Wales. Each knew exactly how to get the media on their side. The Queen Mother regarded them as friends, while Princess Diana once said she treated them as children.

Within the royal household the other departments tend to regard the press office with disdain, and when forced to deal with them, do so with a marked lack of enthusiasm. The good manners that characterizes the royal household prevents anyone from displaying the vexation they frequently feel, but the attitude is usually one of resigned tolerance. As a result a succession of press secretaries has found him- or herself fighting not only members of the royal family, whose antipathy towards the media generally has been passed down from generation to generation, but also their colleagues, who might have been expected to be more helpful towards them in the twenty-first century.

The situation is not helped by the attitude of editors and royal reporters. Knowing that the official sources will not give them the juicy details they are after, the old hands seek out private channels of information. They claim this is because of the lack of cooperation from the press office and that if the Queen's press secretary were a former journalist who understood their problems, there would be more mutual respect. But when Her Majesty has appointed men who have previously been experienced reporters, it hasn't always worked out to the advantage of Fleet Street. The 'poacher turned gamekeeper' philosophy is exemplified whenever anyone joins the royal household, as former colleagues have discovered to their cost. Old friends suddenly find they are not as close as they once thought and are herded into enclosures in exactly the same way as the rest of the 'rat-pack'. But if a press secretary showed favouritism to just one of the journalists, the others would be merciless and no press officer can afford to antagonize the entire media. So even when they get together in an hotel bar during an overseas tour, the barriers never fully come down. Friendliness cannot be confused with familiarity, and when a Palace press officer is briefing reporters on what is going on behind the scenes, he or she never loses sight of the fact that the journalists would not hesitate to quote their words verbatim if they let slip an indiscreet phrase.

While some reporters like to think of their relationship with the Palace as being totally adversarial, the Palace press office does, at times, go out of its way to accommodate the media. There have been many occasions when officialdom has tried to prevent photographers and reporters from getting too close when they are covering a royal event, only for the Palace press secretary to intervene and make sure they obtain what they need.

Many freelance photographers make good livings out of taking pictures of the royals – always without their permission and the more revealing the better. But there is also a small, exclusive group, whose numbers include Lord Snowdon, the Earl of Lichfield and Tim Graham, who are occasionally asked to take official photographs of the family. They are in a different category altogether, but even so find they have their problems. Jayne Fincher is one of the best and most popular of royal photographers, who has been taking pictures of the family since the seventies, including several wedding groups, which are the most difficult if you are not quite sure who all the guests are. Lord Lichfield once revealed that he used to place numbered pieces of paper on the floor and make the group stand according to his plan, so that he could later identify them all. Jayne says her biggest problem was not in identification but in the lack of time they would allow her to prepare. 'Five minutes was the maximum time they would allocate, so forward planning was absolutely vital. There was no lighting test and often, if I was taking a picture which wasn't a wedding group but a commissioned photograph for another reason, I would find that something else had come up for the royal concerned and they would change the time and date. Also they wouldn't allow any extra make-up, which can be quite important to prevent too much shine on the face.'

One of the most prestigious commissions Jayne received was to take the photographs at the wedding of the Earl and Countess of Wessex. Prince Edward's public image is of an arrogant, petulant and spoilt young man who stands on his dignity at all times. Jayne Fincher found the exact opposite. 'He was delightful and is the only royal I've met who didn't demand picture approval. Nothing was too much trouble for him and on one occasion when one of my cameras broke down, he even helped me to mend it.' At the wedding, Jayne took pictures of the behind-the-scenes activity which Edward particularly wanted, and there was one moment when she upset a lamp in St George's Chapel, Windsor. Afterwards, at the reception, the Queen, who thought it was hilarious, drew her attention to it, saying jokingly, 'What were you doing to my lamp?' Jayne found both the Earl and the Countess equally easy to work with and totally relaxed on every occasion.

If Edward is her favourite subject, who is the least liked? 'I'm afraid it's Prince Philip. With him there is never any small-talk, so there's no chance to establish even a working relationship and he always insists on being photographed wearing a suit. Men in suits are notoriously difficult to make interesting. There was one occasion on board the former Royal Yacht *Britannia* when I asked him to join me on deck for a couple of shots, but he wouldn't and there was no negotiating with him. He scared the life out of me, but funnily enough when we had finished, his staff said they thought it had gone very well, while I thought the exact opposite.'

Jayne made her name as one of the favourite photographers of the late Diana, Princess of Wales, whom she photographed many times. 'Diana was a dream. If we were alone she would chat away and even help me pack my equipment afterwards. Though when Prince Charles appeared things became a little more formal. Prince Charles, strangely enough, preferred being photographed by a woman in those days.' Since Camilla came on the scene though, female photographers have largely been banned.

Every journalist worth his salt has a private source of information inside the royal household. They are known as 'moles' and are usually found among the domestic staff, who get tip-off fees in cash. The sums are large, for tabloid papers will pay thousands of pounds for a good exclusive. It depends where they place it in the paper. For example, the person who obtained the first news of Prince Edward and Sophie's engagement (which made the front page of the *Sun*) was paid over £10,000. The average rate for a reasonable story which features in the inside pages is between £150–£500, and this is always paid in cash.

There are also senior members of the household who are prepared to help – not for money but because they believe it is important the right facts are known. Nor are they averse to the occasional good lunch. These contacts are invaluable if used in the proper way: not so much as original sources, but as confirmation of articles the reporter proposes to write. The sources, who are loyal servants, are not prepared to give away any royal secrets, but they are sometimes willing to either corroborate facts, or tell the reporter he is completely wrong. These Palace officials work on the 'Deep Throat' system whereby they do not volunteer information, but they will answer questions honestly – as long as the right questions are asked.

All this presupposes that the press office is always bypassed when journalists are investigating stories. This is not quite true; it's just that often the press office doesn't know the facts. The royal family has a habit of keeping their press advisers in the dark over private matters until it is absolutely necessary for them to know so that they are not forced to lie. It is a proud boast that they never lie – they simply do not always know the whole truth.

Where matters of fact concerning the royal family are involved, it is easy to find out all one needs to know from the press office. Their masses of files contain every item of information about every member of the family past and present and they are scrupulously diligent in returning telephone calls requesting details. If you want to find out who supplies the Queen's gloves and shoes, the press office will tell you in a moment. If your enquiry concerns the names of royal babies christened in the past hundred years, nothing could be easier. But if you ask what sort of under-clothes royal ladies wear, you will receive a polite but icy rebuff, nor will they tell you the favourite foods of any member of the family, even if the enquiry comes from such well-meaning and obviously harmless organizations as the Women's Institute who may want to include the infor-mation in their local newsletter. The reply is always: 'We never comment or give information relating to private matters.'

The trouble is that there is a wide difference between what the Palace wants the public to know and what news-paper editors demand. And it is not only tabloids that increasingly delve into the royals' personal, private life. No longer are people satisfied with the bare details of where the royal family is spending Christmas or their summer holidays. Nowadays they also want to hear who gave what present to whom, why the Duchess of York is still refused entry to the big house when the Queen and her family stay at Sandringham, and if it is true that Prince Charles and Camilla Parker Bowles talk for hours on end in secret tele-phone calls when the Queen has gone to bed. There is a huge difference in what the Palace believes is 'in the public interest' and what the public actually wants to know.

When Princess Diana was at the height of her popularity, her picture on the front page of a newspaper or magazine could guarantee an increase in sales. Today, no member of the royal family has the same effect. In fact, for every photograph that appears in the papers, perhaps as many as fifty are rejected, simply on the grounds of lack of inter-est. When Princess Margaret was taken ill after suffering a number of strokes, the only reason her picture featured in the news was because of the deterioration of her looks.

People love to see the humiliation of others, particularly if they are famous, and even more so if they used to be admired. We all take a vicarious pleasure – which we disguise as pity – in seeing a great beauty, be it film star or royal, brought down to an everyday level. It is one of the less pleasant sides of human nature.

One item of information the press office will never divulge is the private travel arrangements of the royal family. Every journalist knows that the Queen leaves Buckingham Palace on Friday afternoon for her weekend stay at Windsor Castle, returning after lunch on Monday. But the Palace never confirms the time or gives the route. Nor do they say which car Her Majesty will use. Obviously there is a security reason for this secrecy, but the details are also withheld so that press photographers are not given the opportunity to grab that elusive 'scoop' picture they all crave.

If there is one branch of journalism that antagonizes royalty even more than the reporters who write about them, it is the men who take their photographs. Apart from the Queen Mother and the late Princess Diana, both of whom carried on a 'love affair' with the camera throughout their active lives, the royal family regard press photographers as intrusive, aggressive and a thorough nuisance almost without exception. The staff photographers employed by national newspapers are considered slightly less obnoxious than their freelance colleagues, and some, such as Arthur Edwards of the *Sun*, are recognized and held in some affection by one or two of the family, though not by Prince Philip or the Queen.

When one of the royals is undertaking an official engagement, the press office at the Palace gives details of the media arrangements to the press. They then apply for accreditation for their reporters and photographers, who are allocated places where they may stand and watch. They are not permitted to leave the press 'compound' and any that attempt to do so quickly find themselves herded back and refused accreditation the next time they apply. It comes as a surprise to some people, particularly in the provinces, to see the way in which the outwardly gentle and otherwise perfectly mannered press secretaries suddenly become fearsomely aggressive in wielding handbags and elbows when clearing reporters and photographers out of the royal path.

Certain freelance photographers, such as Tim Graham, who has become a wealthy man through his superb pictures of the Princess of Wales and who has been invited to take official photographs of the royal family, are given special places. For the rest, the paparazzi, it's 'anything goes'. They get no cooperation from the Palace and they employ skills more usually associated with the SAS to obtain their pictures. Nothing is too much trouble. They travel on high-speed motor cycles, using the latest technology to maintain contact, and always there is the assistant tagging along with the mandatory step-ladder, without which no self-respecting royal photographer leaves home.

The rewards are worth it. In the days of Princess Diana, an exclusive picture could be sold throughout the world for up to £50,000, and even today syndication rights for revealing pictures of Prince William could easily reach that figure. He is the new super star of the royal family, the successor to Diana the media has been waiting for.

When William started his university studies at St Andrews in Scotland, his father arranged a deal with the press to allow them access for pictures and a carefully scheduled interview, on the understanding that his son would then be left alone to live as normal a life as possible under the extraordinary circumstances. By and large, the media stuck to the agreement, with one exception. Ardent, Prince Edward's television production company, remained behind after all the others had left, and continued coverage. Prince William complained to his father and Prince Charles, justifiably furious, rang his youngest brother to tell him what he thought of him. Edward's company issued an apology, but there was no personal word from him.

Earlier in the year, the most disastrous public relations fiasco also involved a member of the Wessex family; this time it was the Countess, still known to all the media as Sophie. She was running her own public relations company when she fell for one of the oldest tricks in the books. A newspaper reporter, posing as an Arab sheikh looking for a representative, invited her and her business partner to the Dorchester Hotel in London to discuss a possible contract. There she was secretly tape-recorded making indiscreet comments about the Prime Minister and his wife, Prince Charles and Camilla Parker Bowles, and offering to use her royal connections to further the business contacts.

When the subterfuge was discovered, the Palace made the situation even worse by offering an exclusive interview with the Countess as long as the original tape was not published. The interview provided splash headlines, with Sophie being quoted as saying that Prince Edward was not gay – when the subject had not even been raised. If the Buckingham Palace press office was involved – and it has never been revealed if they were – it was arguably the worst kind of public relations advice ever given to any member of the royal family. And the contents of the original tape was still published by a rival newspaper, so the deal could not have had a worse result. It is difficult to believe that an experienced press secretary to the Queen would have countenanced such an agreement; perhaps the advice came from elsewhere. Whatever the truth of the matter, the Earl and Countess of Wessex became the laughing stock of the country.

The main difficulty the media has in dealing with the Palace is that their primary sources, the royals themselves, are not available for interviews and comments. There are occasions when Prince Charles or the Princess Royal will agree to talk to selected journalists about specialist subjects such as architecture, inner city urban development or one of the charities with which one or the other is associated. But these are exceptions. There is rarely an opportunity to talk on the record about their feelings at being a member of the most exclusive family in the world. This is why so much that is written about them is either speculation or has come from 'sources close to the Palace'.

The late Diana, Princess of Wales, broke the mould when she gave that world-shattering interview to the BBC *Panorama* programme and spoke at length about the break-up of her marriage, but Princess Anne would never dream of discussing her first marriage to Mark Phillips and why it went wrong. Prince Charles, of course, did talk with Jonathan Dimbleby for his authorized biography and the accompanying television programme, and spoke honestly about his relationship with Camilla Parker Bowles. Later it was acknowledged that he had made a grave error, as this is the only part of the book – and TV programme – that anyone can remember. Most of the other information, which was intended to portray His Royal Highness in a serious light, has been forgotten.

The biggest mystery of all remains the personality of the Queen. Nobody knows what she thinks or how she reacts to private or public problems. She refuses to be a performer in the way that other members of her family have been: Prince Philip loves to air his thoughts on many subjects; Prince Charles, as mentioned, is equally loquacious when one of his favourite topics crops up. Both the Duke of York and the Princess Royal have appeared on television chat shows, while the Earl of Wessex is attempting to make a living out of TV. But the Queen restricts her media appearances to the annual Christmas radio and television broadcasts, so the magic of monarchy is preserved. She gives no interviews and when she carries out one of her 'walkabouts' chatting to the crowds who wait to meet her, her bodyguards and press officers make sure no hidden microphones and cameras are near enough to catch a royal word. Not that anything indiscreet would ever be heard. Her Majesty is far too experienced to be caught in an unguarded moment.

The Palace press office deals with enquiries from all over the world on a daily basis. The leading television and print journalists have standing requests for that elusive and exclusive interview. It isn't going to happen. The Queen prefers to keep the media at arm's length, and in so doing, preserves the finely tuned balance between friendliness and familiarity. Her feeling is that it has worked well for fifty years. Why change it now?

CHAPTER EIGHTEEN

The Royal Collection

If there is one department within the royal household that fascinates Prince Charles more than any other it is the Royal Collection. He takes an intelligent and enthusiastic interest in every aspect of the work of the department and likes to be personally involved when plans are made for the various exhibitions. He is chairman of the Board of Trustees, with Lord Luce, the Lord Chamberlain, as his deputy; its members also include both the Queen's private secretary and the Director of the Royal Collection, the man responsible for the day-to-day running of the department in which the royal family has the largest financial stake.

It is by far the biggest and most important private art collection in the world with over one million paintings, drawings, items of furniture and priceless engravings, plus a most exquisite group of works by Fabérgé. Sir Hugh Roberts, the Director, is also Surveyor of the Queen's Works of Art. He has overall responsibility for a collection whose total value has been estimated at several billion pounds. Of course, it does not all belong to Her Majesty and there is often confusion over what does and does not belong to her. She does own many valuable items in her own name but the vast majority of the collection is inalienable, which means it cannot be sold by the Queen. In theory, this should mean it belongs to the nation, so the people should be able to decide what and when to buy and sell, and also where and when items from the collection should be displayed. But in practice the royal household control the Royal Collection – on behalf of the Queen – and they alone decide which works of art should be bought and sold, and where they are displayed.

The collection lends many of its paintings and other works of art to museums and galleries all over the world, with the USA, Australia and the Netherlands being among the most frequent borrowers. The conditions are very strict. Those borrowing are required to show they have made sufficient arrangements for security and insurance and have suitable climatic conditions. A painting by Gerrit Dou (1613–75), *The Grocer's Shop*, which was acquired by George IV in 1817 for 1,000 guineas, has recently been loaned to the National Gallery of Art in Washington DC, then to Dulwich Picture Gallery and finally to the Royal Cabinet of Paintings in The Hague in February 2001. While in 2000, to celebrate the Millennium, a touring exhibition of Old Masters depicting scenes from the life of Christ travelled throughout the United Kingdom and attracted 200,000 visitors.

Among the first exhibits in the new Queen's Gallery at Buckingham Palace will be *Portrait of Agatha Bas* by Rembrandt and *The Passage Boat* by Cuyp as well as Thomas Sully's *Portrait of Queen Victoria*.

In 1966 the Queen bought a portrait of Prince Charles

Edward Stuart (1739) by Blanchet but, like all acquisitions made for the royal family, the Collection did not bid itself. The London art dealer, Hazlitt, Gooden and Fox, both buy and sell on its behalf. When the Royal Collection is interested in something they make sure that their agents are bidding for other items and other clients as well, so that the sellers are not aware who is interested in the piece.

Several colourful characters have been in charge of the Royal Collection, including Kenneth (later Lord) Clark, of *Civilisation* fame, who looked after the art collection from 1934–44. But without doubt the most notorious was Sir Anthony Blunt, whose title became Surveyor of the Queen's Pictures when he succeeded Kenneth Clark in 1945, and whose reign lasted until 1972. Blunt was, of course, later revealed to have been a Russian spy throughout the Cold War and a massive scandal followed the discovery. It was after Blunt retired that the three divisions, Surveyor of the Queen's Pictures, Surveyor of the Queen's Works of Art and the Royal Librarian at Windsor Castle, were combined into a single unit named the Royal Collection, whose first Director was Sir Oliver Millar. The amalgamation was on the recommendation of Michael Peat, then a partner in the City accountants and business consultants, Peat, Marwick Mcintock, who had been brought in to advise on streamlining the system.

The department has grown to the point where it now employs more people than any other office in the household. A total of 260 men and women work in the various sub-sections, with the majority belonging to the Royal Collection Enterprises staff. They have 79 at Windsor Castle, 53 at Buckingham Palace and 21 at the Palace of Holyroodhouse in Edinburgh. The curatorial staff includes experts

THE ROYAL COLLECTION

Directorate
Director of the Royal Collection
& Surveyor of the Queen's
Works of Art
Assistant to the Director
Finance Director
Financial Accountant
Management Accountant
Credit Controller
Accounts Assistant
Cashier
Administrator & Assistant to the
Surveyors Receptionist

Works of Art
Surveyor of the Queen's Works
of Art
Deputy Surveyor
Loans Officer (Works of Art)
Assistant to the Deputy Surveyor
of the Queen's Works of Art
Research Assistant, Works of Art
Armourer
Senior Furniture Conservator
Furniture Conservators
Senior Gilding Conservator
Gilding Conservator
Senior Horological Conservator
(Buckingham Palace)
Horological Conservator
Horological Conservator
(Windsor Castle)

Pictures
Surveyor of the Queen's Pictures
Assistant to the Surveyor of the
Queen's Pictures
Loans Officer & Assistant
Curator (Pictures)

Secretary to the Surveyor
Senior Picture Conservator
Conservation Studio Manager
Conservators
Conservator (Structural)
Frame Technician
Secretary, Picture Conservation
Studio

The Royal Library
Librarian and Assistant
Keeper of the Royal Archives
Secretary to the Librarian
Bibliographer
Assistant Bibliographer
Head Bookbinder
Deputy Head Bookbinder
Bookbinder

Print Room
Curator of the Print Room
Secretary to the Curator
Deputy Curator of the Print
Room
Exhibition Co-ordinator
Assistant Curators
Loans Officer
Exhibitions Secretary
Chief Restorer of Drawings
Assistant Restorer
Exhibitions and Maintenance
Conservator
Mount/Framer
Cassiano Project Assistant

Royal Archives
Registrar
Deputy Registrar
Assistant Registrars

258

Paper Conservator
Secretary
Office Administrator
Archives Attendant
Records Manager

Royal Photograph Collection
Curator of the Royal Photograph
   Collection
Assistant Curator
Royal Collection Database and IT
Computer Systems Manager
Assistant to the Computer
   Systems Manager
Junior Support Officer
Inventory Clerk (Buckingham
   Palace)
Inventory Clerk (Windsor Castle)
Superintendent of the Royal
   Collection, Hampton Court
   Palace
Custodian of California Garden
   Stores, Windsor
Senior Indexer
Indexers
Indefinite Loans Officer
Inventory Clerk (Coins & Medals)
Pictures Database Cataloguer
Works of Art Database
   Cataloguer
Print Room Database Cataloguer
Royal Photograph Collection
   Database Cataloguers

**Royal Collection Enterprises
   Limited**
Managing Director
Personal Assistant
Director of Public Relations and
   Marketing
Marketing and Sales Assistant

Public Relations Assistant
   Publisher
Retail Director
Buyer
Head of Design (Retail)
Retail & Publishing Co-ordinator
Assistant Merchandisers
Retail Operations Manager
Stores Manager
Assistant Stores Manager
Storemen
Head of Photographic Services
Picture Library Assistants
Senior Photographers
Photographer
Digital Imaging Assistant

Buckingham Palace
Visitor Manager
Operations Manager
Staff Manager
Administrator
Ticket Sales and Information
   Office Manager
Ticket Sales and Information
   Assistants

The Royal Mews
Assistant Shop Manager
Senior Retail Assistants
Supervising Warden
Wardens and Retail Assistants

Windsor Castle
Visitor Manager
Deputy Visitor Manager
Sales and Information Manager
Cashiers
Information Assistants
Operations Assistant
Schools Groups Assistant

259

Engine Court Shop
Manageress
Senior Retail Assistant
Retail Assistant

Lower Ward Shop
Senior Retail Assistant
Retail Assistant

China Museum Shop
Retail Assistant

Middle Ward Shop
Senior Retail Assistant
Retail Assistants

Admissions Centre
Manageress
Senior Ticket Office Assistants
Assistants
Deputy Head Wardens

Wardens
Casual Wardens
Relief Assistants
Security Cloakroom Assistants
Cleaner
Casual Cleaners

Palace of Holyroodhouse
Superintendent
Shop and Ticket Office
 Manageress
Senior Retail Assistants
Casual Retail Assistant
Retail Assistants
Storeman/Retail Assistant
Cashier
Head Warden
Deputy Head Warden
Wardens
Casual Wardens
Porter

in the fields of pictures, works of art, the library, archives, royal photographs, of which thousands are maintained in the Round Tower at Windsor Castle, and the most recent introduction, the Royal Collection Database.

The Royal Collection is a business and one of its most profitable lines is lending – for a fee – photographic copies of its works of art to book and magazine publishers and, increasingly, television companies. There is a constant demand for accurate information and authentic copies of paintings, furniture and other works, and the man they all have to deal with is the Registrar, who keeps a supply of some 2,500 transparencies which, subject to certain conditions, he will allow to be used for commercial purposes.

The Royal Archives, where the transparencies are kept,

issues a standard set of fees to any would-be clients and an application form which must be completed in advance. A different charge is made for black and white and colour pictures, the lowest fee being for a black and white inside illustration for a book or magazine with a print run of 5,000 or less. This will cost £30 if it is used in one language in one country, rising to £90 for world rights in multiple languages. A jacket cover in black and white for a book with a print run of over 15,000 would cost £360 for all rights. A similar picture from one of the bigger agencies in London could easily cost ten times that amount.

Colour pictures are more expensive at the lower end: £70 for runs of 5,000 or less, but slightly cheaper than black and white at the top end of the scale, where the charge is £320 for all rights in multiple languages throughout the world. It's the same price if you want a royal picture on the cover of your CD album. The Royal Archives charge a £50 deposit on all transparencies, which those who hire them are allowed to keep for up to three months. There are also charges for television and video: a standard picture in one language for one country is priced at £95, rising to £195 for multiple languages and world rights; non-standard goes from £115 to £255; video reproduction costs are from £135 to £315 with the maximum repeat fees being 150 per cent.

Among the conditions the Royal Archives imposes is the stipulation that nothing reproduced from them may be utilized in relation to any scheme of free gifts or induce-ments to purchase other articles, nor may the picture be altered in any way. So if a photograph shows, say, the Queen wearing a tiara or a diamond ring, the publication cannot show just the jewellery without the rest of the picture, unless they submit proofs beforehand which have to be approved. The final condition is that everything supplied by the Royal Archives must be accompanied by one of the following acknowledgements:

The Royal Archives Her Majesty the Queen
(UK & Commonwealth)

or

The Royal Archives Her Majesty Queen Elizabeth II
(all other countries)

The Registrar of the Royal Collection also maintains a unique assemblage of photographs of the tiaras, collars, earrings, cuff-links and other items of jewellery owned by the royal family. Then if a piece is damaged or lost, a picture is available to the Crown Jewellers, Asprey and Garrard Ltd of Bond Street, so that a repair or identical reproduction can be produced. Tales are told of at least two female members of the royal family who, after being given very valuable pieces of jewellery by foreign rulers, sent them to the jewellers with an instruction to make copies in paste, and pay back the difference in value.

The Royal Library at Windsor is a gold mine for researchers and authors seeking information about royalty past and present. The Librarian, with a tiny permanent staff of just eight, arranges lectures and visits by individuals and groups. When the Queen has one of her Dine and Sleep evenings, the Librarian goes to enormous trouble to find suitable articles of particular interest to her guests. If a playwright is among the gathering, there might be a manuscript copy of *The Frozen Deep* by Wilkie Collins, which was presented to Queen Victoria in 1857, when Charles

Dickens was among the cast who gave a command performance. A well-known musician found himself being shown a framed programme of music in the handwriting of King George III, while a famous jockey was intrigued by some prints showing royal sporting activities in the early nineteenth century.

The Print Room in the Lower Library deals with the conservation of items such as old maps, architectural plans and drawings. A dozen men and women work there, supplemented from time to time by volunteers. Students from Camberwell College of Art are among the most enthusiastic, and in a continuous programme of conservation more than 2,000 documents are cleaned, repaired and sleeved in any one year.

Few arts organizations in the world have more skilled and varied talents at their command. The Royal Collection includes among its employees picture conservators, gilding, furniture and horological conservators, bibliographers, print room curators, restorers of drawings, framers, an inventory clerk for medals and coins, designers, photographers, plus dozens of wardens and casual wardens at Buckingham Palace and Windsor Castle to assist with visitors. They organize the retail shops at Windsor Castle, open all year round (and whose biggest single seller is still a slim book about Princess Diana), and the temporary shop in the garden at Buckingham Palace, which trades for the eight weeks of the year when the Palace is open to the public. The ticket office at the Palace of Holyroodhouse comes under the umbrella of the Collection as do the thirteen wardens and the one senior porter who work there.

Perhaps the attitude and dedication of those who work in the Royal Collection is best summed up in the words of a young lady who was restoring a number of ancient royal documents at Windsor Castle. When I asked her how long she had to complete the task, she replied: 'As long as it takes.'

CHAPTER NINETEEN

❧

The College of Arms

When the Queen decided she wanted to change the name of the royal family to Mountbatten-Windsor, she informed the College of Arms who registered the change and prepared the necessary documents.

The College is the main, but not sole, receptacle for all such documents and has been since the charter by which it functions was issued in 1555 by Mary I. Although an earlier charter was issued by Richard III in 1484, to all intents and purposes, the later date is accepted as the one from which the College of Arms traces its foundation. Today its work is associated in the public's mind as being concerned solely with royalty and the aristocracy; but while it is true that much does revolve around royal ceremonial or establishing coats of arms for the nobility, the bulk of the day-to-day routine involves genealogical research on behalf of the general public.

Every day, scores of enquiries are received from all over the world from people seeking information about their families. The records of the College stretch back many centuries and include not only thousands of British entries, but many from all the countries that were once part of the British Empire and those that still belong to the Commonwealth. The records relating to America date back to long before there was a United States; as far back as 1586 in the case of the city of Raleigh in what is now the state of North Carolina. These records have been maintained right up to the present day and include the period of the American War of Independence (1775–83).

Canadian registrations began in 1763 with the City of Quebec, and the College receives many enquiries from both English and French speaking Quebecois seeking help in tracing their family trees.

The examiners at the College have become expert in discovering fakes when people attempt to prove they are descendants of a noble line – or, in more recent times – heirs to a substantial fortune. Before genealogies are accepted for registration they are subjected to rigorous investigation which can take several months to complete, though most are finished in weeks. It is vitally important that a registration is correct, not only because the credibility of the College has to be maintained, but also because their verification of a claim could be used as evidence in a court of law.

The College of Arms or, to give it its full magisterial title, the Corporation of the Kings, Heralds and Pursuivants of Arms, is based in the City of London, on a site granted to it by Mary I in 1555. The original building was destroyed by the Great Fire of London in 1666, and the present premises, still at the same location, Victoria Street, were built in the reign of King Charles II by Morris Emmett, whose title was 'His Majestie's bricklayer'. Mr Emmett never actually soiled his hands with bricks and mortar; his post derives from the days before architects were known. He worked in partnership with his brother, William, who was responsible for the elaborate wood carving at the College.

There are thirteen members, all appointed by the Queen to be her Officers of Arms-in-Ordinary with responsibility for all matters concerned with armorial, genealogical and ceremonial affairs. Together they comprise the sovereign's heraldic office and they are all members of the royal household.

They are divided into three categories: kings (3), heralds (6) and pursuivants (4), all under the supervision of the head of the College, Garter Principal King of Arms, Peter Gwynn-Jones. His title, which is taken from the association with the Order of the Garter, the senior Order of Chivalry, dates from 4 July 1415 and was first granted by Henry V to William Bruges. The holder of the post remains a senior officer of the Order of the Garter today.

Garter is by far the busiest member of the College. His duties include parliamentary responsibilities, where he has to be present for the introduction of all new peers to the House of Lords, and, under the Earl Marshall, the Duke of Norfolk, supervises the ceremonial arrangements for the State Opening of Parliament. He is also responsible for the secular sequences at royal weddings, funerals, the Investiture of the Prince of Wales; and he proclaims the accession of a new sovereign from the Brick Balcony at St James's Palace.

The three kings of arms, Garter, Clarenceaux and Norroy & Ulster, exercise the royal prerogative on behalf of the Queen in the granting of armorial bearings. But only Garter is the official inspector of regimental colours and the College retains the badges of all British service units.

Clarenceaux is the senior of the provincial kings of arms and his title dates from 1334. He has jurisdiction over all England south of the River Trent. The third king of arms, Norroy & Ulster, although the junior, bears a title older than either Garter or Clarenceaux, dating back to 18 March 1276. His 'parish' stretches from the River Trent north to the Scottish border, and after the creation of Eire as a republic the office of Ulster King of Arms was joined in 1943 to Norroy in order to continue the role. Norroy & Ulster has two claims which make him unique in the College of Arms: he remains King of Arms, Registrar and Knight Attendant to the Most Illustrious Order of St Patrick, although no new appointments to that Order have been made since Eire became a republic, and he was the first Officer of Arms to perform his official duties in tabard on mainland North America, which he did in New York during the Queen's Silver Jubilee year, 1977.

Of the six heralds, Windsor, Lancaster, Chester, Richmond, Somerset and York, five take their names from the great families they once served; the exception is Windsor, which is named after the castle. The four pursuivants: Rouge Croix, Bluemantle, Portcullis and Rouge Dragon, are named after royal badges. Rouge Croix is derived from the red cross on the national flag of England, St George's Cross, while Rouge Dragon comes from the Red Dragon of Wales, originally found on the flag of the seventh-century Welsh King Cadwalader. Bluemantle has existed since 1484 and his title comes from the blue cloaks worn by Knights of the Garter. There have been seventy-four holders of the title and the most recent is the last officer from the College of Arms to have conducted an heraldic ceremony on Canadian soil. He did this in 1987 in the city of Surrey, British

Columbia before the establishment of the present Canadian Heraldic Authority.

The fourth pursuivant, Portcullis, was instituted by Henry VII. The date is unknown but generally accepted to be shortly after his coronation in 1485. The name comes from the badge now used by Parliament, but originally inherited by Henry from his mother, Lady Margaret Beaufort. The various holders of the office have had some intriguing and historic tasks to perform. In 1837, the twenty-fifth Portcullis arranged the first South African coat of arms for Sir John Andrew Truter, Senior Justice of the Cape of Good Hope, while in 1874, the first Tasmanian grant of arms was made to Sir Philip Oakley Fysh. Portcullis included a flying-fish in the design, which proved to be a fortunate premonition as, many years later, Sir Philip's great-nephew founded Australia's national airline, Qantas.

The most common image of the officers of the College of Arms is when they appear attending Her Majesty at one of the great ceremonies of State. The Garter service at Windsor is probably the most spectacular and familiar, when the officers wear their colourful, magnificently embroidered tabard tunics bearing the sovereign's shield of arms. One way in which it is possible to distinguish the degree of the wearer is by the material of the tabard: damask for a pursuivant, satin for a herald and silk for a king of arms. Underneath the tabard, the officers wear a military style uniform dating from 1831, consisting of a gold embroidered scarlet jacket, black knee breeches and black silver-buckled shoes. The heralds also wear a sword and a black cocked hat adorned with black feathers. The three kings of arms wear black velvet hats with white feathers.

The everyday business of the College is conducted by the officer-in-waiting, one of the members (the three kings are exempt) who take it in turn to be duty officer for a week at a time, during which their personal banner is flown. For this time they answer all queries that arrive either by post, telephone or, frequently, in person. The only enquiries they do not deal with are those addressed to an individual officer.

The College of Arms is not part of the Civil Service, nor does it receive money from any source apart from the fees it is able to charge for the research it carries out. Officers do receive an annuity from the Privy Purse, but it is hardly one that would cause too much of a dent. Garter is paid £49.07, Clarenceaux and Norroy each receive £20.25, the heralds, £17.80 and the pursuivants £13.95 each – and this is for a year's work. But they are allowed to use the facilities of the College for private, professional, genealogical and heraldic research. They are allocated a set of rooms and access to the records and extensive library. So if someone wants to find out if they are related to a noble family, perhaps even entitled to a knighthood or earldom, they can approach one of the officers directly and a fee is negotiated depending on the amount of work involved. One man decided to give his wife an unusual Christmas present by researching her family tree. He had a budget of £500 and the College managed to trace the lady's family back as far as the early seventeenth century. The College does not overcharge for its labours and its fees compare very favourably with those of commercial organizations.

As we have seen, the research is not confined to notable families, although the majority of enquirers are optimistic about finding they belong to a great house. Records are kept relating to even the most humble of ancestors and some of Britain's most important families have been surprised and occasionally delighted to discover they come from modest beginnings.

When the research has been completed and verified, documents are prepared for the client adorned with the most intricate artwork. The College employs the finest heraldic artists in the country and the hours of labour spent by the letterers illuminating the parchment scrolls is testimony to the years of apprenticeship they have spent acquiring their skills.

In addition to the Officer in Arms Ordinary, there are also a number of Extraordinary Officers. They do not constitute part of the establishment of the College and receive no salary or fees. Their main task is to support the Officers in Ordinary on ceremonial occasions, and most take their titles – which can be heralds or pursuivants – from the family names and titles connected with the Earl Marshal's family, the House of Howard. These are currently: Arundel, Beaumont, Fitzalan, Maltravers, Norfolk and Surrey. Others use titles associated with the regions they represent: New Zealand and Wales, which had its own King of Arms until the end of the fifteenth century.

Scotland has its own college of arms known as the Court of the Lord Lyon, who is also secretary of the Order of the Thistle. Their headquarters are located in Her Majesty's New Register House in Edinburgh but some of the work of researching family backgrounds is carried out by the officers at home or from their private offices. There were originally thirteen Scottish Officers (the same as their English counterparts) but since 1867, when the Lord Lyon Court Act was passed, their numbers have been limited to seven: Lord Lyon, three heralds and three pursuivants. Lord Lyon is paid a realistic salary but the others receive purely nominal annuities: Heralds, £24 a year and pursuivants £16.67. The officers respond to genealogical enquiries from all parts of the world and they are also accepted as the definitive authority on all matters relating to clan history and Scottish tartans.

The uniform of the Scottish heralds differs from that worn by English officers in that the tabard has a Scottish lion rampant in the first and fourth quarters, with the leopards of England in the second. And unlike their English colleagues they do not wear swords while in uniform. Lord Lyon has a gold stripe down the outside of his tight-fitting trousers – called overalls – which, to distinguish him from his officers, is a quarter of an inch broader than the stripe on theirs.

Whereas the English heralds are seen mainly in attendance on the sovereign, in Scotland they are much more often in evidence, parading frequently on many public occasions such as the installation of the Governor of Edinburgh Castle, when Lord Lyon demands the ceremonial surrender of the keys.

The system of heraldry is based on the custom of decorating the shields of warriors before they entered battle in the Middle Ages. There is nothing peculiarly British, or English about it; most other countries had similar customs. Heraldry came into its own when jousting tournaments became popular. The squires attending their knights were required to organize the events and each vied with the others to provide more elaborate designs by which their masters would be recognized. From these beginnings the present system of heraldry emerged. And although the heralds no longer have responsibility for arranging military tournaments or tattoos, their role in State ceremonial remains an integral and picturesque element.

Between them the heralds have accumulated years of experience in dealing with Court protocol, and many people, aristocrat and artisan alike, have cause to be grateful to them for the courteous and knowledgeable manner in which they guide newcomers in the right direction. A state occasion can be very intimidating to the uninitiated; a friendly word of encouragement from a gentleman (there are no lady heralds) in a medieval costume, can relieve the tension quite dramatically.

Their task is to make the event run smoothly and enjoyably for all concerned. So, in a sense, it hasn't changed all that much in over five hundred years.

✑

CHAPTER TWENTY

Royal Travel

During the official working year ended 31 March 2001, the royal family between them undertook some 3,000 engagements, ranging from visits to housing associations in central London, to trips to many of the provinces and a few long-haul journeys overseas. Their combined travel expenses amounted to just over £5 million, and all this activity was coordinated by the Director of Royal Travel, a senior RAF officer who has the services of just thirteen other staff to assist him. The majority, nine, are personnel of the Queen's Helicopter Flight: four pilots, an operations officer and four landing site officers. The others are administrators.

They use aircraft (both fixed wing and helicopter) of No. 32 (The Royal Squadron), based at RAF Northolt in London; commercial aircraft for longhaul flights; the Royal Train, which is now owned and operated by an American company, English Welsh and Scottish Railways, and, for short visits to nearby venues, vehicles provided by the Royal Mews. Two exceptions to this last provision are the

Prince of Wales and the Princess Royal, who, when they are travelling from their country homes, prefer to use their own private Bentleys.

There is no longer a Queen's Flight and the number of aircraft and service personnel has been reduced considerably since the move from RAF Benson in Oxfordshire to Northolt. Now there are just two BAe 146 jets, each capable of carrying up to 25 passengers, and five smaller HS 125s which have a capacity of seven passengers.

The squadron flies Government ministers and senior service officers as well as the royal family, and in the year aforementioned, the Queen and her family used the fixed-wing aircraft for only eight per cent of the squadron's total flying time. They did, however, use the six-seater helicopters a great deal, and spent some £1.887 million on them. Their fixed-wing flying was only slightly less at £1.793 million. When aircraft of No. 32 Squadron are not available, or if it is thought to be more economical not to use them, the household charters commercial aircraft, which are cheaper to run than those of the RAF. In 2000–01, the royal family flew 121 hours in small fixed-wing aircraft.

The largest single expense comes when the Queen is involved in an overseas tour that involves lengthy air travel. For these they charter full-size jets such as a Boeing 747, and air travel costs go through the roof. In 1999, there were three State visits outside Europe costing £807,000. In 2000 there were none, so the expenses came down accordingly, but in 2002, the Queen visited Australia in the spring for the Commonwealth Heads of Government Meeting, so the travel bill for that year went up again.

Before any flight is undertaken, the Director of Royal

Travel liaises with the Fleet Directors of the airline, which is usually British Airways although occasionally the relevant national carrier is used, such as Qantas on a trip to Australia. They always carry out at least one reconnaissance flight to survey the proposed route, along with representatives of the royal household, who check the various timings and arrange the Queen's programme accordingly. Then, if the Queen is flying British Airways, three separate teams are used to ensure the food and drink side of the operation is successful. There is a Controller Aircraft Catering, a Route Catering Manager and a Manager Menu Development, each with their own staff. All are paid by British Airways, the cost incorporated into the package deal.

Apart from the catering teams, scheduling coordinators, operations controllers and operations planners, all work under the supervision of the BA Manager, Operational Contingencies. While on the flight itself, a back-up team consisting of representatives from customer services, security, engineering and the company providing the aircraft, either Boeing or Lockheed, joins the crew.

The flight crew is specially chosen. The pilots are the senior captains in the airline with hundreds of flying hours to their credit. Wherever possible cabin crew who have attended the Queen before are chosen, and pen pictures are provided of everyone on board.

The senior navigation officer has prepared the route and made all necessary clearances with the many air traffic control areas through which the aircraft will pass. Three security officers, apart from Her Majesty's own personal bodyguards, travel with the party and remain with the aircraft at all times. If the flight is due to make refuelling stops along the way, the local British Airways manager will make the arrangements and often travels with the royal party through his sector. While on a flight to Australia or New Zealand, when there may be one or more stops en route, the airline's senior maintenance engineer joins the crew and liaises with his colleagues on the ground to make sure any engineering requirements are provided for. A supply of mechanical spares has already been positioned at convenient depots along the route.

A three-man security team supervises the loading of the royal baggage, and they do not leave the aircraft at any time. Once they have reported for duty, they remain at their posts until the aircraft has landed and its passengers and luggage have been disembarked.

If the Queen is to travel farther by air, to smaller airports where the giant jumbo jets cannot land or take off, one of the BAe 146s of No. 32 Squadron will take over. It will have been positioned some days before Her Majesty arrives and appropriate advance preparations will have been carried out. Runways will be measured, terminal facilities inspected to see if they are suitable for entertaining the sovereign, and a dozen other details investigated. It's all done to ensure the smooth path of the Queen. The entire operation appears seamless and unhurried simply because attention to the smallest detail is checked over and over again. Nothing is left to chance, and the Queen, who has now travelled to every country of significance in the world during her fifty-year reign, notices immediately if anything is wrong.

Being selected for a royal flight is the pinnacle of a flight crew's career. The cabin crew go through an intensive grooming session and are fully briefed about the special requirements of their VIP passengers days before the flight, and they stay at an hotel at Heathrow Airport the night before, instead of turning up just a few hours before the flight. They also check in three hours before the flight rather than the usual two. In addition a back-up crew is ready at a moment's notice in case of illness or some other unforeseen circumstance.

The proposed menus have already been sent to Buckingham Palace for the Queen's approval and a wine list has been selected from Concorde's reserves. The catering manager is aware that the Queen does not care for heavy meals, particularly when she is travelling, and she hates waste in any form so he consults her personal chef before making his suggestions. And even when the destination is in the Caribbean or Far East, local dishes are rarely included. Her Majesty has to put up with enough exotic foods prepared for her by hosts anxious to share their native products, so she does not welcome anything out of the ordinary. During one tour of Belize, a local delicacy was placed in front of her called a Gibnut. She ate it – or at any rate managed a few mouthfuls – without realizing that it was a rodent, looking, and presumably tasting, not unlike a giant rat.

British Airways has special Royal Flight equipment, including bone china and the finest crystal glassware. They provide flowers, menu cards and a supply of in-flight reading material, including their own airline magazine, and during the flight the latest news is electronically transferred from Britain so that Her Majesty and His Royal Highness can be kept up to date with world affairs. Prince Philip, an experienced pilot himself, likes to visit the flight deck from time to time, and the captain periodically issues bulletins for both his royal passengers and those accompanying them, showing where they are at any given point, and also giving advance information of the weather expected at the destination so that the Queen can change into appropriate clothes before she lands.

Before any long overseas tour, the Lord Chamberlain usually makes arrangements with the authorities at Heathrow Airport for the families and friends of the staff travelling with the Queen to have special places to see them off and welcome them home.

The Chief Clerk to the Master of the Household sends out a letter with a pro forma reply informing the staff that they can invite two relatives or friends to a particular area on the south side of the airport. The time of departure and arrival is given and the staff member has to give the names of those he would like invited. No changes are permitted. It is a thoughtful gesture instigated by the Duke of Edinburgh and approved by the Queen, and it is appreciated by those who will perhaps be abroad for several weeks.

Staff are also informed of the various currencies used in the different countries they are visiting and the current rate of exchange, with two members of the household made responsible for the issue of all money. They then debit the person concerned and an account is issued by the assistant treasurer when they return home.

Any mail for members of the royal party is forwarded immediately by diplomatic bag. Staff are told the address is (Name), Royal Party on Tour, c/o The Court Postmaster, Buckingham Palace, London SW1A 1AA. If members of the party want to send letters home, they have to place them in the post bag in the private secretary's office (one is provided at each stage of the journey) and no postage stamps are required. Members of staff are enthusiastic shoppers on overseas trips and during the return flight the household issues customs declaration forms which have to be handed in to the member of the household responsible for seeing that the necessary duty is paid.

The Master of the Household allocates the seats during a royal flight and the rule is that everyone must arrive at the airport wearing suitable clothes: suits and ties for the men and dresses for the women. Once on board, they are allowed to change into more comfortable attire until they are ready to land, when they change again. There's always a rush to get to the lavatories and exchange suits for track suit trousers and trainers; on one occasion the queue stretched back half the length of the economy section. After waiting for twenty minutes one of the 'less than manly' footmen was next in line when the Queen's Mistress of the Robes, the Duchess of Grafton, moved up from Club class and politely asked if she might jump the queue. The footman stood back and, as she went into the lavatory, he sniffed: 'That must be the first time a duchess has taken precedence over a queen.'

An important addition to the party is a Queen's Messenger, who can be despatched at any time to bring back to London any messages of a sensitive nature which cannot be transmitted by other means. The messengers have special passports in red covers, embossed with the words Queen's Messenger and, inside, 'Charged with Dispatches'. Based at the Foreign and Commonwealth Office, they receive full diplomatic immunity although they are not members of the Diplomatic Service. Most are former service officers and among their other royal duties is acting as ushers at the annual Diplomatic Reception held at Buckingham Palace every November.

Before the main party leaves for the homeward journey,

a small advance group, which always includes the Palace Steward, flies back to London to prepare Buckingham Palace or Windsor Castle for the royal couple's return. So by the time the Queen and Prince Philip arrive back home everything is as they expect. Nothing is ever left to chance where the comfort of Her Majesty is concerned.

As one of the busiest members of the family, the Princess Royal uses helicopters, aircraft of the Royal Squadron and private charters. A glance at the log for the period 2000–01 shows that on 16–17 March she flew in a HS125 from RAF Lynham to Edinburgh and back, to watch Scotland play Italy at rugby. The cost was £11,467. On 21 March she again used the same aircraft to fly from Northolt to Coventry, where she had several engagements, including opening a Salvation Army residential home for the elderly. The cost of the away-day fight was £10,625. There was no suitable aircraft available on 27 March, for her flight to Newmarket from RAF Kemble, near her home in Gloucestershire, so she chartered a plane at a much reduced cost of £4,414. On 29 March she used both a HS125 and a Sikorsky S76 helicopter to get from Northolt to Manchester then East Midlands and home to Kemble. The total cost was £10,370. She again made use of a helicopter on 5 September to fly from Cirencester to Southampton and home to Gatcombe Park at a cost of £7,422.

The Duke of Gloucester made an official visit to Kazakhstan in September to 'foster British relations'. He flew in a chartered aircraft for which he was charged £55,060.

Princess Alexandra was on holiday in Scotland when she was invited to attend the Air Force Board dinner to commemorate the Sixtieth Anniversary of the Battle of

Britain. A BAe 146 of the Royal Squadron was available to fly her from Aberdeen to London and the cost was £20,541.

Prince Charles needed to get home to Highgrove after attending a reception at the Globe Theatre in London, so he commandeered one of the S76 helicopters at a cost of £5,016. During the same month, his staff carried out reconnaissance visits to the Czech Republic, Slovakia and Switzerland. They travelled Business class on scheduled flights at a total cost of just £2,923. When the actual four-day visit of the Prince of Wales took place, a chartered aircraft cost £64,457.

A similar 'recce' exercise to Warsaw on behalf of the Duke of York was carried out for £562. His staff also carried out another 'recce' to Germany, costing £586, but the proposed official visit to Dresden was subsequently cancelled.

Quite often, a number of engagements are undertaken in a particular area on the same day. For example, in April 2000, the Queen and Prince Philip flew from Northolt to Aldergrove Airport in Belfast. The primary purpose was to award the George Cross to the Royal Ulster Constabulary. However, Her Majesty and His Royal Highness made full use of their limited time in Northern Ireland to fit in as many other engagements as they could. When the Queen travels, she is always accompanied by several members of the royal household, so the cost of using a BAe 146 (£17,000) for the one-day trip was fully justified.

The Princess Royal is Patron of the Scotland Rugby Union Team and she attends all their matches. So when, in April 2000, she flew up to Edinburgh to sit in the stand at Murrayfield, she also accepted an invitation to a charity sporting dinner to make it all worthwhile. She ran up a travel bill of £11,467.

It didn't cost all that much more for the Duke of Edinburgh to fly to Copenhagen for the Queen of Denmark's sixtieth birthday party. Since he used one of the smaller seven-seater HS125s, the bill only came to £15,290.

The biggest single bill for air travel in the year 2000 was incurred by the Princess Royal. On 20 November she flew from London to Delhi in India at the start of an extensive tour lasting ten days. She travelled by scheduled airline, out and back, and the first class fares for the Princess, her lady-in-waiting and her private secretary amounted to £19,916. This did not include the fare of her bodyguard, whose expenses were paid, as always, by the police. Between 21–28 November, the Princess moved between various destinations in Bangladesh and Nepal in her capacity as President of the Save the Children Fund. The total cost, excluding the fares to and from India, amounted to £213,930.

Until fairly recently the most expensive form of royal travel was by rail. The Royal Train is an ultra-exclusive 'palace on wheels' that is the sole prerogative of the sovereign and her family, though nowadays it is supposed to be available for use by Government ministers on official business. It is greatly loved by royalty, and both Prince Charles and the Princess Royal have often said that their idea of a perfect way to start a holiday at Balmoral is to journey north on the train.

Since 1 April 1997, the royal household has been responsible for the costs of royal rail travel. Prior to this, it was all paid for by the Department of Transport. But it's really only a matter of accounting. The difference is that instead of the department paying the cost directly, they now provide the necessary funds.

Today the Royal Train is the only personal train service in Britain, and while it does not compare with the luxury of royal trains of earlier days, it lacks nothing in the way of comfort. Queen Victoria was the first monarch to have a train of her own, and although the locomotives that pulled the carriages were pathetically slow compared with the high-speed engines of today, the inside of her coaches were ostentatiously opulent in the extreme: thick carpets, silk curtains and feather beds. The only items missing were kitchens and bathrooms. The old Queen believed it was unsafe to eat on the move and insanitary to bathe or use a lavatory while travelling. Which is why there were so many small halts on the route from Windsor to Ballater in Scotland, all fully equipped with what passed in those days for luxury 'facilities'. The Queen would insist that the train stopped whenever she felt like it; timetables meant nothing to her, or to the railway companies operating the same routes. Everyone, rail barons included, accommodated the Queen.

Today's Royal Train and the way it operates is far removed from not only the trains of previous reigns, but also the Royal Train of just twenty years ago. Until fairly recently there were fourteen royal carriages, but there was no such thing as 'The' Royal Train. You might see more than one on any given day in different parts of the country; it all depended on the make-up of the rolling stock. Now the Royal Train has been reduced to nine coaches, which includes accommodation for household, railway staff, who always travel with the royal family, police, communications equipment and their own electricity supply. Depending on which member of the family is travelling, and how many, five to eight of the coaches are used at any one time. When the number of coaches was reduced from fourteen, two were retained to be used for spares and the other three were sold on 31 March 2001 for £236,000, the proceeds going to the Department of Transport, Local Government and the Regions.

Although the train is still a very popular mode of transport with the royal family, helicopters have replaced it for many journeys. They are both quicker and less expensive to run. In 1999, the train was used for a total of twenty-four journeys. The following year the number had dropped to seventeen, with an average distance per trip of 550 miles.

The total cost of running the Royal Train in the year 2000–01 was £596,000, which included £100,000 for maintaining the coaches, £101,000 for storing the coaches when they were not in use, £72,000 for using the railtracks and paying for the out-of-the-way sidings that are occupied when a member of the family stays on board overnight, and £8,000 for catering, which is not provided by the royal kitchens but by the usual Inter-City service available on most train journeys.

The Royal Train is easily recognizable as the exterior of the carriages is painted a distinctive shade of 'Royal' claret. Inside, the Queen's personal quarters are decorated in light pastel shades of beige, and in her saloon, which extends to the full width of the train, there are easy chairs and a sofa upholstered in pale blue with hand-stitched velvet cushions and a small coffee table. Around the walls are paintings reflecting a more glamorous age of rail travel in the age of steam. Next door to the saloon is Her Majesty's bedroom, with a single bed, and an adjoining bathroom, complete with full-size bath.

The Duke of Edinburgh is one of the most frequent users

of the train and the largest of his private quarters is the dining room equipped with a full-size table capable of seating ten people. This is where the Duke holds many business meetings; he does not believe in wasting time, so rarely is a lunch held which is not also a working occasion. The colour scheme is plain brown and even the armchairs are designed to be functional rather than comfortable. Visitors are not encouraged to stay too long.

At No. 32 Squadron (the Royal Squadron) specially picked aircrew fly the Queen and her family, but strangely, the same selection process does not apply to the Royal Train. There is no 'Royal Train Driver' as such. Whoever happens to be next on the duty rosta takes his turn. At least that's the official line. But the stewards who wait on the family are usually chosen time after time.

The Royal Train is not cheap to run. A glance at the programme for 2000–01 shows that when the Queen and Prince Philip travelled from Slough (Windsor) to Lincoln for the annual Maundy Service, a journey which included an overnight stay on board, the cost was £34,263. And when they journeyed from London to Bodmin in Cornwall, the one-way trip cost £36,474, with a further £12,750 added when they flew back the following day in a BAe 146 of the Royal Squadron.

On a number of occasions it has not been considered worthwhile to keep the train waiting, even if the royal couple spend the night on it. For a trip from London to Cardiff in June 2000, the total rail costs were £33,619, but the Queen and Prince Philip did not use the train for the return journey. Instead a helicopter was positioned in Cardiff to fly them direct to Buckingham Palace at a cost of £7,353.

The Prince of Wales has always enjoyed the Royal Train and in September 2000 it was brought up to Aberdeen (he was on holiday at Balmoral) to carry him to a number of official engagements in Northampton. The cost was £36,700. In February 2001, His Royal Highness opened Shrewsbury School's new music department, and while he was in the area, he also carried out several other public duties. The train was brought into use for the two-day visit at a cost of £33,106.

In addition to these journeys by the Royal Train, members of the royal family also use normal scheduled services every year. For example, if the Princess Royal is travelling up to London from her home, Gatcombe Park, in Gloucestershire, she will often join the train at Kemble, the nearest station. It doesn't make a special stop for her and no particular arrangements are made, apart from reserving seats for her and her police bodyguard. The days when a top-hatted station master was on hand to see off and welcome important passengers are long gone. The only time it happens these days is when the Royal Train itself is expected.

In the travel year 2000–01 some sixty journeys where the tickets cost less than £500 were taken by members of the royal family, who travelled around 8,900 miles by scheduled train service at a cost of £7,359, a considerable saving on what would have been spent if they had used the Royal Train for the same journeys. The royal household are always required to use scheduled rail services when they travel on Palace business, and in the same period they spent £16,964. So the total cost of rail travel for the Queen and her family, and their staff, amounted to £620,000, with £596,000 attributed to the Royal Train and the remaining £24,000 to other rail journeys.

The Keeper of the Privy Purse, in his annual report on the Grant-in-Aid for Royal Travel by Air and Rail – the Grant-in-Aid is the amount voted for Parliament to cover these costs – lists the cost of each mile travelled. By air it is just £18 per mile, while by rail it rises to £42. So it is quite easy to see why using helicopters and aircraft, even when they have to be chartered, is much more economical than calling on the Royal Train.

The Royal Family have the choice of some of the most privileged forms of transport in the world: a private (well, almost) fleet of aircraft, helicopters, luxury limousines and, when the occasion demands, those fantastic horse-drawn State carriages in the Royal Mews. I've spoken to most members of the family and asked them which they prefer. Without exception the answer is the same: the Train. Now that the Royal Yacht is no more, the train seems to be the one place where, when away from home, the Queen and her family can truly relax out of the public gaze. It may not have quite the same romantic image as when Queen Victoria rolled in majestic style from Windsor to Balmoral, insisting that the driver never exceeded thirty miles an hour, but there remains some of the glamour of bygone days. In an age of world-weary cynicism, when jet travel has in most cases reduced the longest journeys to a single day, Prince Charles says he gains a lot of pleasure just looking out of the window at the countryside of Britain passing by.

CHAPTER TWENTY-ONE

✑

Royal Shopping Lists

If the Queen wants half a dozen fresh eggs and the dairy at Windsor has run out, she – or the man in the Master of the Household's office who does the shopping – orders them from Deans Farm of Tring in Hertfordshire.

If Prince Philip ruins his waxed jacket when out carriage driving, a new one is supplied by Messrs J. Barbour & Sons of South Shields, and on those odd occasions when Prince Charles feels like riding a bicycle in the country lanes around his Highgrove Estate in Gloucestershire, there's a local shop on hand in Tetbury, called Thames and Cotswolds, to provide the necessary conveyance.

All these companies, and a further eight hundred, share the privilege of belonging to the Royal Warrant Holders Association, an exclusive organization of tradesmen and women who supply certain members of the royal family with goods and services and have been rewarded with the right to advertise that they have done so by displaying a Royal Coat of Arms. It is shown on their premises, on vehicles and packaging and on headed writing paper.

There's nothing new in the practice of royalty allowing their names to be used for commercial gain. They have always known their value as a marketing commodity and successive sovereigns down the ages have actively encouraged trade by lending their names to commercial undertakings. Royal patronage can be traced back to the twelfth century, when Henry II granted the first Royal Charter to the Weavers Company in 1155.

In the sixteenth century, Henry VIII, having drawn up the 'Statutes of Eltham' to govern the 'good order of his household', gave permission for one Thomas Hewytt to 'Serve the Court with Swannes and Cranes and all kinds of Wildfoule'. He also appointed the first Court Laundress, a lady by the name of Anne Harris, who was required to 'weekly wash the pieces as need shall require, and for her paines be paid £1 10s a yeare, without further charge for wood sope, or any other thing'. There is still a laundry appointed by the Court; it is now Sycamore Laundry of Old Town, London, founded in 1865 by a Mrs Buckland, who used to take in washing for the gentry. Her great-great-grandchildren still run the family business and their proud claim is that they have never lost a single item of royal laundry. Prince Charles has appointed his own launderer, Anton Laundry Ltd. He also has a butcher who is entitled to display his coat of arms: Amberley Vale Foods, while Ainsworth's Homoeopathic Pharmacy provides him with the alternative medicines he swears by and without which he never travels abroad.

Henry VIII's daughter, Elizabeth I, had a supplier of 'Sea and Fresh Water Fish' who received '£10 a yeare entertainment and £22 11s 8d a yeare for losses and necessaries'. In the seventeenth century, James VI of Scotland, who became

James I of England when he moved south of the border in 1603 – and in doing so, is credited with introducing the game of golf to the English – appointed one David Gassiers to be 'Goffe-club Maker'. The present Duke of York is a self-confessed golf fanatic who likes to play with some of the world's leading professionals, but he does not have an appointed golf club maker for the Duke is not in a position to award warrants.

Not all members of the present royal family are entitled to award warrants: only the Queen, the Duke of Edinburgh and the Prince of Wales. The Queen gives permission, and so far she has decided that, to maintain exclusivity, these three should be the only members of her family able to make the awards. So, no matter how long a firm or individual has been supplying, say, the Princess Royal, they cannot receive any official recognition. Even the late Diana, Princess of Wales, at one time the most famous woman in the world, was denied the privilege, much as she wanted to reward some of her favourite dress designers and milliners.

Every century has seen the sovereign awarding Royal Warrants, usually claiming, at the same time, either massive discounts or, more commonly, free goods on the grounds that, by allowing the suppliers to advertise their royal connections, they substantially increase their trade.

Many sovereigns have been notoriously mean and reluctant to pay their bills. Charles II has the record for holding out for the longest period. His Master of the Great Wardrobe once wrote to him, pointing out in suitably tactful language, that some of the bills had been outstanding for as long as two years and that the tradesmen were 'very necessitous persons'. The amount owing was £1,348 18s 4d

– equivalent to a couple of million pounds today. There is no record of His Majesty acceding to his aide's suggestion and settling the account.

In Queen Victoria's time there were a number of picturesque royal warrant holders such as the Household Spider and Rat Catcher and the Official Cobweb Cleaner, and royal coal merchants were appointed to every royal residence in England and Scotland. These have now largely disappeared with their places taken by central heating engineers, air conditioning mechanics and suppliers of industrial vacuum cleaning equipment.

While for most appointments to the royal household one has to wait until asked, this doesn't apply to a firm or individual who wants to be considered for a royal warrant. There are strict rules, before joining and afterwards, but the basic qualification is to have supplied goods or services satisfactorily for at least five years. Once this is achieved the warrant is usually awarded. Warrant holders then get preferential treatment when it comes to quoting for contracts. They still have to be competitive – the Keeper of the Privy Purse always makes sure of that – but all other things being equal, a warrant holder will be chosen to do the job.

A glance through the booklet listing the names and trades holding royal warrants shows what an eclectic bunch they are, and not all are the household names one normally associates with the High Street. Sixty years ago the firm of Temple and Cook Ltd, the only ironmongers in Belgravia, came to the rescue of the royal household when they managed to find in their stock a couple of old keys that fitted an ancient lock at Buckingham Palace. They were eventually awarded a royal warrant and theirs must surely be a unique relationship with royalty: the friendly neighbourhood ironmonger to the Queen and her family.

Without doubt the town with the highest percentage of royal warrant holders is Ballater, the town closest to Balmoral. Almost every shop boasts the royal coat of arms and a 'By Appointment to . . .' Florists, butchers, grocers and game dealers all have reason to be thankful to the members of the royal family who award warrants, and to those others who do not, but shop there anyway. Royal patronage is never more obvious than at Ballater and there is a very real commercial advantage as the thousands of tourists who visit the area every year flock to buy in the shops used by the Queen and her family. One shop is literally outside the gates of Balmoral Castle in the tiny village of Crathie. It is owned by George Strachan, who has a main store in Arboyne – where they claim to stock the largest selection of Scotch whiskies in the world – 400 different brands – and further shops in Ballater and Braemar. Strachan's can claim to be the business closest to any royal residence to hold a royal warrant.

Women have been allowed to hold royal warrants for centuries, but it wasn't until the beginning of the twentieth century that they were permitted to attend meetings of the Royal Warrant Holders Association. Until that time, from its formation in 1840, a female individual or a company owned by a woman was allowed to 'appoint a gentleman to represent her' at their functions. In the nineteenth century the Association's name was the cumbersome 'The Royal Tradesmen's Association for the Annual Celebration of Her Majesty's Birthday', and the celebrations took the form of banquets at which much drinking accompanied numerous loyal toasts to various members of the royal family, and even to the Archbishop of Canterbury and members of the Established Church.

All the firms and individuals who belong to the Royal Warrant Holders Association are British. In theory at least the royal family does not grant warrants to any foreign companies, though, in reality, some of the companies which still trade under their original British names are now owned by overseas corporations. The Bentley cars driven by Prince Charles and the Princess Royal, although arguably among the oldest of British marques, are today owned lock stock and barrel by the German firm of Volkswagen. The Rolls Royce limousines used by the Queen, now come courtesy of BMW, and the Jaguar cars favoured by several of the younger members of the royal family, may still be made in the United Kingdom, but under the aegis of their American owners, the giant Ford Company of Detroit.

Obviously there is tremendous 'snob' appeal in being able to claim one drinks the same tea or coffee as Her Majesty, has one's hats made by her milliners, Freddie Fox and Sophie Mirman, wear similar raincoats supplied by Messrs Thomas Burberry, drink the same brand of gin or even write with the same make of fountain pen. It's a Parker, so is the ink she uses, and even though the company was founded by an American, George S. Parker in Janesville, Wisconsin, they have been making their pens in England since 1941.

The Queen's gundogs at Sandringham and Balmoral sleep in specially constructed kennels made for her by Neaverson's of Peterborough, who have held their royal warrant since 1970. The kennels are built of Russian timber and, because the Queen likes her dogs to have plenty of space, hers are made a foot larger than the standard size.

Neaverson's haven't benefitted all that much from having a royal customer; they were already selling all they could make before the Queen bought from them.

The garden parties at Buckingham Palace mean good business for a number of companies, not just those who supply the cakes and tea. Since the days of Queen Victoria, Black & Edgington of Tower Bridge in London have been supplying and erecting the tents and marquees on the lawns. Theirs is an enormous undertaking, with a stock of thousands of tents in all shapes and sizes. They will arrange everything from a children's tea party in your back garden to the corporate hospitality tents at Wimbledon. And, as flag makers to the Queen, they will also sell you a standard to fly on top of the tent.

Royal warrants are normally granted for a period of ten years, but unless there has been a serious problem – the supplier has gone into receivership or the person awarding the warrant has not used their services for three years or more – the warrant is usually renewed.

In recent years the most publicized withdrawal of a royal warrant was when the Duke of Edinburgh decided not to renew the warrant he awarded to Harrods. The official reason was that he no longer bought anything from them; unofficially, it is believed that an allegation made by Mr Al Fayed, the owner of the store, that Prince Philip had been responsible for causing the death of his son Dodi (killed in the car crash that also killed Diana, Princess of Wales in 1997) was the reason for the break. Harrods had royal warrants from all four members of the royal family who at that time awarded warrants; and the four coats of Arms were one of the most distinctive displays in Knightsbridge. But on Mr Al Fayed's orders Harrod's surrendered those of the Queen, the Queen Mother and the Prince of Wales when the Duke withdrew his support.

One peculiar aspect of the system is that no matter how large the business that supplies the goods or services, the royal warrant is always awarded to an individual: either a partner in the firm or a director, who must be resident in the country.

Strict rules intended to 'preserve the dignity of the warrant and prevent commercialization' govern both the display of the royal coats of arms and the conduct of the suppliers. However, there is no doubt about the enormous advantages to any business able to show that they supply the royal family. The advertising may be ultra-discreet, but customers know full well that the dinner service they are buying, or the vacuum cleaner or the bottles of champagne, are the same as those enjoyed by royalty. And that is a feeling many people are willing to pay dearly to experience.

Conclusion

In the early days of the Queen's reign, membership of the royal household was considered akin to belonging to a gentrified profession, and even in the lower reaches there was an air of cradle to grave paternalism. The word meritocracy was unknown, and only in the past ten years or so have qualities that in the past would have immediately disbarred anyone from entering royal service, such as driving ambition and a willingness and ability to make public presentations of Palace policy, been accepted. Not only accepted but demanded. Long-term careers are becoming a thing of the past. A huge social shift is happening, and that sense of security, once so vital a part of life in the royal household, now has to be found somewhere else.

Some of the older, more long-serving servants depend on that old protective blanket, and cannot cope when they are eventually forced to live outside in the real world. They have become used to the private post office, the cosy subsidized bar, the laundry that is collected twice a week and returned free of charge; the fact that a maid will clean your room and also that you can invite friends to visit you inside the Palace.

In the past, working for the royal family was regarded as a privilege by those employed – and also by those who employed them. The question of money never arose; the royals refused to discuss it and the servants wouldn't dare. It is still felt to be an honour by most of those working at the Palace, but now the royals have to accept it is one that must be rewarded with hard cash. The era of low pay, long hours and servile deference has ended. There is still a tradition of bowing and curtsying within the Palace walls, but now the staff have to achieve 'performance targets' to get a rise. Consequently, they are slightly more challenging than before and less inclined to subsidize the royal family.

The Queen has described Buckingham Palace as a small village and it does have many of the same features. The love affairs, hetero- and homosexual, are talked about in the same way, the staff – and not just the domestics – love to gossip about the latest scandals, promotions and wages. If someone is given a better Grace and Favour home than his colleagues on the same level, there is the same bitchiness you'd find anywhere; and while ambition is restricted to climbing the social ladder rather than monetary rungs, the closer a servant gets to the Queen, the more his associates resent him. This is where the power lies, in access to the sovereign. It doesn't matter what grade of servant you are, footman, housemaid or private secretary, if you are promoted to the tiny personal group that surrounds Her Majesty, everyone knows that you enjoy a special position and will try to cultivate you. Even the Lord Chamberlain, the titular Head of the Household, uses the services of the Queen's Page to gauge her mood when he wants to raise a particular topic with her. And even he, exalted as he is in royal circles, dare not simply poke his head around the door of her sitting room. The curious mixture of informality and Court protocol that exists in every corner of the Palace, means that whenever he wants to see Her Majesty, he has to enquire of her Page if she will grant an audience. He is rarely refused, but he has to go through the same rigmarole every time.

In years gone by the only way anyone could get a job in the royal household was to be invited. You couldn't apply and they never advertised. Things have changed to such an extent in recent years that when the Queen needed two new assistant press secretaries, an advertisement was placed in a professional journal and the successful candidates interviewed – not by her personally, she merely rubber-stamps the choice of her private secretary – and duly appointed. Although background is still important, employees no longer have to come from a particular school or family. The household has at last become a meritocracy. But the very top posts such as Lord Chamberlain and private secretary are still filled by men known to the incumbents, even if not to the Queen herself. And their positions are highly unlikely to be advertised on the open market, though the post of assistant private secretary to the Queen was advertised in the national press in March 2001 – the first time this had ever happened, and much to the dismay of some of the 'old guard'. There was even more alarm when a firm of professional headhunters was engaged to find a new Keeper of the Privy Purse to replace Sir Michael Peat when he moved to become the Prince of Wales's private secretary. His successor, Alan Reid, came from Sir Michael's old firm, KPMG. Generally speaking, the 'old-boy' network still operates at this level, but to be fair it works. In her fifty years on the throne the Queen has yet to employ a failure as either Lord

Chamberlain or private secretary, though there was one head of the household in recent years who didn't last very long and who was not the most popular of men.

Farther down the scale, in the kitchens and servants' hall, it was invariably a closed shop, with jobs handed down from father to son, mother to daughter. Countless stories tell of generations of footmen and cooks from the same families. The system had worked for over a hundred years. The young men and women knew what to expect from their parents and had been brought up 'knowing the form', the most important lesson for anyone in royal service.

These days the Master of the Household, who employs all the domestic and liveried staff, and the Crown Equerry, who is responsible for the chauffeurs, grooms and staff in the Royal Mews, actively encourage applicants. They periodically organize recruiting visits to areas of high unemployment and they see anyone who bothers to knock at the side door of Buckingham Palace seeking work. No one is ever turned away without the courtesy of an interview, and as there is usually a vacancy or two somewhere, more often than not, a trial period is offered. But references are always checked and the Royal Protection Department will look into the applicant's background to see if there is any criminal history or mental illness. Applicants also have to take a medical carried out by the Palace's own doctor, and their size is important. If they are being considered for training as a footman, they cannot be too short or too tall.

The household has been criticized many times for its employment policy. It has been accused of not taking on enough blacks, Asians, Jews, women or Catholics, and certainly all these groups are under-represented. But this is not because of any particular prejudice – though one private secretary thought the idea of the Queen having a Roman Catholic press secretary mildly amusing. Her Majesty is probably the least colour conscious person in Britain, and if she thought that a man or woman of African or West Indian descent was the best person for the job, she would never object. She does have reservations about appointing women to the top posts, but this is because she is more comfortable working with men. She has been surrounded by men all her adult life and even though she relies on her ladies-in-waiting for companionship, they do not figure largely in the business of monarchy. It is mentioned occasionally that of the three hundred-odd people working for the Queen at Buckingham Palace, less than ten per cent are women and that there is only a handful of women members – including one assistant private secretary, the press secretary and two assistant press secretaries. There are very few black or brown faces, though the Princess Royal does have a black woman as her personal dresser and a black woman is a senior member of Prince Charles's press team at St James's Palace.

When senior members of the household are asked why ethnic minorities are so poorly represented, the usual reply is that such people do not often apply. That may be the case, and positive discrimination just to be seen to be politically correct would do no one any good – either the Queen or those seeking to involve Her Majesty in a controversial issue. Taken to its – seemingly – logical conclusion, those who advocate change for change's sake, would perhaps like to see a black, female, lesbian Lord Chamberlain who would breast-feed her baby at a State Banquet. Perhaps in years to come we shall see a more multi-cultural face of the royal household. But it is much more important that the present efficiency is maintained and that the Queen is served by men and women who recognize that working for the sovereign is a privilege.

The royal household is far from perfect, and there are still too many servants who believe that royalty is infallible and completely trustworthy in all things, when in fact they are just as unreliable and prone to error as the rest of us. Many of the changes being implemented are painful to people who have served loyally for many years. The ruthless way in which long-established practices are being abolished may seem to be the only means of propelling the household into the twenty-first century, but there must be some sort of happy compromise. Ancient titles and picturesque posts may appear to be anachronistic but, in a world which is increasingly run by accountants, there should be a place for those who, above all, take a pride in their jobs, regardless of how much they are paid.

Perhaps it might be more efficient and cost productive if Palace staff were recruited from a wider spectrum of the British working and middle classes. This does appear to be the tendency at the present time, and many people will applaud the efforts of those in charge to streamline. But if they go too far and remove all the eccentrics and personalities, it won't be nearly as entertaining to those of us who have enjoyed looking in from the outside – or as frustrating to those men and women on the inside who like to think they are already doing a good job for the Queen. As one long-serving and very senior courtier put it, 'Although we are a team here, we have always prided ourselves on being able to cope with the individual odd-ball. The occasional eccentricity is tolerated and even welcomed. That's what has been so special about working at the Palace. Is there really a need to impose uniformity in all things?'

Index